CHEATING AND DECEPTION

CHEATING AND DECEPTION

J. Bowyer Bell
Barton Whaley

With a New Introduction by
J. Bowyer Bell

Transaction Publishers
New Brunswick (U.S.A.) and London (U.K.)

New material this edition copyright © 1991 by Transaction
Publishers, New Brunswick, New Jersey 08903
Originally published in 1982 by St. Martin's Press.

Library of Congress Catalog Number: 90-45018
ISBN: 0-88738-868-X
Printed in the United States of America

Library of Congress Cataloging-in-Publication Data

Bell, J. Bowyer, 1931–
    [Cheating]
    Cheating and deception/J. Bowyer Bell, Barton Whaley.
        p.   cm.
    Reprint, with new introd. Originally published: Cheating. New
York, N.Y.: St. Martin's Press, c1982.
    Includes index.
    ISBN 0-88738-868-X
    1. Deception. 2. Deception (Military science) I. Whaley, Barton.
II. Title.
  BJ1421.B69   1991
    179'.8—dc20   90-45018
                                                          CIP

Contents

Introduction to the Transaction Edition   ix
Acknowledgments   *xxxv*
Preface   *xxxvii*
Prologue   *1*

PART I: THE NATURE OF DUPLICITY

1. The Prevalence of Guile: The Ruses of War   *15*

2. The Structure of Deceit: A Theory of Cheating   *45*

3. Applied Theory: Wily Warriors   *75*

4. Deceivers and Dupes: Profiles   *97*

PART II: CHEATING—THE EIGHTFOLD WAY

5. Magic   *129*

6. Games and Sports   *171*

7. People and the Everyday World   *224*

8. Public Cheating: Politics, Espionage, and War   *254*

PART III: CHEATING THE CHEATERS

9. Illusion and Reality in the Arts   *285*

10. Hoaxes and Self-deception in Art and Science   *303*

Epilogue: Counterdeception   *327*

Index   *333*

Introduction to the Transaction Edition

"DECEPTION" is one of those garden variety words, often used but rarely defined, that tends to summon up unpleasant connotations; "deception" is a polite variant of cheating, and cheating is wrong if not wicked. Even those deeply involved in cheating–cheating at cards, cheating at love–must often find what have become standard rationalizations to comfort themselves: I am driven by necessity, there is no alternative, others do it, and, of course, no one will know. Particularly for Americans and much of Western civilization, official cheating–government duplicity, cheating as policy, conscious, contrived deception–is usually beyond excuse except as a last resort in response to the threat of extinction. Deception tends to be considered a distasteful tool to achieve even vital national interests unless it is used in conjunction with the deployment of military force.

Even in war, some oppose deception as beneath national dignity, the means of lesser powers or immoral ideologies. Still, a general may deceive a dangerous enemy under certain conditions without fear of public condemnation: War is hell. Thus, surprise achieved through deception is not only accepted, but often praised. In fact, there are far more studies of "surprise," which is merely a byproduct of effective deception (or at times self-deception, an entirely different matter not being consciously shaped to purpose and to advantage), than there are of military deception or strategies of deception. Surprise is seemingly more valid than deception in strategists' eyes. All other policy, however, should avoid recourse to deception. War may be hell and deception needed, but the same is not supposed to be true for elections or income tax rates or farm policy.

Not only is this aversion to deception understandable, given the Judeo-Christian heritage of Western society, it is also praiseworthy. There are enormous benefits of honesty, including a Western conscience made easy. No apologies or qualms need arise from denying recourse to deception. What is curious is that such denial extends to the very examination of the nature of cheating–cheating being, so to speak, the dark side of deception. Apparently, to study deception is to advocate the practice, so that for some, or many, it is better to inspect other matters or other facets of the subject, like surprise.

In fact, this book arises directly from the general, if often unarticulated, assumption that any venture into deception can contaminate. It seemed to the authors that often the very study of cheating was assumed by many to be dangerous, perhaps immoral, certainly not worth funding or patronage or even a kind word. This attitude should not have been–although it was–unexpected: Who in Washington wants to study the advantages of assassination? Which foundation would underwrite an investigation into the positive returns of racism? The authors deceived themselves about the prevalence of value-free research for the responsible. Still, this innocence, in time, led to *Cheating and Deception*.

A very long time ago, while at the Center for International Affairs at Harvard, I met one Dr. Barton Whaley, then working at MIT with Professor Ithiel de Sola Pool and teaching at the Fletcher School at Tufts, who was concerned with deception. At Harvard, MIT, or within the Cambridge academic community, someone is always working on some intriguing bit of esoterica–why not deception? Since my own concerns–terror, assassination, insurgency–were only slightly less peculiar, although then far more trendy in practice if not in analysis, deception seemed a not unreasonable academic arena. Whaley's recently completed dissertation, long postponed, had been a study of Operation Barbarossa, the German invasion of the Soviet Union in 1941, surely a longago and therefore proper subject. He had, as well, completed a variety of studies in various areas of policy communications, including a massive mimeo tome entitled *Stratagem, Deception, and Surprise in War* that seemingly placed deception under the rubric of strategy studies. Deception, however, if treated at all by strategists, was considered as an aside, an adjunct to battle, a technique, not even a tactic. There was a feeling that any investigation of the subject probably lay outside the major concerns of strategists, who were involved in nuclear exchanges at one end of the spectrum or anti-insurgency on the other and not much in between. That was left to the hand of military historians.

In those days, if deception could be analytically slotted at all (and few bothered), it should have been slotted in intelligence. It was, after all, a means of creating an alternative reality to confuse an opponent's analysis. In those longago days of the Vietnam War, as a field, even a small subfield, intelligence did not really exist. Old spies and popular authors wrote about intelligence. There were a couple of professors working in places such as Vanderbilt and Brown and a few scholars interested in bits and pieces of the subject, but there was no concept of a proper field, such as the study of federalism or bureaucracy or even the physical health of national leaders. Perhaps within the classified world of the intelligence community, there were those so involved; however, in the outside academic world, in Cambridge, intelligence, and so deception, were esoteric and peripheral interests. The national security analysts, the new strategists, and certainly the military historians had only peripheral interest in the matter.

Thus, no one was interested in deception research. Any practical applications of such work could produce results that many on campus would assumed to be an intrinsic part of the war industry of imperialist "Amerika." The declining number of academic hawks had other issues. the purely theoretical in communications theory or military history found no potential in the area. Deception fit no fashion. Thus, very few were interested in Dr. Whaley's work which as in my own case, seemed peripheral to real concerns, an analytical by-road.

In any case, I moved on to other distant wars and rebellions, travels that distracted me from a passing interest in deception, seemingly, in my work, a minor facet of revolutionary strategy–an analytical aside, if a necessary means for those denied conventional assets. George Washington might not have lied as president, but as rebels, his army, if not his cause, might well have served as a deception example. Rebels need every extra edge they can forge; they must cheat if need be. Still, revolutionary cheating was the least of my analytical worries while wandering about in Eritrea, Cyprus, or the Yemen. Deception was filed under curious, Bart Whaley under old friend, and there, for some time, matters rested.

In time, as the decade of the seventies ended, with students no longer roaring at the gate, insurgency out of fashion, terror all the rage, change everyplace, and the focus on new conflicts and crisis in Lebanon, Ireland, Cyprus, and Israel, with Vietnam quiescent and Iran on the brink–little had changed regarding matters of deception. Small wars come and small wars go, but deception research, apparently, remains static, stable, undone, and ignored.

There was, as before, some interest in strategic surprise; a few more people were concerned with intelligence as a policy matter, but there was no rush to fund work on cheating. In fact, as far as I could determine, the only folk who paid money for deception were the audiences for magicians, those who purchased their own delighted confusion–mostly children or their parents. Real magicians, rather than those who practiced social science sorcery, had very little leverage with academia, even though Whaley had insisted that they knew more about deception than anyone else. One magician had actually been deployed by the British as a deception planner during World War II and had even hidden the Suez Canal from German bombers by the use of a dazzle technique that may have confused the pilots but won no hearts in the universities. There, often, good deeds gain no laurels, only published words shaped in proper style. Deception had very little to offer, being undesirable as policy, irrelevant to major issues, marginal to the major disciplines, and requiring, to date, the unfashionable methodologies of the historian. Whaley and his few scattered friends seemed to be hobbyists, but no worse for that.

It was, thus, not so much that Whaley was working in a fallow, academic vineyard as that he had focused on a subject seemingly without analytical merit. No one, or rather no one important, saw the importance, anymore than anyone could imagine why a major scholar would seek a career investigating the literary merit of children's book–blurbs or the evolution of elite newspaper formats. There might be something there for the cunning mind, but not much, and only as a single exercise. A case might be made to study the intelligence community, although none had, but not really to study deception. It was consequently with some surprise that while between wars I received a telephone call from Whaley indicating that someone in the Washington think-tank world not only had some money to spend on deception–a crucial factor to those analysts who wander the fringes of legitimate academia–but also wanted to assemble a panel of specialists. For the first time in a decade of concern, someone had shown serious interest in Whaley's field, in his barren little acre.

Just how barren that acre was became clear when I was approached to be a member of the panel. All my revolutionary friends were assumed to be devious as well as dreadful, and, hence, as chronicler of revolts I, too, was assumed to be intimate with deceit. Experts have been created with fewer credentials, although not often,

I had at least kept up with deception for a decade, which simply meant that I talked about Whaley's enthusiasm when our paths crossed. So, emboldened by ignorance and curiosity, tempted by Washington, and lured by Whaley's enthusiasm, I agreed to be a deception specialist.

Although all was not clear at the time, apparently Mathtech, a subsidiary of the prestigious and arcane Mathematica, had acquired a contract to investigate deception. Neither Mathematica nor Mathtech had deception specialists, much less a deception program, but then who did? In November 1976, there had been a Deception Workshop in New York City that attracted a variety of individuals from the defense-research establishment, with a scattering of academics as well as the professional magician James Randi. The conference touched on all sorts of practice, from polygraphs to problems in computer simulation. Then, apparently, deception had disappeared from everyone's agenda until the Mathtech project started up. While literally billions of dollars had been spent by the government on technological deception, hiding missiles, tanks, and submarines, nothing had gone to social science work. In a very small way, Mathtech was to find out what could be discovered in this direction.

The Mathtech people had early on tracked down Whaley in Cambridge. In turn, Whaley added me to the panel, which included a sampling of the intelligence community, retired, a specialist in the Middle East from Harvard, the assigned Mathtech people, and a representative from the patron agency. The Mathtech contract was not, surprisingly, with CIA; the involved specialists would work as consultants for Mathtech. The arrangements in such matters were novel to me but were quite conventional and appeared academically reasonable. In order to protect unintentional leakage, but mostly to make the government happy, all those involved had to have appropriate security clearances. Both the process of our investigation and our results were, however, open and unclassified. This was often the arrangement for those who migrated between Washington and academia, filling the Eastern shuttle and, later, the pages of academic journals.

The only peculiarity for me was the need to be security cleared. For the others this caused no great problem—several had clearances and except for one or two of the academics the remainder had merely to be brought up to date. Since I had spent the major part of my grownup life associating with gunmen, terrorists, and active revolutionaries in some of the least savory parts of the globe, my career required an extra effort. The clearance problem postponed my advent in Washington as a fully classified expert for some time.

Still, time moved along. The troubles in Ireland and Lebanon continued. There was terror in the cities of Italy and Germany. I was in and out of more wars, unwittingly involved in various deceptions. Eventually, my clearance came and the panel met and found that no one, except Whaley, knew very much about deception. This had not kept Mathtech and Whaley, who knew the most, from producing several small studies on aspects of deception. Still Whaley felt, and I agreed, that, perhaps, a small typology of the subject might be useful, and might even be essential if we were to talk about deception at all. Mathtech agreed.

The two of us decided to do the typology of deception in Dublin, where I intended to spend the summer of 1979 attending, still again, to the Irish Troubles. This meant associating with subversives—my old friends, gunmen active and retired. A little analytical thinking between interviews appeared appealing, so Whaley and I spent the summer in Ireland involved in deception, one way or another. Arriving with a blank mind on deception matters, I became fascinated with the subject. Were there categories of deception, general steps in the deception process, and ways to evaluate results across time and in different modes? What, indeed, was deception: card tricks, false eyelashes, practical jokes, military maneuvers, delusions of grandeur, a fake punt in football, a clown suit, a while lie, any lie? In a sense, we began at the beginning, an exercise enormously rare in an analytical world often crowded with models and theories. In deception matters, however, no one had thought to extend social science methods to the subject. Perhaps this was for good reason; perhaps it was not worthwhile to be serious about the subject. My interest was captured in any case, thinking about such matters made a pleasant change from sitting in nasty places talking to those who possessed the absolute truth and smelled slightly of cordite. My life was beginning to smell slightly of cordite, and, hence, categories and models were very welcome.

What evolved we called *The Dublin Papers*, one on the structure of deception and the second on the process. Just as Whaley had always suspected, only magicians had bothered to examine the nature of deception. Analysts had rarely written on the matter and then only as historians. Others, the deception planners, had been more concerned with the effect than detailing the method or the varieties of means. And, understandably, magicians, when they published at all, had a rather narrow scope, an arcane language, and a reputation that would prove counterproductive in the world of the academic mandarins and social science analysts.

The most important examples, then, were mostly to be found in military applications, in which, to a large degree, the Western cultural distaste for cheating was overcome by the perceived need for national survival: All was fair in war. There, in one form or another, the practitioners, many in every way brilliant, recognized that deception was largely divided into hiding the truth or showing the false even if both qualities were always present. We took matters further along, finding other categories and various stages. The summer was fascinating, since once our attention was focused on the phenomena endless examples and curiosities emerged. For the two of us deception might not have evolved into a science, but for two months it certainly became a consuming interest. Whaley had at last found not only a use for his massive, accumulated data, but also someone as concerned as he was.

Once we were back in Washington, Mathtech was still interested, but not very. The project directors were mostly concerned with tidying up details, instead of pursuing a general theory of deception and further research. Other priorities began to appear for me and the major interests of my new International Analysis Center were elsewhere, although deception remained a prospect. In turn, Mathtech found that the intelligence community had seemingly lost interest in the subject. Why, after years of neglect in the public domain in any case, there had been any interest by the covert world in the first place was never made clear. Anyway, the only deception patron was about to withdraw. Apparently, the money for next year would go into projects dealing with hard imagery. There would be no more money spent for theory or social science analysis or, more to the point, for the Whaley-Bell-through-Mathtech work. Very little money had actually been spent and so we assumed there would be other money about other patrons. The ending of funding for social science research at the very moment that results seemed to be coming through was, we thought, a momentary matter, an oversight soon corrected. Times were changing in Washington, but not quite in the way we assumed.

Election years are special, especially in Washington. Seemingly, for a year before the event nothing can be done. Since the campaign may take a year, this often appears to mean that no one wants to make an unnecessary decision between the first stirring of the candidates in midterm and the great decision in November. After the election, there is a long pause while the administrators settle into office, find the key to the restroom, and fill out forms. Sometimes it seems that Washington only works ever so briefly for a few months in midterm. In the case of President Jimmy Carter, the election pause was certainly more pronounced. This was, first, because his likely opponent, Governor Ronald Reagan, appeared to be a winner and one likely to dismantle everything that came before. Second, the Iran hostage crisis had left the President isolated in the White House and put everything else on hold. In 1980, very little seemed to happen; certainly no one rushed to fund deception research.

With the election of Reagan in November, however, much, if not everything, seemed likely to change, for here was a president who, in his concern with countering the plots and plans of the evil Russian empire, would surely favor an investigation of lying, cheating, and stealing. Perhaps all might not even be fair, or at least a little tactical deception might be considered, if not adopted, in a potential anti-Communist crusade. Some policies might be unfair. Even if this were not the case surely his administration, straight-arrow or not would want to counter Soviet deception. The hawk Republicans would want to oppose Communist lying, cheating, and stealing with the tools of counterdeception. Who would be better to help in matters of counterdeception than Whaley and Bell? Wrong again. When Reagan said he opposed big government, he seemingly meant any government at all. For the first time in a generation, we had a president who did not want to play with the empire, who was in no rush to nominate many key national-security players. When those vital assistant secretaries and deputy assistant secretaries, who actually run the government—and, more to the point, arrange contracts—were appointed at last, they were often ideologically sound but administratively innocent and almost always unknown. They were new. They were suspicious. They proved especially suspicious of plans to spend government money and thus extend government power.

Reaganite Washington in 1981 was a very different arena, and the new players wore no numbers, took no names, and knew a new truth. Of course, neither Whaley nor I knew very many of the old players, nor the rules of the contract game, nor how to go about learning.

Apparently, we should have been retired flag-rank officers who had spent a decade circling the Beltway around Washington, buying drinks in motel bars, and making good buddies. Now it was too late for old academic dogs to learn new tricks or the new names. Our old academic patrons had always shown marginal interest in international-relations projects with policy implications, and were still not at all interested in deception as a subject. The only likely consumer remained the federal government. Now, no one could find the government, and when an appropriate administrative ideologue could be discovered there was no interest in spending taxpayer money.

The "government" was, of course, enormous, filled with brilliant people who often expressed analytical interest in deception but seemingly always lacked access to funds. The administrators, the new and especially the old, were also used to dealing with familiar people and with the conventional, especially in matters of money. There was no place that we approached in the great bureaucracy that revealed someone with a perceived need for work on deception. Deception might be a wonderful subject, but no one felt a need to examine it. A basic Washington rule was that without a perceived need, there would be no money, however trifling the sum.

To make matters more complicated, deception seemingly should have been an obvious area of interest for many. In the State Department, there was rarely any money forthcoming for research in any depth. The agency had already opted out. The Pentagon would spend great sums to thwart the Reds, but not on the likes of us. Surely, elsewhere in the intelligence community, there might have been interest, but there was not. Everywhere we tended to find glazed eyes, which might have indicated only that all this had been done long ago and classified, or else that nothing had been done and so nothing could be admitted. We did not despair. After all, someone had sold LSD and others psychic research and laser beams and reports on rare poisons or ground-nut schemes had found patrons.

Deception proposals that thus should have been of interest proven barren, at least for Bell and Whaley. Perhaps we were not expert enough. Perhaps deception was of prime interest to someone but we could not be told. In fact, this problem reappeared again and again as we wandered the corridors of power's agents. Our product, deception research, might well be all sewn up between classified covers. The deception conference in New York back in 1976 had, indeed, indicated that scattered through the government were at least a few concerned with deception, but in 1980 and 1981 we could find no public hint of ongoing deception research. No one would tell us anything. Perhaps there was not much to tell. Certainly outside of the government no one was interested, and no one who came out of the government into the world of academic analysis showed evidence of any exposure to the subject. Therefore, we were left without even winks and nods to sell what might already have been bought to those whom we knew not, and who neither knew us nor cared for the product.

Long ago in Dublin, while we were hot on the trail of theory, all had seemed easy. We had been deceived. In retrospect, our blundering through the bureaucracy did not help the cause of deception research. Perhaps nothing could have done so, since America abhors authorized cheating. Yet we tried, and persevered for what we felt to be a good cause.

At DARPA, the Defense Department's research branch, in which most in-house scholars and administrators tend to think in numbers, charts, and graphs, the distance between our concerns and the real world of contractors was apparent even to us. Although it was not then of public concern, any sensible person would have recognized that deception in space would have a real-world role, would fall within the purview of national security policy, and would be, in part, a DARPA matter. There, deep within the Pentagon, we found a significantly placed bureaucrat who expressed an interest in the problems of deception in space. The problem from DARPA's point of view, we were told, was that space was so big, empty, and visible that, surely, deception would face awesome technical problems, i.e., need diodes in untold numbers and in complex configurations. I suggested that since a magician could hide an elephant on stage in full view of an audience, in theory, at least, there should be little serious problem in hiding things in space or, if the proper theory could be deployed, in finding them in all that empty space. Apparently, not since Hannibal had elephants been a consideration within defense bureaucracies, and our argument was not simply ignored but disdained.

Generally, no matter where we went within the government, the response tended to be the same: (1) if deception were a good idea, we would have done it and (2) if deception research has been overlooked and is needed, we will do it ourselves. The one crucial factor that might have overridden these basic and not unreasonable principles remained. No one we contacted felt a need for such work.

Mostly, it appeared that the government tended to turn to external analysis for a variety of purposes. Often a need was felt to be on record, to show interest, to have, by contract, acquired bits of paper in case questions arose. To the cynical eye some contracts seemed to be rewards for past service, golden handshakes for old appointees or those recently retired, or simply ways to maintain contacts with friendly contractors and even to keep those contractors in business in case of need. Occasionally, there was an instant need, the pressure of an unforeseen crisis that required the work of specialists not on the government payroll. Sometimes these experts created themselves to fill the demand, cobbling together an instant capacity. Sometimes the expert was real, but had been previously an unmarketable esoteric focus on Shi'ite Moslems, the Bulgarian Communist Party, or the atmospheric implication of nuclear explosions.

Mostly and properly, the bureaucrats were content with their internal capacities. After all, they had good people, the enormous physical and intellectual resources of the government, and a steady stream of classified documents to read. External aid and comfort was seldom necessary except to go on record or, every so rarely, to fill unforeseen gaps. "Deception" need not be put on record and was not considered an emergency need. Moreover, it was a curious subject.

Americans, individually and collectively, dislike to resort to deception, except in military matters or to maintain the secrets of the national security apparatus. Even a theoretical study of deception was seemingly risky and, for many, unsavory. Deception also seemed to fall within the area of the intelligence establishment, in which everything worth knowing was classified. How could external research cope without a steady flow of top secrets? Thus, our subject was curious, unsavory, dubious, and classified. Worse, it engendered no interest.

Our complaints, justified or not, were not going to change matters, so we accepted that the bureaucrats would remain tied to their immediate focus, and suspicious of speculation and speculative research. This was true when the research was especially without promise of immediate practical return, and funding it carried the risk of being caught out supporting unsavory, un-American research. Thus, the bureaucracies would not be patrons at all unless mattered shifted.

If the inherent nature of government-sponsored research made life difficult for the aberrant, then conventional academic support was all but impossible. At all times, foundation money was difficult to raise, since so many academics sought this limited funding. (By the Reagan years there was very little academic money in any case.) The foundations also had a tendency to suspect projects that appeared to have a policy input unless they involved doing visible good in the Third World. Seemingly, the government should pay for government matters, a perspective shared by the Reagan appointees who did not feel that funding deception research was their proper responsibility. Like the government, the foundations funded what they knew. They seemed content to underwrite more studies of NATO force levels, reviews of deterrence in nuclear matters, and further looks at a new economic policy.

Beyond the foundations, the normal academic response remained normal and academic. Deception did not fit in the appropriate divisional categories, had no major figure or department as champion, could hardly be approached with appropriate methodologies, and might well bring the contamination of the real world into the groves of academe. This was fair and true. The unconventional have a difficult time in academia because an academy is by nature conservative, attracting the conventional and structured for standardized achievement that is easily judged and easily taught.

One exception was Tom Schelling who had, as a Yale economist, applied game theory coupled with wry humor and vast insight to international behavior (bargaining among nations with poorly understood rules), and presented academics with what they truly love–a new methodology. This meant that many had a new means they could use to address their own analytical problems. So Schelling ended up admired and respected at Harvard, justly so. However, he was neither fish nor fowl, only famous and useful.

Whaley and Bell were not Schelling, had no new methodology to offer, were involved with a fishy subject, and did not have a base at Yale. In the past, when money in the relevant areas was available, academic barons could sponsor their own projects but there was less money and little interest available to us. There was no room at the academic inn, nor, from the first, any real reason to suppose that there would or should be.

A government uninterested, publicly at least, in deception was a bit of a surprise, but an academic world concerned with purely academic matters was not. Our concerns were considered academic, and our reputations were not judged sufficient to impose our interest on institutional priorities. We were interesting but marginal academic figures without tenure or real prospects, nice to have about the house but not likely to blossom as late stars. So what was next?

There was always the unpleasant fact to consider–our problem might not have been the nature of existing institutions nor their priorities and agendas, but rather that deception was not worth researching or, worse, that we were not sufficiently competent to do it. We did not have and never had access to classified material, making us less appealing to the government and, as academics we were merely untenured research scholars adrift on a marginal enthusiasm. Whaley, a deception buff, and Bell, a gunman fancier, neither of them serious nor a stayer, might themselves be the cause of the lack of concern in all quarters.

This possibility, of course, had to be ignored. We preferred to consider our investigation too unconventional and our careers simply too irregular for the orthodox: Self-deception in our theory, and in most practices, lies outside the scope of our investigation. Thus, it seemed not unreasonable, like my revolutionary friends who, whatever else, had learned to persevere, for us to wander Washington preaching the gospel of deception research. We might yet win, though, by deploying a guerrilla strategy of persistence, undertaking a campaign of attrition. Such a protracted war requires not only determination but money, so we came full circle again.

Within Washington, there are a constant round of seminars, conferences, meetings, and analytical square dances crafted for various purposes: to make money, to lobby a cause, to find a patron, to expose the truth or reveal evil, to further careers, or to sell a program, a candidate, an institution, or an idea. There is always a forum to spread the word, whatever the word. There is always a conclave driven by a hidden agenda. We went on the road, or around the beltway, or whatever, to pursue deception funding.

Mostly the audiences seemed interested. Cheating on a grand scale has a certain attraction. I spoke in smoke-filled rooms of retired flag officers, to rows and rows of defense contractors and middle-rank government administrators, to academics, and even to most of the patrons of Nathan's Saloon in Georgetown. I was asked to lecture to an interested group of government people by a new enthusiast and was picked up, driven to a nondescript glass office building somewhere in northern Virginia (much of northern Virginia is filled with nondescript glass buildings housing God knows what), and spoke for hours to a collection of middle-aged men who, one suspected, had made a living by practicing what I was preaching. For all I know, they were shoe salesmen awaiting a new line, but, whatever they awaited, it was not a quick-fix lecture on the theory of deception, my line of the moment.

One of the more disheartening, if enlightening, forays occurred early on in the Reagan administration. For some months after the election, the city teemed with transition teams staffed by the ambitious and honored who, often with an axe, smoothed the way for the anticipated revolution. Some members hoped to stay in place after Reagan was in the White House, others, often mistakenly, knew that they would be retained. Once Reagan was in office, these transition groups existed briefly in limbo before being replaced by the regulars. At this stage, we ran into an old Harvard friend who had disappeared into an analytical black hole, (an elegant think tank in California). He now, unexpectedly had emerged as the *de facto* transition administrator of a small but significant part of the national security apparatus. Over drinks one Friday evening, he agreed that since deception was, indeed, important to his mission and we wanted very little money, arrangements would be made on the next Monday to fund our work. The weekend papers, however, indicated that his transition team had been disbanded, yea, even as we spoke, and the members dispatched back to their old desks. By the time we finished reading the bad news, he was deplaning on the West Coast, an unexpected event. Monday was a dim, dark day, and our proposal was now as transitory as the momentary administrator's hopes.

Our campaign gradually began to wind down as our limited list of contracts exhausted. We did find all sorts of interesting people and projects along the way, however. A personal favorite, hidden away in the Pentagon, was the National Warning staff, which was concerned with analyzing ways to avoid unpleasant surprises. Composed largely of people from other places, the group had existed for years–doing classified work, of course, so we had no way of telling how mutual our interests might be. It was a comfort to know that, even if disregarded, there were those specifically charged with protecting the policymakers from unpleasant and unexpected news, although if the powers-that-be took as long to find those analysts as we had, then they were still in for unpleasant surprises. For us, there *were* no more surprises.

We continued our search for deception-research patronage. There was a deputy assistant secretary who felt that much of the political establishment had been deceived by liberal claptrap, but who needed no aid on Soviet deception since this was a given. Why fund research that would only open Democratic eyes? Some other responses were very practical, more or less asking when we had last hidden a warship or advised on the camouflage. All in all, our journey through the defense bureaucracy proved fascinating, if not profitable. There was a whole world hidden in anonymous offices, often filled with very bright people indeed, engaged in long-term and serious research but without the elegance and recognition available in universities. Often their work focused on the margins of defense concerns. Such focuses may well, then and now, have included deception; if so, the efforts were and remain classified. The suspicion remains that this probably was not the case. There were all sorts of good bureaucratic arguments against such work.

Most interesting of all was the establishment's feeling that deception was not an appropriate tool—not simply that it was politically unwise to be caught investigating deception and thereby, perhaps, advocating it, but that truth was an American weapon and the contemplation of deception might well endanger national interests. There was thus some expressed and serious concern with counterdeception. This concern became our second option, once the penny had dropped on the probable fate of our deception projects. Even then, the concept that work was needed to counter deception attracted no takers. Comforting to us as citizens, if less so as researchers, was this persistent, universal distaste for lying and cheating in the nation's name.

Years later, "Irangate" would illustrate that however seductive the idea of lying for the public good may be, the American public prefers truth in governance. The Iran-Contra affair also showed how poorly Americans manage deception. Officials had trouble practicing duplicity. Americans would have preferred open covenants, openly arrived at. Americans suspect the covert; even hard-core anti-Communists want to expose, not to deploy, deception. Obviously, in our search for funding, we were not simultaneously engaged in survey research on national attitudes. Still and all, the impression created, then and later, was that Americans within the defense establishment were loath to fund our research because in some serious degree it was un-American, counterproductive, and a tool of undesirables, as well as having no practical utility, since truth was the best strategy.

There were surely those in Washington who might advocate deception but, alas, they felt no need for theory. There might even have been a disinterested concern with theories of deception hidden away. It might simply be, therefore, that we had missed the one waiting patron or that more capable and connected researchers would have found a haven. The immediate reality for us, however, was that there would be no governmental aid and comfort. The tour through the world of the Beltway had, in the end, proved as futile as forays into the formal government. No one wanted our orphan.

Reluctant to give up entirely on such matters, we decided on an alternative strategy. We might well reach the desired audience by a side entrance, fashioning our work into a more popular mode that could be read seriously by the serious and for amusement by most. We could write a popular book on *How To Cheat*, incorporating the *Dublin Papers* and many of the examples that Whaley had been collecting in massive numbers over the years. In order to protect the guilty authors' tattered academic credentials, we decided to deceive the readers, if not our friends, and publish under the name of J. Barton Bowyer. My editor, Tom Dunne at St. Martin's in New York, felt that the idea had merit, if not the actual promise of a bestseller. He was willing to offer a small advance, considerable enthusiasm, and a free hand. Thus, while I was again attending foreign wars for some months, Whaley collected himself and arranged his examples in chapters so that when I returned I could add bits and pieces. We thus produced, not without contention, the book. If nothing more, we decided that collaboration was probably not worth the hassle as each of us was deprived of his most cunning contributions, each style cancelled the other, and we each became a reluctant compromiser for the greater good.

In the meantime Dunne had discovered, just as we had at the Pentagon, that cheating and deception were un-American. One of the largest bookstore chains would not carry a book entitled *How to Cheat*. Still, this might indicate that the American public would gobble up an illicit subject. The book chain said, "no." We pointed out that there had been a volume entitled *Steal This Book*. The book chain said, "no." We were thereafter working on a book called *Cheating*. In time we had finished using our old typology and curious examples, plus such idiosyncrasies as oddly numbered pages to deceive the unwary reader and cartoon illustrations. No effort was spared. Dunne felt that either the book would sell well or not at all. He was not quite right, but he was nearly so.

The work did not disappear without a trace, for it was generously, even widely, reviewed. Mostly it was considered an amusement that some reviewers found marred on occasion by academic intrusions–the average reviewer often found all the neat names in our typology academic in tone (a blow to our cunning)–but worthy. Academics were not amused by the humor. There was no rush to buy. The potential readers remained largely illusory. Insufficient purchases led to the conclusion that impulse buying did not extend to cheating. We did get one letter demanding a refund for overpayment given that our page numeration had cheated him, a sly by-product that subsequent editors removed for fear of more serious results.

Other than the brief post-publication flurry of interest, there was little visible result. In fact, outside our narrow circle of deception buffs, old friends, and close relatives, there was only one serious response to the work. *Cheating* came out as *La meravigliosa arte dell'inganno* in Italian, a quite unexpected occurrence that led, if nothing else, to a publicity descent on Rome for me and my Irish wife Nora. My impression was that while deception research in Italy might be little different from that in America, cheating as an aspect of the human condition fit more comfortably into society there than it did in America. Still, there was no time for cross-national reflections, since the Rome venture was simply the last hurrah for our joint deception work.

Whaley discovered some people at Monterey who were concerned with strategic deception and he soon moved to the West Coast in pursuit of aid and comfort. If there was not a rising concern with the subject of deception on either coast, at least the more general area of intelligence had begun to be considered as a proper field of study. Academic journals appeared, panels at conferences met, and books and anthologies were published, including one by the Monterey people entirely on deception. In the meantime Whaley had published both an article and a book on Nazi Germany's rearmament–a wonderful case of strategically hiding the truth and showing the false while the watching world thought the reverse was occurring. The fact that the Whaley book was included in a Foreign Intelligence Book Series indicated the process of normalization: Intelligence was proper. Frank Barnett's National Strategy Information Center sponsored a series of anthologies on intelligence that included deception segments as a matter of course. Intelligence as a subject had become proper and academic. The uses and misuses of intelligence, the structure of such services, the impact of perception on judgment and analysis, and the failures and surprises all generated a substantial intelligence literature often included under my traditional category titles. Deception remained on the margins.

In the decade after the New York deception conference in 1976 and a RAND report by Herbert Goldhamer (*Reality and Belief in Military Affairs*, commissioned by Andrew Marshall at the Pentagon's Office of Net Assessment, finished as a first draft in June 1977), very little theoretical work had been done, even though the subject was becoming, if not more popular, at least more proper. Most studies were either focused on the nature of Soviet deception or on case studies. Everyone seemed to assume that the process was understood or irrelevant to their own analytical interests. Thus, a whole literature on surprise, especially surprise military attacks, evolved without addressing the proposition that surprise was nothing more than a stage in the deception process. Theorists list kinds of surprise, but ignore the secondary nature of the phenomena; they have not moved up a generalizational level to deception. In Ariel

Levite's *Intelligence and Strategic Surprise* (New York, Columbia University Press, 1987) there is an extensive bibliography of works that, in title and often in subject, focus on deception, although usually on a single example of interest for nontheoretical reasons or a facet of the subject in general. Most contemporary analysts are not interested in the nature of deception, but only in the implications for their particular policy recommendation, or in the reasons that particular institutional responses are flawed, or on the strategic implications of the process. Their prime focus is on the players and their policies, not the process.

An enormous amount of rich and rigorous work has been done. There has been a special interest in deception during World War II, in Soviet deception, and in deception within the intelligence community. One of the key scholars has been Professor Michael Handel, at Harvard in the old days, currently a professor at the United States Army War College in Carlisle who has edited or written a recent collection of books on such matters, including several published by Frank Cass in London: *Intelligence and Military Operations* (1989), *Leaders and Intelligence* (1989), *Strategic and Operational Deception in the Second World War* (1988), and *War, Strategy and Intelligence* (1988). He is also co-editor, with Christopher Andrew of Corpus Christi College at Cambridge, of *Intelligence and National Security*. This, along with Reese Brown's *International Journal of Intelligence and Counterintelligence*, indicates the gradual institutionalization of the subject as an appropriate field.

In fact, as the Eighties closed there was a growing set of works entitled in some way "deception," but neither further theoretical work nor as far as Whaley and I can determine, serious theoretical comment on his article in the March 1982 special issue of *The Journal of Strategic Studies* on military deception and strategic surprise that built on the original work in Dublin. New work like *The*

Art of Deception in Warfare (London, David and Charles, 1989) by Michael Dewar, formerly of the British army and now with the International Institute of Strategic Studies in London, tend to quote the Whaley article, but are still content to start off with an ad hoc introductory chapter of middle categories and unanalyzed processes.

Everyone seems in a hurry to get beyond the assumed agreed generalities into the specific. Mostly those who address deception at any length are those technicians concerned with narrow, if fascinating, military applications, readers of intelligence anecdotes, and those who look with deep suspicion on Soviet intentions and actions. It is a mix of fans, buffs, and ideologues.

The serious people seem to remain focused on perception and foreign policy, or perception and politics, as well they should, for there lurks the real power to act on events. Deception is interesting to them because the practitioners manipulate perceptions to policy ends, a subject far easier to address than self-deception, and a subject far more important in the analysis of great events.

In matters of deception, however, there are rational planning, specific maneuvers and results that can be weighted and measured–self-deception probably plays no greater role (unless factored in by the deception planner) than it does in any other human activity. Thus, the target's hope to get something for nothing becomes an axiom of deception–planning for the con man rather than an ill-defined psychological quirk of the victim. Reading the victim, whether as in Hitler's analysis of Stalin or the three-card-Monte player's weighing of his audience, is a reasoned and explicable act, far more accessible than a probe into the delusions of the deluded. Deception should be, but is not, a more amenable subject of investigation; it is not divorced from either power or great events. No matter; perception and misperception have their advocates and explainers, which, at present, deception lacks.

Thus, more than ten years after the genesis of *Cheating*, in matters of deception the state of the art has been little advanced even though there is growing interest in the subject, at least in contrast to the early years. With the expansion of scholarly interest to intelligence matters, other facets of deception have come under scrutiny, although most strategic analysis has remained directed at surprise, especially but not entirely military surprise, especially, but not limited to, the Israeli experience. A sign of the times was the study made by Professor Robert Jervis of the Institute of War and Peace Studies at Columbia University, who has fashioned a brilliant career on studies of perception in international relations, which analyzed the CIA's failure to grasp the nature of events in Iran during the last days of the Shah. The American intelligence community, and so the administration, was most unpleasantly surprised.

The Iranian Shi'ites had their own delusions. They, like a great many of those who believe they possess the absolute truth, seldom sought to deceive their prospective victims as to their ultimate intentions. Washington was deceived by unchallenged assumptions and procedures rather than by a ruse. Global deception by those few individuals or governments that have the capacity to act, like Hitler and Stalin, is actually rare although strategic deception, as when Germany hid the planned invasion of Russia, Operation Barbarossa (see here Whaley's landmark study of that deception ruse published by MIT Press, 1973), is common.

Thus, a second emerging strand of investigation, as noted, has been woven by very committed Western conservative scholars and their allies around Soviet deception. The Soviets have none of the Western hesitation about the deception, but are compulsively secretive (note *Soviet Secrecy and Non-Secrecy*, edited by Raymond Hutchings for Barnes and Noble, 1987) thus making investigation difficult. Soviet deception has, during the Reagan years, inspired several, mostly polemic, books; it has generated a more general concern for the concept. There is, then, at present, an ocean of interest for deception work to swim about in that did not seem to exist when we went off to work on Mathtech's project. Most of those concerned, however, have indicated specific rather than general interest. No one yet has focused on the nature of the currents, the process of deceiving, how cheating is everywhere done. For it *is* everywhere done.

Acknowledgments

IT MAY WELL BE that this small growth in analytical interest attracted the attention of the ever-perceptive Irving Louis Horowitz at Transaction Publishers when he urged republication, almost without modification, of the original *Cheating*. I have my doubts, however, for it is more likely that his taste is universal and includes the marginal and esoteric as long as it is sound academically. Still there have been solid, not to say massive, volumes written on bribery and lying, giving insights into the nature of man and society, so why not cheating? Certainly, unlike lying, an aspect of deception, or bribery, a special if ubiquitous case, deception is a more important aspect of the human comedy. That is why, of course, the reader will find all sorts of examples, from love to money, even if, in truth, the authors are really only concerned with policy matters, politics, and wars and rumors of wars-the stuff of analysis. This need not dissuade the lay reader, beloved of authors all, since part of the fascination of deception is that cases may everywhere be found.

I keep a file of examples selected from comics, solely, I suspect to mail off to Whaley, who, in residence again in California, handles West Coast deception. Who else still would care? In any case, Professor Horowitz has taken the risk, and *Cheating*, transformed once again, still lives as *Cheating and Deception*. His conclusion has been that our venture into both humor and trade publications was ill advised, and that our despair of analytical and academic interest was premature and shortsighted and that our *Cheating*, from the first, should have had an appropriate tone and serious publisher. There is no reason to suppose him wrong. So we all agreed to go into Transaction paperback.

Deception research may best be served by appearing within Transaction covers rather than emerging as government policy or as an analytical hot topic. It is comforting to know that in an era of egotism and cynicism those in power within and outside of the government, the Reagan government, regarded deception as unacceptable. Perhaps other, more qualified or better connected analysts might have found a patron in Washington, but I doubt it. Cheating and deception thus have remained until very recently a minority interest, a field for buffs and fans, clippers and pasters of examples. One of the few and early interested scholars, Professor Marcello Truzzi of Eastern Michigan University, an expert on the bizarre, threatens to produce a newsletter. Surely, this is often the last resort of the microspecialist, but it is yet an eventuality that all deception mavens anticipate with delight.

All the deceptions research veterans hope that the new and rising analytical interest will flourish. Perhaps the times are really changing and Transaction Publishers and Professor Irving Louis Horowitz have roles to play. So everyone–authors, publisher, and editors–hopes that the text will both enlighten and perhaps even amuse. The authors, especially and despite all, somehow continue to keep the faith and believe that out of sight over the horizon someone, someplace has a perceived need for work on deception, will find our credentials adequate or will find someone else's attractive, and will underwrite a theoretical analysis of deception – serious stuff. In this, however, we may well be entering the analytically forbidden arena of self-deception. Quite another matter, quite another book.

J. Bowyer Bell
New York, New York

Preface

♦ ♦ ♦

I did send for thee to tutor
thee in stratagems . . . .

—SHAKESPEARE, *Henry VI*

"STRATAGEM" does not sound too dire; but "cheating," although much the same thing, has a bad reputation. Few enjoy being cheated, duped, or swindled, although the odd surprise is usually acceptable, even—especially—at the hands of Houdini. Cheating is, of course, an aspect of deception and deception is a significant part of all human behavior. Yet "cheating" is little understood and rarely studied. Some know how to cheat successfully at cards, considerably more how to cheat on their spouse, and lying—white or black—is all but universal. At least in the field of military-diplomatic deception, some experts recognize that basic principles and procedures may be involved; but investigation has been scanty, as neither soldiers nor scholars like to admit to funding cheating (some sort of violation of the Judeo-Christian or Protestant ethic, it is to be assumed). Deception is *unfair*—note President Jimmy Carter's outraged indignation at the Russian invasion

of Afghanistan and a whole American generation's searing
memory of the Japanese *sneak* attack on Pearl Harbor on December 7, 1941. Deception is un-American, even when the
advantages of cheating are patent. So it appeared that it was
time to take the deception skeleton out of the closet and display to a broader public the nature of cheating, if even for no
other reason than to create in the totally honorable a mind
prepared to counter deception—for after the fact, counsel is of
no value.

Tom Dunne of St. Martin's, who over the years has tolerated an inordinately large number of splendid book ideas [for
scripts that flowered over the first martini only to wilt and die
by the last brandy] this time felt that *Cheating* had a future.
Of course, he insisted that there must be no cheating, that the
reader must *really* learn how to cheat. This seemed fair
enough. Unfortunately for that year's potential cheaters, a
highly theoretical work on deception modeling took prece-
dence, resulting after months of Irish contemplation in *The
Dublin Papers,* which form the structural basis of this book.
Thus, while *Cheating* is a popular excursion through human
nature's back alleys, a very real and most elegant map does
exist.

In the course of tracing this map of deceit, a considerable
amount of honorable aid and comfort has been proffered,
wittingly or no, by a great many persons of every ilk: Dr.
J. Bowyer Bell, theorist of deception; Major Ladislav Bittman, former deputy director of the department of disinformation, ministry of the interior, Prague, Czechoslovakia; Nora
Browne of the Kingdom of Kerry; Maureen Browne of the
Donnybrook/Ballybunion Brownes; Jeffrey W. Busby, Oak-
land, California, a magician's magician; Dr. Richard N.
Christie, professor of psychology, Columbia University, inventor of the Mach(iavellian) test; Mrs. Megan Clark Sweet,

proprietor of the no name bar, Inc., Sausalito, California, and astute realist; Cedric Clute, former manager of the Magic Cellar, San Francisco, California; General Moshe Dayan; Dr. A. George Gitter, professor of social psychology, Boston University, authority on hypocrisy and deceptive body language; Alec Guinness; General Yehoshafat Harkabi, former director of military intelligence, Israeli army; Ms. Sara Harned, Sausalito, California, bridge and poker buff; Dr. William R. Harris, the RAND Corporation, Santa Monica, California, coiner of the word *counterdeception;* Jasper Johns, New York, New York, of symbols, flags, and the bronze beer can; Dr. R. V. Jones, World War II deception planner for the RAF bomber command; Dr. Amrom H. Katz, Los Angeles, practical joker and military deception expert; Michael Kelly, Nathan's Saloon, Georgetown, Washington, D.C., bartender and handicapper; The Honorable Henry Kissinger (retired); Ms. Delrae Gunderson, Washington, D.C., wise to the ways of clowns; the late Professor Harold Lasswell, who could always distinguish the woods from the trees; the late Professor Dan Lerner of MIT, a pioneer in the study of communications, and bon vivant; Dr. Barbara Levy, Phoenix, Arizona, clinical psychologist; President Abraham Lincoln, on the statistics of democratic deceit; Il Maestro Sigfrido Maovaz, Rome, Italy, who transmutes paint into marble and the like; Richard M. Mitchell, Detroit, Michigan, late master of the con; Ms. Clarellen Morrell, Sausalito, California, cocktail waitress and raconteur; Professor Ithiel de Sola Pool, MIT, Cambridge, Massachusetts, communication theoretician; Lewis Reich, Washington, D.C., lawyer and investigator of military deception; Dale C. Scott, Sausalito, California, sailor and gentleman; Pádraig Ó Snodaigh (and his collaborator, Oliver Snoddy), Dublin, Ireland; Eamon J. Timoney, New York, New York, former O/C Derry, Irish Republican Army; Ms.

Mary Walsh, Washington, D.C. and Dr. L. Daniel Maxim, patrons of deceit research; Dr. Barton Whaley, San Francisco, and elsewhere, father of the study of deception; General Eliahu Zeira, former director of military intelligence, Israeli army. There were as well a great many people who were of no help at all but that is another matter.

—JBB

no name bar, Sausalito, California
Pembroke Lane, Dublin 2, Ireland
Riggs Place N.W., Washington, D.C.
Nathan's Saloon, Georgetown, Washington, D.C.

Prologue

◆ ◆ ◆

IRATE GENTLEMAN: You're a fraud, a charlatan,
and a rogue, sir!

W. C. FIELDS: Ahhh—is that in my favor?

THE CHARLIE BROWNS of the world, and they are legion, without guile and yet hauntingly addicted to great expectations, seem destined, always, to encounter W. C. Fields in his various guises. They are perpetually deceived and invariably surprised and our hearts go out to them. And yet, our fondness for W. C. Fields as scoundrel—fraud, charlatan, and rogue—is undeniable. In much of real life and art, few who deceive become the hero of the moment. The hero must be heroic and is punished by one means or another if he falters. The true hero or heroine may be tempted and succumb but swiftly returns to the fold of the respectable: George Washington, hewn cherry tree to one side and ax behind his back, soon remorsefully confessed his unauthorized tree surgery. He could not tell a lie and neither should we. This great theme in Western history always deplores the cheat, the liar, the fraud and fake, and favors the true, the noble and good: the frontal joust over the surprise foray. Honesty is the preferred policy but not necessarily the best one.

Much cheating of the day-to-day, common variety, is inordinately dull: shortchanging at the checkout counter, padding the expense account, lying to small children, or peeking at examination papers. It is no more than background noise to the major movements in contemporary society, at best oil on roiled waters, at worst mean and rarely worth contemplation or analysis. Some cheating gives almost universal pleasure and is institutionalized and harmless: card tricks, sleight of hand, the whole spectrum of the magician. Some deception now seems so logical and necessary as not to count as cheating at all: wartime camouflage, the illuson of three-dimensional space in a two-dimensional painting, or trick plays in football. All such activity is and remains an aspect of deception, and cheating is deceitful, if nothing else.

Most writers deplore cheating in all its forms, from simple lies to grand strategic deceptions. They exclude, if they consider them at all, only those forms like magic tricks that are without malice. These moralists treat cheating as if it were something fit only for outlaws, criminals, or depraved tyrants—tyrants in war, politics, business, and even in personal relations. They imply that cheating is so deplorable that it is a defining characteristic of bad guys. Good guys, to their narrow way of thinking, should not cheat, *do* not cheat. In their romantic mythology, heroes and heroines are good and God-fearing, always truthful, patient in adversity, all but naive, impulsive, and often a bit dimwitted. They are the Noble Savage, Othello, Juliet, Horatio Alger, pious pilgrims all on the road to salvation without a map, often doomed by honesty from the start. Their opposite number, the villain, is evil and Godless, often satanic, a weaver of lies, quick to revenge, cynical, calculating, and always astute: Iago, not Othello. It is permitted to cheer the wise and clever pranksters such as Puck, Eulenspiegel and the Good Soldier Schweik; but it is not permitted to mistake them for models of personal behavior. Of course, alas, a great many splendid heroes, like George Washington, at one time or another cheated a bit, lied, stole and generally deceived those near them for good cause or bad. Benjamin Franklin busied himself in the patriotic forgery of "Black" propaganda against the Hessians; the young Thomas Jefferson and most if not all of America's splendid generals tended to sly indirection. Decent fellows, all, they recognized that there are two major motivations for cheating: there is no other option but disaster, or there is no other option that is so cost-effective. In the first case, why lose a battle if stealth will give victory? In the second, why lose soldiers if stealth will give swift and cheap victory? Even the defeated enemy, bested elegantly and quickly, may find that having been cheated saved lines.

The need to cheat arises out of the nature of power. Power is the ability to set priorities that may be economic, social, military, or political. In fact, political power is the ability to allocate priorities among these other forms of power. Power is based on brute force, threats of force, persuasion, authority, charisma, deception, or any combination of these. Two of these components of power stand in a peculiar relationship to each other, a reciprocal relationship in which one tends to balance the other. Plutarch expressed this by means of the symbols of the lion and the fox. If we lack the strength of the lion, we can make up for this deficiency by using the cunning of the fox. Machiavelli described this relationship in detail, emphasizing "force" versus "fraud." Hobbes agreed. The question is one of brute force versus dissembling, cunning, guile, fraud—in short, force versus deception.

The principle of force versus deception applies at all levels of human organization. It is as true of the relationships of individuals in small groups as it is of large orgzanizations or whole nations. Whenever one person or group has power over another, whether parent over child, husband over wife, teacher over pupil, employer over worker, master over slave, or tyrant over subject, their relationship is unevenly predictable. On the one hand, the child, worker, or subject is uncertain about the actions of its parent, employer, or tyrant, because the more powerful person always has the luxurious option of being arbitrary. On the other hand, all major actions (mainly reactions) of the weaker person in the relationship are highly predictable. The dominant person controls the punishments and rewards that enforce the obedience of the weaker. Exceptions can arise. Children will sometimes challenge the authority of their parent or teacher; employees occasionally change jobs; and slaves sometimes rebel. But these are only episodic exceptions.

The weak have only four options. They can run away or, in final desperation, escape into insanity or suicide. They may gamble all and openly rebel. They may submit abjectly.

Or they may cheat.

By cheating they adopt a strategy of deception to counterbalance brute strength and thereby gain leverage, giving them an "edge" and enhancing their freedom of action. By deceiving they make their own rules by lying, stealing, cheating. But to be caught out in a lie or fraud is to lose and at a cost. The wise deceiver, therefore, learns to use deception with suitable caution.

In theory few have as little power as the slave and hence as few options in the face of brute force. In the American pre-Civil War South, few slaves revolted and only some escaped to free states or for that matter into insanity or suicide. The only apparent options appeared submission or deceit. Most Blacks, by necessity, accepted their role as slaves, but such acceptance of this surface role was accompanied by a sustained individual and collective effort to carve out a rather large area of personal freedom within that larger role. The slaves' strategy, called "masking," involved projecting a false personality to deceive the masters. Most slaves deliberately feigned passivity, laziness, stupidity—the Sambo image. This largely successful strategy constitutes a type of passive resistance.

A far more complex—and far more aggressive—response to brute power began in Asia in the ninth century when simple "masking" evolved into centuries of intricate deception taught by Chinese political defectors who fled to Japan. Among the refugees were some monks who settled in villages and hills outside Kyoto and converted several local clans of commoners to their particular sect of Buddhism. As this faith was not tolerated by the official Japanese Shinto religion, government persecution began. These Buddhist converts became hunted men, and the original clans fled to the mountains. From this point on they began to practice various survival skills. As these techniques were honed and codified they came to be called collectively *ninjutsu*, literally "hiding-art," or "art of invisibility"; and the clans became known as the ninja ("hider").

Ninjutsu is one of Japan's martial arts, but it differs from all the others in that it was developed and practiced exclusively by the common ninja and not by the aristocratic samurai warrior class. As commoners with literally no family name to disgrace, the ninja had no use for the samurai's heroic ritual man-to-man duels. They pragmatically preferred to get the job of life and death done as effectively as possible. And, as deception is the most cost-effective way to survive or kill, that was their technique of choice.

Masters of concealment, ninjas *never* appeared outside their own clans without disguise—as priests, craftsmen, itinerant tradesmen, enemy soldiers, anything but what they were. Moreover, disguise extended beyond the mere donning of costume to careful mastery of the customs, gestures, postures, and jargon associated with the role. The ninja also mastered camouflage, blending with the night in black coveralls with all-black equipment or blending with the snow in white uniforms with white equipment. Motionless, they could melt into the landscape as just another tree stump or rock. Of necessity, the ninja were superb escape artists, hiding under floors, above ceilings, in wells, and in trees. They could remain submerged under water for hours by breathing through reeds. They could scale sheer cliffs and walls. Training began in early childhood and was physically far more arduous than that of any samurai.

For four centuries the ninja survived by pure deception in a hostile world. Then, beginning in the thirteenth century, they turned defense into attack and profitable attack at that. It was a period of civil war and the ninja simply rented themselves out as mercenaries to any warlord who would pay their high fees. The two very special services only they could or would supply were espionage and covert operations, particularly sabotage and assassination, services that the samurai disdained.

The ninja freely borrowed the weapons and techniques of the aristocratic martial arts *(bujutsu)*, particularly *kyujutsu* (the art of archery), *bojutsu* (the art of the staff), and *iaijutsu* (the art of the quick-draw sword). But these traditional weapons were adapted to lethal surprise. In addition they developed their own specialized weapons of stealth—darts, star-shaped throwing knives, brass knuckles, caltrops, daggers, dirks, rope ladders, and grappling hooks. Each ninja also knew how to make smoke bombs and prepare a variety of poisons.

The ninja guarded their secrets fiercely. They recruited few outsiders. If they were about to be captured, most committed suicide, which was logical, since the samurai's typical "straight" nondevious thinking led him to kill the hated ninja immediately on capture by the most terrible means—boiling alive or skinning to death. The samurai made no effort to use the ninja. The few ninja who tried to defect or turn traitor would be hunted down and killed with a Mafia-like vengeance by loyal ninja, often their own brothers or other close relatives.

Japan's reunification in 1638 brought two centuries of peace to the country and ended the ninja's value as mercenaries. The art of ninjutsu was banned. In a peaceful and more tolerant world the ninja clans had no further need to hide, and only a very few continued to teach and practice their art. Today there are only a handful of practicing ninja, and the old ways are relics, not a means of survival.

For the American slave, masking was a means to gain personal and social privacy, a secret world away from the master's eye. For the ninja, matters were more serious, for their array of ruses and techniques had to guarantee them survival in a hostile world—until those ruses and techniques became sufficiently valuable to be sold on an open if brutal market. What real choice did either group have but to cheat, to hide the real and to offer the false. What choice did the Jews of Europe have during the years of Adolf Hitler's Final Solution but to hide as did Anne Frank in an attic or to pretend to a false identity. What choice but to go gently into the ovens as most did, confused, unbelieving, incredulous. Some like those in the Warsaw Ghetto in 1943 did rebel, not in hopes of survival but as witnesses to institutionalized horror. Some few escaped into madness and suicide. For the survivors it was dissemble or die—and so they cheated the ovens.

Not all ruses are in response to such lethal and unpalatable alternatives, but for the deceiver the existing present may truly seem murderous. For many, the authoritarian systems of Eastern Europe are intolerable. Rather than stay, they climb the Berlin Wall at enormous risk, smuggle themselves in secret compartments, or hijack airplanes. Yet large portions of their private life are private, their employment is productive if not as rewarding as it might be in the West; if they eschew subversion or treason, there will be no concentration camps or death cells. They need not create an invisible society like the ninja or disappear into the attic like Anne Frank merely to survive. They must only accept the system. But for some this is beyond their capacity, such mere survival is a living death.

In Communist Poland one of these was Jerzy Kosinski, a young, rebellious intellectual. He constantly skirmished with the bureaucrats. He just could not, would not, accept the official Marxist-Leninist doctrine of a Communist state. He was twice suspended from state-controlled universities and threatened with expulsion. Nevertheless he used all his cleverness as a brilliant doctoral candidate in social psychology to rise to a regular teaching post. Meanwhile he planned his escape, one man alone against the power of the whole state bureaucracy. To get abroad on some official excuse, he would need prestigious sponsors. But he was not willing to endanger his family, friends, or colleagues by using them to further his scheme. As a prize-winning photographer he had access to certain government printing offices. From these he stole official stationery, rubber stamps, and seals and proceeded to create four entirely fictitious members of the prestigious Polish Academy of Sciences to act as his sponsors. If he had been caught, his tricks would have cost him fifteen years in prison. His four "sponsors" began an active correspondence with official bureaus, seeking permission for Kosinski to travel to the States for postgraduate study at an American research foundation, a fake foundation that he also had created on paper.

For two years the correspondence continued until, finally, the ponderous system authorized a passport. While waiting for his visa from the American Embassy, often no less ponderous a process, he carried in his pocket a cyanide capsule. He had decided that one way or another they would not be able to keep him in Poland against his will. For Kosinski Poland was intolerable. In 1957 the visa finally arrived, the passport allowed him across the frontier. On 20 December 1957, he arrived in New York City at the age of twenty-four with $2.80 in his pocket and a name to come. He began to write and became one of the most acclaimed new writers in his adopted country. The critics raved and the reading public made his books, *The Painted Bird, Being There, Cockpit, Passion Play* best sellers. These strange and shocking novels are by nature highly original artistic creations, but Kosinski considers the most creative act of his life to be the way he arranged his passage to the States, cheating the system with pure deception, presenting the guardians of the state with his cunningly false sponsors and foundations to hide his real intentions.

Deception, cheating the system, need not be a matter of life or death, a situation where only the sly survive. It need not even be the weapon of the weak, although it often is. It can be, rather, a means toward an end not easily achieved by brute force. In point of fact, leaving aside whether the serpent cheated Adam and Eve or Eve Adam, events difficult to date, the first recorded example of cheating occurred on or about 2500 BC in the Nile valley—and it was, as is so often the case, an act of greed. Now, Lake Nasser spreads beyond the Aswan Dam on the Upper Nile, drowning Nubia and many of the ancient temples. Since 1966 Beni Hasan has been under water and with it the first evidence of cheating. There on the wall of a forty-five-centuries-old burial chamber is a tomb painting that depicts the oldest known con game. The hieroglyphic text with the painting tells us the Egyptians called this the "up from under" trick. When modern con artists do it to separate a sucker from his money, they call it the shell game. When magicians perform it for your entertainment, they call it cups-and-balls. Whatever name it goes by, this wall proves it is a true classic.

Our sleight-of-hand man kneels on the left. He has just been seen to place a small object under one of the four cones. He has shuffled the cones about on the flat ground. The sucker on the right thinks he has followed this razzle-dazzle and the performer has taken care that he can just barely do so. The sucker points to the cone he thinks conceals the ball, and the performer is about to lift it. It will be empty.

The sucker can't win, not ever, unless the "nut man" lets him. And he will only do that as a come-on to entice larger bets. The reason why the ball is never under the chosen cup or the pea under the walnut shell is that it is not under any of the shells or cups. Not until the performer places it there, because the last time the sucker sees it is the last time it's there. The sleight-of-hand artist has "palmed" it the instant he seems to place the shell back over the pea. And it stays in his hand until the moment he chooses to seem to show it had been under one of the shells all the time.

Anyone who thinks this proves the hand is quicker than the eye is wrong but in good company. In fact, a prestidigitator doesn't even try to be fast. He depends instead on only two things. They are simple but require much practice and skill. First, he makes the sleight itself, the tricky hand manipulation, appear as natural as possible. Second, he uses the psychological principle of "misdirection" to distract your attention at the crucial moment.

Next time you are walking downtown and are lucky enough to find a shell game in progress on the sidewalk, stop awhile and watch. Or try to catch the similar three-card monte game, which is more popular nowadays because word has finally gotten around after forty-five centuries that the shell game is somehow rigged, although few know exactly how.

In the old shell game, in order to earn a small but dishonest profit, the con man has allowed the sucker to perceive that the pea has been hidden—and that he the sucker knows where—when in fact he is being presented with three equally empty shells. The shells, akin to Kosinski's "sponsors," hide the real—in this case the pea in the palm. The inevitable result for the ancient Egyptian or the chap on the corner of Broadway is a dishonest living, not as vital an aspiration as Kosinski's or Anne Frank's but still no small matter in the light of present brute economic forces.

Although deception is the last or at times even the first resort of the weak against the powerful, the latter also cheat as a means to control their enemies or their subjects or their allies. The powerful do not *have* to use deception because they have other powers, other means of control including naked coercive force. Generally, the greater the relative degree of naked power an individual has over others, the less he will tend to rely on deception. Why bother? When the striving General Bonaparte became the established Emperor Napoleon, he forgot his guileful and most successful use of armies and came to depend on the sheer force of his big battalions. It is generally true of individuals that the more force they command, the less they will resort to fraud. Conversely the weaker one's position is relative to others, the greater will be the real power gained by using guile. It is thus no wonder that the chroniclers of Western order, the artistic apologists for the Tudors or the Church or Industry have long urged stern morality, flaying the liar, the cheat, the rebel against conventional morality, perceived wisdom, or the System. Cheating is subversive. It is not playing the game. It defeats honest effort and decent men. And worst of all for the threatened, it works today just as it did in Beni Hasan all those years ago.

PART I

THE NATURE
OF DUPLICITY

CHAPTER 1

The Prevalence of Guile: The Ruses of War

♦ ♦ ♦

All warfare is based on deception.

—Sun Tzu,
The Laws of War (Fourth century BC)

WHAT THE ancient Chinese military philosopher Sun Tzu really means is that all warfare *should* be based on deception. Alas for the common soldier or the daring officer this has not always been the case, for the commander with the big battalions often finds it more comfortable to rely on honest, brute force. Much, much later Lawrence of Arabia noted acidly that "deceptions . . . for the ordinary general were just witty hors d'oeuvres before battle." History is replete with ordinary generals who nibbled on deceit and sent the troops into the cannon's mouth or against the longbow. Yet throughout history some extraordinary generals, and some even less exalted warriors, used deception to win out over superior force or to cut their own casualties. Since war, unlike a con game, is a matter of life and death, often for the victorious as well, the advantages of guile to avoid defeat or crippling losses have held an attraction that stretches back through time and across most cultures.

Even before the rise of complex civilizations, there is some evidence of prehistoric guile. For example, a 17,000-year-old cave painting in the Pyrenees depicts a Cro-Magnon hunter in the skin of a reindeer with the antlers as headdress. This was an elaborate form of camouflage that not only hid the man but presented the innocent reindeer victim with a false and fatal reality. Thus, despite the lack of adequate evidence, it is reasonable to suppose, if Stone Age hunters used stealth and camouflage to approach and surprise their prey, that these techniques of the hunt were applied when man first hunted man, the most dangerous of all game. Yet deception and guile appear to have played a rather minor role in the institutionalized war that came with civilization. In Egypt and the eastern Mediterranean, the highly ritualized mode of fighting pitted two heroes in a duel featuring strength and sinew. There were also examples of surprise attack, but these appear to have been the result of sheer speed on one side and poor intelligence on the other more often than of calculated deception. There were also some clumsy ambushes and the occasional ending of a difficult siege by some genuinely clever ruse. But these exceptions were sufficiently infrequent and consequently so marveled at by their chroniclers that it is now apparent that most commanders preferred force to guile. Still, it is the guile that was remembered.

The earliest example of deception in warfare from ancient records occurred around 1450 BC, when the Egyptian general

Thot captured the city of Jaffa. He gained this major victory by feigning defeat and hiding two hundred soldiers in baskets that were supposed to contain "surrender" gifts to the city's gullible governor. Like good conmen ever since, Thot realized that the easiest way to lull suspicion is to appeal to greed. The governor rushed the baskets into Jaffa to find the goodies inside were false but the soldiers were real.

One of the earliest examples of guile in the Bible occurs in about 1300 BC; soon after Joshua seized and sacked the city of Jericho, he moved on against the nearby Canaanite city of Ai. The tactics he had used to breach the double walls of Jericho did not work against the triple walls of Ai. Instead of settling down to a prolonged and costly siege, he fashioned a lure, displaying before the watching Canaanites a false reality that hid his assets and intentions. He simply ordered his army to lift the siege and withdraw in disorder. Then, when the delighted Canaanites rushed out of their city to fall upon the retreating army, a concealed force easily entered and seized the virtually unguarded city, leaving the cheated Canaanites in disarray.

At almost the same time, a somewhat more elegant ruse nearly allowed the Hittites to inflict a decisive defeat on the invading Egyptian forces, under the personal command of Pharaoh Rameses II, around 1290 BC. Bad Egyptian intelligence had permitted the Hittites to deploy their entire army unnoticed behind the city of Kadesh on the Orontes River in the Lebanon. Seizing that opportunity for a strategic ambush, the Hittite king sent two Bedouins posing as deserters to meet the slowly approaching Egyptians. These two agents reported the Hittite army still in the far north, and Rameses believed this planted lie. Believing Kadesh to be weakly defended, he decided to take it in one quick stroke. Leaving

three of his four divisions behind with orders to continue their
slow advance, Rameses rushed forward toward Kadesh with
only his second division.

Just before the Hittites could spring their nimble trap,
Rameses' scouts captured a pair of their spies. Under torture
(depicted in the tomb reliefs commemorating the battle) the
two scouts revealed the nearby presence of the Hittite army in
time for Rameses to summon up his third division. Even so,
the Hittite chariot attack caught the second division on the
march and cut through it to surround the pharaoh in his
headquarters camp. Rameses only just managed to escape to
rally his forces and turn a near defeat into victory, however
costly.

The most famous ruse in military folklore, showing star-
tling similarity to the one the Egyptian, Thot, had used at
Jaffa, is the Trojan-horse ploy, used when Troy fell to the
Greeks, in 1183 BC. This spectacular ruse was celebrated by
Homer, Virgil, Apollodorus of Athens, Dictys of Crete, and
Dares the Phrygian. The story may seem trite today, but it
conceals a subtle theme, first presented around AD 350 by
Quintus Smyrnaeus in his *The Fall of Troy*. This theme is that
of force versus fraud, of naked coercive power against guile as
alternate ways to win.

The situation the Greeks were caught in was that they had
spent ten costly years in their cruelly fought siege of the Trojan capital. There seemed to be no possibility of a breakthrough. At that point the prophet Calchas assembled the
weary Greek chiefs and heroes and told them: "Stop battering
away at these walls! You must devise some other way, some
ruse. . . . We cannot take Troy by force alone, so we must find
some cunning stratagem." At first none of his companions
could suggest a suitable plan. Then the ever wily Odysseus
spoke up. He proposed: "If Troy is to fall to guile, then let us

fashion a great horse in which our mightiest warriors shall hide in ambush."

Odysseus explained his daring plan. They would place the horse outside the city walls, burn their camp, embark, and sail away—but only just over the horizon to await developments. Their secret agent, Sinon, would explain to the astonished Trojans that the Greeks had given up and had left the horse as an offering to appease the goddess Athena for having looted her sacred image from the city. The Trojans could then be expected to drag the huge horse into their city as a victory trophy. That night, while the Trojans slumbered, drunk and gorged from the celebration, Sinon would light a signal fire to summon back the Greek fleet while the thirty hidden warriors would slip from the Horse to spread havoc and open the city gates.

Calchas approved this scheme. But Neoptolemus, the blond "battle-eager" son of Achilles, was disgusted. He argued: "Brave men meet their foes face to face! Away with such thoughts of guile and stratagem!" On and on he ranted, denouncing cheating as unworthy of heroes. In traditional terms, he was of course right and very Greek. It was not the Hellenic fashion to cheat in war. Their reputation before gods and men would suffer. The soldiers, however, hungered more for victory than for further heroic displays, and so they voted to build the great horse of guile. And, as planned, the Trojans took the lure and the Greeks the city. And as Neoptolemus foresaw, ever after, even in lands and languages then unknown, the unwary were advised: "Beware of Greeks bearing gifts."

Perhaps an even more elegant form of deception is the apparent deployment of nonexistent force. Exaggerating one's strength in order better to intimidate the enemy creates the impression of "dummy" units. The deceived opponent accepts as real the illusory effect and acts accordingly—withdrawing in haste or attacking inappropriately, cheated by the wily. The father of the dummy, or "notional," army is Gideon, judge of the Israelites, who faced with scant resources an unappetizingly large opponent. His target was a Midianite force, but his own band was too small to intimidate them into flight or surrender, much less to defeat them by any conventional means.

Gideon ordered his weak force to assault the enemy under cover of night. To pretend that he had been heavily reinforced, he ordered the approach be heralded by blowing as many extra battle trumpets as could be found, each simulating a new unit. To add to the illusion of numbers, he had his few soldiers bang away on pitchers to simulate the noise of a large force in motion. Thinking they were being attacked by an overwhelming host, the Midianites fled in alarm. Not only had Gideon created an effective dummy army, he had created this illusion entirely by deceiving the enemy's sense of sound.

In all of these cases of deception, the cheated is surprised by the false and the hidden—nonexistent soldiers or the all-too-real Greeks. In other cases the victim is cheated by his own conception of the limits of reality—he knows the rules of the game and thus is surprised when his opponent violates them. He in fact cheats himself of options and opportunities because he refuses to change the rules of the game. His conservatism may be the result of simple stupidity or of true belief. Neoptolemus truly believed that guile was unworthy of Greek heroes. In Japan, the samurai believed that the tactics and the techniques of the ninja, effective or not, were not honorable. Ultimately, the samurai were no longer surprised at the ninja. At first, however, innovation is almost inevitably surprising. One repeated reaction is indignation—the new is not only strange but also unfair. Another reaction is despair and defeat at the hands of those who did not play the game, who would not act as anticipated, as was considered proper and right. Better the heavens fall than we soil our honor by using the cunning weapons of the ninja or the tactics of Odysseus. It is simply difficult, often impossible, for people—individually and collectively—to accept and adapt to swift changes.

Innovation and swift change may apply either to procedures (new tactics and methods) or to technology (new weapons or gadgets). Modern military theorists recognize a special category of "technological surprise" and rate it as a highly effective means for defeating an unprepared victim. One of the more notable examples occurred about 1013 BC, when David slew the giant Goliath with a slingshot. David forthwith became the father of technological surprise and Goliath the victim of his preconceptions about the nature of battle. It had not been a *fair* fight, strength and valor being discounted by skill. The future king of Israel simply had not played by the rules of the time. He had introduced the novel when Goliath had anticipated the normal.

While there were stratagems of deception scattered throughout the battles of the ancient world, the theorists of cheating in war only came into view with the rise of historians. Around 370 BC Xenophon, citing historical precedent, advises the wise general always to take ruthless advantage of the enemy's off-guard, weakened, and disorganized moments. By a remarkable coincidence, at nearly the same time similar counsel was proffered by Sun Tzu in China and the epic poets of the *Mahābhārata* in India. The Hellenic world offered increasingly imaginative examples of deceit in war, some quite elegant indeed. For example, during the siege of Syracuse in 212 BC, the Greek defenders constructed a false beach by using a flimsy straw-covered frame leading from the shoreline out into shallow water. The first Roman assault

wave disembarked onto this dummy shore and was slaughtered as the soldiers foundered toward the real one.

Actually, the level of tactical deception and strategic indirection remained at a relatively moderate level until the
Carthaginians and Romans struggled for hegemony of the
Mediterranean. The level of war stratagems jumped suddenly
to a higher plateau during the century and a half between
Hannibal's invasion of Rome in 216 BC (when he introduced,
albeit with little effect, the elephant into the campaign) and
the assassination of Julius Caesar in 44 BC (when his opponents took advantage of his arrogance and assurance by
changing the rules to their advantage—as men were wont to
do in eras of deceit). The Roman world in this period between Hannibal's invasion and Caesar's death was marked by
a very high level of deception in diplomacy and domestic
politics. Everyone felt potentially threatened. The rules were
changing. The importance of brute force was declining. Military and political innovation was rampant. And then came
Octavian and with him the transformation of the Roman
Republic into the Roman Empire. The emperor who succeeded him could deploy big battalions; imperial military institutions were established and generals needed no recourse to
guile. Stratagems passed into virtual oblivion as a common
military practice, although guile in politics was long maintained.

This sudden disappearance of deceit from military practice
was not novel in the ancient world. Generalship everywhere
was singularly personal. The commanders of Egypt, Persia,
Judea, Greece and early Rome were seldom military profes-
sionals. Whatever guile they brought with them derived from
their political and diplomatic experience and disappeared
with them. The armies they commanded, particularly the
Greek phalanxes and Roman legions, were efficient profes-

sional, disciplined, shock instruments but lacked any strategic doctrine except that of their temporary commander. In an era of guile and deceit, he was guileful and deceitful from necessity, and uncertainty, and weakness, but with the advent of the Roman Empire conservatism and brute force triumphed. With big battalions and weak enemies there was no need of a doctrine of deception.

Oddly enough, the first military manuals urging more elegant and deceptive manuevers began to appear just as the Empire discarded guile. In *Strategemata*, written about AD 90, Frontinus revealed some theoretical understanding of deception with his typology that included such psychological rubrics as "On concealing plans . . . [and] finding out the enemy's plans," "Distracting the attention of the enemy," "Creating panic in the enemy's ranks," and "Inducing treachery." The next effort was the *Strategemata* of Polyaenus, written hastily in AD 162 or 163, composed of 900 ruses of war intended to aid the co-emperors Marcus Aurelius and Verus in the war with Parthia. The most cogent and influential work came much later, around 390, at the twilight of the legions. *De Re Militaria* of Vegetius stressed surprise and stratagem in defense as well in offense, urging the use of luring in defense and of baiting in offense. He noted that "surprise, ambuscades, and stratagems" are the *only* hope of success for a much weaker protagonist and that "stratagem and finesse," along with "famine, surprise, or terror," are always preferable to general engagements. The former makes it possible to "destroy the enemy . . . in detail and intimidate them without exposing our own forces," while in the latter case, "fortune has often a greater share than valor." For Rome, whose commanders had so long depended on the brute force of the massed legions, it was too late: their enemies had the weight of numbers. The barbarians were at the gate.

The eastern Empire—the Byzantine Empire with its capital at Constantinople, escaped the onslaught of the waves of barbarians out of Asia. Created at the end of the fourth century, this Eastern Roman Empire had other problems with the Persians but also sufficient resources to defend itself. The Byzantine Empire had inherited the political and military traditions of the old Greco-Roman world and preserved much of its literature, including works of Frontinus and Vegetius, the theorists of stratagems. This meant that just when it was too late for the West to seize upon military deception, the time was right for the East, sorely pressed by greedy neighbors, to do so. Even more important, the emperor Justinian found a great commander in Belisarius. At the very outset of his first campaign against the Persians, in AD 530, this twenty-five-year-old general of the East showed his deep understanding of deception by declaring in his unsuccessful negotiations with his enemy: "The best general . . . is that one who is able to bring about peace from war." And in the following year, by a series of creative, bloodless maneuvers, Belisarius quickly balked a Persian-Saracen invasion and herded the invading army back to the Euphrates River. And yet again, in 542, he cunningly bluffed a far more powerful Persian army into retreating to its homeland without joining battle. This extraordinarily cost-effective stratagem was continued, if not as successfully, by the successors of Belisarius.

As in the West, the theorists came after the great battles that had been won by deception, but in this case they came in time to influence the future. The plagiarizing emperor, Leo the Wise, if he cheated in writing his *Tactica* around AD 900, was the most sophisticated of several Byzantine scribes that taught the army to cheat others. For him, a campaign won without battle was the best because it was the cheapest and least risky. And, when it was unavoidable, battle was merely a means to a political end and not a test of honor, chivalry, courage, or heroism. These qualities he disdains as the clap-trap of barbarians or fools—fatal to victory. Instead, Leo stresses the need to understand one's enemy in order to play against him the panoply of ruses that constitute the essence of generalship. He urged such ploys as insincere parleys and dis-patching forged compromising letters to sow unwarranted suspicion.

Not all generals and commanders understood or accepted Leo's principles. The bumbling emperor-general Romanus Diogenes returned to conventional offensive tactics and was promptly and decisively beaten in 1071 at Manzikert by the devious Seljuk Turks, who had apparently bought the crucial services of one Byzantine general. Fortunately for the empire, ten years after this castastrophe began the long reign (1081–1118) of Alexius I Comnenus, who brought high intelligence and a full measure of cunning to Byzantine palace politics, diplomacy, and war. A professional soldier, he usurped the throne by a military coup, kept it for thirty-seven years by agilely dodging constant plots and betrayals, conducted di-plomacy with consummate insincerity, and fought his many wars with guile and imagination. Having outwitted many assassins, he died a natural death at the age of sixty-two. This was, perhaps, the most remarkable feat of all, for, as in the West, even when the use of military deception and guile de-clined, the use of deceitful politics did not. Byzantine politics involved complex plots, constant deceit, unending intrigue, and intricate, deadly betrayals. Of the 107 emperors who reigned during the empire's 1,058 years (AD 395–1453), only 42 died in office of natural causes, including eight deaths by accident or in battle; the other 65 reigns ended violently as a result of 65 successful plots: 23 emperors died by assassina-tion, 18 were mutilated and dethroned, 12 died in prison, and

12 were forced to abdicate. Lacking any regular rule of succession, the beckoning throne was an almost constant target of intrigue. Thus, while the butcher's bill for emperors was horrendous, that for their unfortunate and perhaps ambitious families was worse—brothers were blinded and cousins murdered, parents lived in dread.

No wonder that most Byzantine commanders understood guile. No wonder that the very active diplomatic service had as its main task lying to potential enemies, embroiling neighbors with one another, and cheating in the service of an ever weakening state. One of the last effectively devious players on the Byzantine stage was Anna Comnena, 1083–1150, daughter of Alexius I Comnenus, who made it plain that she admired her father more for his sharpness than his bravery. Adopting his methods, she attempted to engineer a palace revolution to steal the succession from her hated younger brother, John. Her intrigue failed, and Anna was forced out of politics to become, from her comfortable confinement in a convent, the West's first woman historian. Emperor John became known as John the Good, and given the rising threat to the borders of the empire this was hardly good for Byzantium. The empire needed guile not goodness and the decay became irreversible. In 1453, the dying city of Constantine, all that was left of the once huge empire, fell to an unimaginative but sufficiently ponderous Muslim siege. The great invasions out of Asia finally swept away the Eastern Empire as they had the Western a thousand years before.

The older barbarians—the Huns and Goths, Vandals, and Visigoths—had disappeared from history, their kingdoms long absorbed by others. They had mingled with the old Romans, with the new Scandinavians, and with each other. In 800 a new, European empire was born, when the Frank, Charlemagne, was crowned Holy Roman Emperor by the Pope on

Christmas day. There was no golden age but only centuries of internecine strife among competing commanders, aspiring monarchs, between emperors and popes. Yet there were universals: the Christian religion, the new institutions of feudalism and chivalry, and a host of shared attitudes and assumptions.

One universal was a disdain for the practice of guile in combat. The Christian religion imposed a moral command that turned the minds of the governors and governed to otherworldly values at the expense of secular considerations. Pragmatic considerations, even *raison d'etat*, could seldom be offered as a ready excuse for recourse to fraud. The etiquette of chivalry did not allow for cheating on the field of combat, on the field of honor. There is scant evidence of deception for eight hundred years. The European strove for victory by hard fighting. A noble who could sit on his charger and manipulate his lance and shield was ready for war. The joust for pleasure was simply war written small—two ponderously armored knights thundering toward each other. No manuevering, no deception, no retreat—they simply ride into each other. As Leo the Wise observed caustically, "The Frank believes that a retreat under any circumstances must be dishonourable, hence he will fight whenever you choose to offer him battle." Ignorant of theory, these Frankish commanders knew only chivalrous brute force, and their rigidly stereotyped style of battle made them easy prey to unfamiliar foes.

Over the long medieval centuries, the West faced various alien challenges. For example, in the eighth century the Arabs came out of Arabia, spreading militant Islam with the sword. Fanatic, determined, totally dedicated, they swept across Africa and into Spain without recourse to guile or delay, dependent on the great, swirling cavalry charge, certain of instant access to heaven in case of death. Fortunately for the West, their impetus ran out at the Pyrenees. Unfortunately for the West, the leadership of the Islamic world would move into more guileful hands as the centuries passed. Much later, in the fourteenth century the greatest of Arab historians, Ibn Khaldūn, would note approvingly that "trickery is one of the most useful things employed in warfare. It is the thing most likely to bring victory." This the Europeans could not understand. When the ponderous, mindless, hack-and-slash feudal armies undertook crusades to wrest the Holy Land from the infidel, they were promptly and decisively defeated, as they always had been by the clever Byzantines. Again and again the feudal mob faced an alien enemy using very different and more cunning tactics. Yet they persisted, and in the course of time the crusaders actually *learned* from their betters. Eighteen years after they had blundered into the Holy Land in 1097, they finally learned to avoid costly pitched battles with the Saracens. When battle proved unavoidable, they initiated surprise attacks or resorted to feigned retreats to lure premature Saracen attacks.

Another great and very alien challenge to the West came again out of the East. At the center of the Eurasian heartland lay a unique culture that erupted from time to time in raids upon the great urban agricultural civilizations along its fringe. These were the nomadic tribes of Central Asia. Their style of warfare consisted almost totally of cavalry tactics and strategy limited to raiding, except in the rare dramatic periods when they were united under leaders such as Jenghiz Khan or Tamerlane. Unless united, the separate tribes were too small to threaten seriously their civilized neighbors.

The invention of the armor-piercing compound reflex bow, by perhaps 1000 BC, made the nomad's horse a powerful weapons platform, and the later invention of the stirrup, which spread from China around AD 300, made it a stable one as well. The magnificent reflex bow was not only the most powerful nonmechanical bow ever invented, it was also short enough to permit the archer on horseback to swing and fire to either side or to the rear without his limbs or weapon becoming entangled with the horse. A shot to the rear was called the Parthian shot; this term was corrupted to *parting shot,* and became the stock English phrase for the surprise last word.

Among the most effective of the horse warrior's tactics was the feigned flight, a carefully rehearsed "panic" retreat to lure the enemy into a precipitate charge. The nomad force would charge the enemy's organized position and then pretend to have been put to flight. Their unsuspecting foes would take off after them, soldiers breaking ranks in eager pursuit of booty. Then, on command, the nomad cavalry would turn back in unison to launch their real charge against a now thoroughly disorganized mob.

With only two exceptions, the clumsy medieval European knights never managed to cope with these surprise tactics. In the first exceptional case, the Germanic knights, after suffering two decades of repeated large-scale raids from nomadic Magyar horsemen, finally mastered their enemy's tactics of feigned flight and ambush. Thus, Henry the Fowler (in 933) and his son, Otto the Great (in 955) ambushed, surprised, and routed the Magyar invaders. Elsewhere out of Asia came first the Seljuk Turks and then the Ottomans smashing through the decaying defenses of Byzantium and sweeping up into the Balkans. Other of the Asia raiders spread out to the east instead of the west, into southern Asia, into any settled and tempting border land. Of them all the most impressive proved to be the Mongols who reached a new level of competence in warfare. Their successes during the thirteenth and fourteenth centuries were closely connected with skilled and systematic use of deception by Jenghiz Khan and his immediate successors. Tight organization, rigid discipline, extreme mobility, great striking power, effective tactics, rigorous training, and constant battle experience combined to make the Mongol army an enormously powerful fighting machine. Because of its sparse nomadic population base, however, it was a small army even for its time—only 129,000 at the time of Jenghiz Khan's death in 1227—one that could not afford heavy casualties. Yet, between 1190 and 1292, the Mongols unified all the Central Asian steppe tribes, conquered China, Korea, Persia, Afghanistan, Iraq, and Russia and raided Burma, Annam, Japan, Java, India, Syria, Poland, Bohemia, Hungary, Serbia, and Austria. To sustain this long series of campaigns, often against stronger foes, sheer force had to be bolstered by deception.

At the tactical level, the Mongols' vast repertoire of ruses included feints, demonstration attacks, camouflage by raising dust clouds to conceal movement or exaggerate strength, stuffed dummies on spare horses, false campfires, ambushes, and especially the carefully rehearsed feigned flight intended to lure the enemy into a precipitate charge.

Mongol strategic intelligence was superb. Their campaigns were planned and launched only after detailed political and military information had been obtained, information that gained them many bloodless victories through bribery, treason, or alliance. This fine intelligence also enabled the Mongols to design highly effective strategic psychological warfare programs, by means of which they panicked, demoralized, and terrorized their prospective victims, again sometimes inducing surrender without battle. Psychological operations typically included two specific techniques of presenting false information: forged letters that discredited or destroyed prominent enemy officials were a propaganda device that could be fine-tuned to specific targets; spreading rumors calculated to mask their intentions or exaggerate their numbers and strength was a more general device used by the Mongols.

None of these tricks were new in the thirteenth century, and all would be used again by other armies in other places. What was new was the high priority the Mongols gave to deception in all phases of their operations. They were not beyond being deceived, however. The mighty Kublai Khan learned that his ambassadors had been mistreated by one of the several small kingdoms of Java and ordered a punitive expedition. When the Mongol-Chinese fleet arrived off Java in 1293, the navigator was uncertain of his landfall, so the admiral put in at the nearest harbor to get sailing directions. The local officials courteously directed him a bit farther down the coast. The Mongol horde sailed off and dutifully wreaked havoc on the designated kingdom. Fortunately for the admiral, Kublai Khan never found out that his admiral had been twice duped. First, his genial hosts had selfishly and shamelessly used the Mongols to destroy *their* own private enemy. Second, by ironic navigational luck the "helpful" hosts turned out to be the target the Mongols had originally sought. Mostly, however, the Mongols came out of battle as winners. Fortunately, very fortunately for the West, they were spread thin on the ground, campaigning in Java or China instead of slashing into Western Europe.

In Europe the few victories won by deception did not nourish the mainstream of medieval military lore. Brute force remained the order of the day; but at least the Mongols were elsewhere, the Magyars were settled in Hungary, and the Turks were busy with the Byzantines. With few outside distractions, the European knights could display their valor among themselves in set-piece medieval battles that even improvements in arms did little to change. The mounted knights would be encased in increasingly heavy armor,

hoisted aboard huge horses, and would then ponderously attack each other. If unhorsed, they were unable to move and
were prey to lesser soldiers; they would be held for ransom or,
if apparently lacking in fiscal resources, gutted on the spot.
This was "proper" war. All else—unruly mobs wandering
through Europe on peoples' crusades, yeomen bowmen, hard
young men with pikes—was beneath notice, beyond the pale
of chivalry. The knights only wanted more of the same: more
armor, longer lances, more thundering hooves and swirling
banners. No changes and no cheating. When changes came,
they were ignored. At the battle of Crécy, in 1345, the flower
of French chivalry, the shimmering knights on chargers,
charged into an unanticipated shower of shafts from English
longbowmen. The knights were slaughtered but their leaders
remained unrepentant. They were surprised, of course, by this
technological innovation but not sufficiently to make them
change their ways. In 1415 at Agincourt, the English under
Henry V once again deployed longbows and once again the
packed charge of the French knights collapsed into a slain
generation, slaughtered because the French refused to admit
that the rules of the game had changed.

In fact elsewhere there already was some evidence that the
weak were finding means to avoid certain defeat at the hands
of the strong. Thus, Robert Bruce employed "unfair" means
against the English at the battle of Bannockburn in 1314 in
Scotland. Bruce had his Scots dig stake-lined pits and surrounded them with concealed caltrops (small, four-pronged
spikes). The English charge took their troops into the pits and
their horses onto the caltrops. Meanwhile, Bruce's cavalry
emerged from concealment in nearby thickets and fell upon
the disorganized English mass.

There was another notable early example of guile to the
south, when the Venetians made use of dummy installations

during the siege of the city of Ragusa (now Dubrovnik, Yugo-
slavia) in 1171. The crucial ploy was the Venetians' construction of a cardboard fort in a position that apparently
threatened the defenders. By and large, however cunning and
cheating in war were practiced, if at all, on the edges of
Europe.

Almost four centuries later, in 1513, the Flemish defenders
of Tournai set up large strips of painted canvas that simulated fortifications in order to deceive the English concerning
the extent and location of their defenses. This was a harbinger
of a new era of Western guile, for increasingly, the old re-
straints on deception weakened with the rise of a new secular-
ism: the vitality of feudalism, the moral authority of the
Roman Church, and the charm of chivalry were eroding. No
place did this happen sooner than in northern Italy. There,
the Renaissance meant not only a kindling of interest in the
glories of Greece and Rome that inspired magnificent art and
literature but also burning pursuit of political power by any
means. There was an almost continual struggle for power
among the various city-states, ministates eager to fashion a
local hegemony. Venice created a sea empire. Milan and
Florence, Pisa and Lucca struggled for more power, more
control. Under princes disguised as popes, the papacy was
equally involved in such temporal matters. Conspiracy, bribery, treachery, assassination, revolt, and usurpation were accepted, if often publicly eschewed, political means. Where for
centuries in the West there had rarely been an assassination,
now in Italy assassination became a method of statecraft.
Elsewhere, theologians might argue on the virtues of tyran-
nicide; in Italy, where there was no dearth of tyrants, the
assassin became a tool of the powerful, the ambitious, and the
weak alike: poisoners were available for hire, murderers paid
by uneasy princes.

Yet, while Italian Renaissance politics and diplomacy were permeated with guile, duplicity, and cheating on a grand scale, the warfare of the time was not. Usually political guile paralleled military guile—and continued longer after the princes could depend on brute force—but not in Italy. The art of war was gradually monopolized by the *condottieri,* mercenary troops concerned only with their pay and the odd opportunity to loot a city or switch sides for profit. At best the condottieri cheated with low cunning, padding their muster rolls, concealing deficiencies in equipment, and avoiding battle—really the white-collar crimes of their day. In the field, with little training and less interest in sacrifice, when an unavoidable confrontation with another mercenary army occurred or a siege was forced, the condottieri responses were clumsy, all but ritualized chessboard pageants, clashes without elegance or guile. This comfortable state of affairs, busy but stable, was disrupted in 1494 by the French invasion of Italy that triggered the intervention of the Spanish Hapsburgs. In the French-Spanish war the Italian city-states became pawns in an enlarged and increasingly deadly game. The Italian cities shifted and maneuvered, making and breaking alliances (Milan switched sides a dozen times), seeking advantage or evading disaster.

Warfare was again deadly serious, too serious for condottieri. Cities were cruelly sacked and prisoners of war murdered rather than ransomed as before. The Italians realized that their desperate situation needed a new military doctrine. They actively debated the merits of alternatives to the unreliable mercenary system, experimenting with new formations, new weapons, and new tactics. But time was short and little came out of this theoretical analysis. The disadvantaged Italians did turn in a few cases to military stratagem, limited mainly to maneuvering to *avoid* risky battles and purchase treason to gain victory without battle. In response to the times, theorists produced increasingly realistic writings on politics and war, a trend culminating in the early fifteenth century with the works of Machiavelli and Guicciardini.

Niccolò Machiavelli, 1469–1527, was a shrewd, jestful, secular, pagan Florentine diplomat and moderately successful politician. He was the first Western theorist to address explicitly the problems of power, force, and stratagem in politics, diplomacy, and war. He understood and explored the manipulative psychological techniques involved in deception in his *The Prince, Discourses,* and *The Art of War.* He even treated the theme of gullibility and guile in his farcical play, *Mandragola.* This was at a time when military deception—cheating on the battleground—was not done. As late as 1512, for example, in the battle of Ravenna, adversaries were still accustomed to beginning battle with chivalrous challenges and to conducting war, at least in theory, in accordance with agreed rules and fixed means. It fell to Machiavelli to point out most explicitly the very intimate interactions of war, politics, and economics, and to apply to military theory the then common practice of political deception. He urged that any and all means were justified to defend the state or ensure its victory: efficacy was the only sensible criterion. Recognizing that an army was an economically precious commodity, he urged that the wise commander "never attempt to win by force" what he "was able to win by fraud."

Francesco Guicciardini, Machiavelli's young friend, was equally candid in his maxims on statecraft and equally harsh on the simple-minded moralists who doubted the virtue of lying for the state.

Men who are of an open and genuine nature and, as they say in Florence, "frank," are very praiseworthy and pleasant to everyone. Deception, on the other hand, is odious and disliked. But deception is very useful, whereas your frankness tends to profit others rather than you. Still, . . . I would praise the man who is ordinarily open and frank and who uses deception only in very rare, important matters. Thus you will have the reputation of being open and genuine, and you will enjoy the popularity such reputation brings. And in those very important matters, you will reap even greater advantage from deception, because your reputation for not being a deceiver will make your words be easily believed.*

Relatively swiftly, Machiavelli's and Guicciardini's ideas won the day, and deception and guile in politics and war spread across Europe.

From 1611 until 1806, deception gradually but steadily came virtually to dominate warfare in all its phases from grand strategy down to tactics. Thomas Hobbes noted in *The Leviathan* in 1651, "Force and fraud are in war the two cardinal virtues." The printing presses churned out manuals on military affairs replete with ruses and stratagems, advice, and discussions of deception. And the generals, some at least, adapted and adopted the text. The French *Jeune École* school of naval strategy, for example, later elaborated in the eighteenth-century *guerre de course,* according to which one should shamelessly "attack the weak, fly from the strong" as a means of winning a cheap victory by unorthodox means over superior forces. The eighteenth century provided ample examples for those who would later seek means to counter brute force. Surprise was in, fair warning out.

Whenever possible, the wise did the "impossible." This *always* produces surprise. What one person rejects as an impossi-

* Francesco Guicciardini, *Maxims and Reflections of a Renaissance Statesman* (New York: Harper Torchbooks, 1965), maxim 104.

bility, another may not only think possible but sometimes make real. The impossible—as perceived by the victim—may mean an impossible time or place or any of the other types of things that people can misperceive and be deceived about. A classic case occurred in the eighteenth century in Canada. Quebec fronts on an open plain and is backed by a formidable bluff high above the St. Lawrence River. In 1759, the besieged French commander, the Marquis de Montcalm, deployed his army to the front, feeling that he was protected by the topography to his rear. The attacking British commander, Major General James Wolfe, learned from scouts that a narrow and very difficult—but not strictly impossible—goat trail led up the bluff. He thereupon scaled the "unscalable" Heights of Abraham with his army. The advance unit spoke French to the few unsuspicious enemy guards and quietly overcame them. Thereby Wolfe surprised Montcalm and fought and won the Battle of Quebec on the killing ground of his choice.

The "impossible" option, like technological innovation, assures surprise. The fact that a victim is surprised does not necessarily mean that his opponent intended to deceive him. David simply meant to kill Goliath by recourse to his slingshot. Goliath was simply surprised at the novelty. At Quebec, Wolfe hid his intention to attack by maneuvering *beyond* Montcalm's conception of the battlefield. Montcalm was deceived by his own perceptions. To assure that the deception would last long enough to be effective, Wolfe resorted not only to the invisibility of his army, hiding the real, but also to presenting in the van the false, French-speaking advance units. Thus, the impossible assured invisibility that was protected by the visibly false. It was a long way from the plunging knights of chivalry or the challenge before the battle.

The culmination of the long years of deception in politics

and war came with the advent of Napoleon Bonaparte, who
made frequent and effective use of guile in his political maneuvers and on the battlefield. For him, battle was only the
culmination of a carefully laid strategic plan.

And his grand strategy made full use of a carefully orchestrated plan of deception to confuse and mislead his enemy even before the campaign was launched or a battle
joined. Thus, prior to a campaign, a thick curtain of security
would descend: the press would be muzzled to prevent leaks
and his counterintelligence efforts would protect against
penetration by enemy agents. Information about the target was assiduously collected both from public sources and
through the secret service. Deception was promulgated
through planted articles in the controlled press. Then when
the campaign was underway, various ruses were systematically used to deceive the foe about the timing, direction,
strength, and nature of Napoleon's blows: unit designations
were continually changed, deployments were shuffled about,
and feint attacks constantly mounted. This was Napoleon's
practice. Yet, oddly, while some of this practice is expressed in
the earliest and most widely known collection of his maxims,
it does not really appear there in any coherent structure. And
after 1804 there was no longer any coherent practice. Possessed of the big battalions of brute force, Napoleon discarded
guile in practice and theory. As emperor he became too proud
to cheat. Maneuver gave way to ponderous and costly assaults by large forces and initiative to mere precipitateness.
And in time, when the big battalions ran out, victory gave
way to defeat. The lessons that Napoleon had learned and
then discarded were ultimately and elegantly presented in
General Carl von Clausewitz's great book, *Vom Kriege (About
War),* published in 1832, the year after the author's death.

But by then, the orthodox soldiers of the West had largely

dropped the notion of psychological deception as an important aspect of military doctrine in favor of the new and fashionable mechanical and scientific principles of the nineteenth century. And with the machines came a reaction, exemplified by concepts of romanticism, that demanded prideful heroic display as a necessary proof of manliness. Odysseus was forgotten and the Light Brigade charged into the cannons—it was not effective, but it was magnificent. There were those, such as Colonel Garnet J. Wolseley, who grumbled about romantic sentiment. In 1869 Wolesley, in *The Soldier's Pocket-Book for Field Service,* wrote: "As a nation we are bred up to feel it a disgrace even to succeed by falsehood; the word spy conveys something as repulsive as slave; we will keep hammering along with the conviction that 'honesty is the best policy,' and that truth always wins in the long run. These pretty little sentences do well for a child's copy-book, but the man who acts upon them in war had better sheathe his sword for ever." Nevertheless, the generals preferred honest magnificence to such advice. They sought to bring overwhelming force to a decisive point, breaking the enemy army's morale and then his ranks. Rigid discipline, élan, and quality of will were stressed. Soldiers were expected to fight to the last man.

Deception, however, was not quite dead, for across the Atlantic in the United States the American Civil War became too serious a matter to be left entirely to muddled generals who ordered clumsy frontal assaults or fought on one line until they had frittered away their army. The good generals, and seldom have so many appeared simultaneously, employed all the classical ruses, depending upon surprise and deception, and devised novel techniques and tactics. The impact, as always, was the same; the impossible astounded, innovation surprised.

For example, although mines had been used in siege warfare almost since the invention of gunpowder in China in the late 1100's, they were used only to breach fortifications by direct assault rather than by stealth. Then, in 1862, Confederate Brigadier General Gabriel Rains invented the land mine. The land mine, concealed by surface cover, is just a big booby trap. Unlike standard booby traps, whose use is limited to minor tactical situations, land mines can serve a larger strategic role when used en masse in vast mine fields. In early May, a Union cavalry regiment pursuing Rains's withdrawing infantry up a muddy road from Yorktown toward Williamsburg suddenly found itself in the world's first mine field. Casualties were light, but not realizing they had already detonated the only four mines in the field, the Union force cautiously left the road and detoured through the wilderness while the Confederates escaped. Union commander McClellan denounced this infernal device as a violation of the laws of war, and even Confederate General Longstreet wanted Rains courtmartialed. However, Rains's wily commander, General Magruder, got the inventor transferred to the munitions bureau.

McClellan was able to be surprised because of what he assumed were the laws of war. Much more interesting are strategies that consciously intend to deceive, hiding the real or presenting the false. Curiously, it is possible to confound the same enemy repeatedly. One of the more stubborn myths about deception is that you can't work the same trick twice. In fact, you can often play the same trick again and again, often even on the same dupe. All that is required for one of the most elegant of all deceptions, is an either-or option: here or there, left or right, up or down, back or forward. Each pair embodies symmetry of choice and the points in a geometry of place. In military theory they are the basis of the principle of "alternative goals."

This general type of deception can be a one-shot affair, as in a single battle. Or it may be repeated, as when a single target is attacked again and again with only the direction of approach varying, as in the conjurer's cups-and-balls routine. Finally, and most impressively, it may be serial, a fluid operation of movement from one place to another, as in a ground campaign or a series of downfield plays in football. Serial deception involves feinting first one way and then the other.

In 1864 General Sherman made his decisive 180-mile drive to Atlanta. Together with the three hundred-mile follow-through to the sea, this campaign sliced the eastern Confederacy in two. From that point forward the rebels were doomed.

Throughout his drive to Atlanta, Sherman's logistic tail was tied to a single railway line. He had to advance and attack along that line, a fact that the Confederates knew and that he knew they knew. Yet in every engagement but one, a frontal attack at Kennesaw Mountain, he surprised his enemy as to the place of attack and consequently defeated them each time. How was this possible? Sherman had the old left-right option, and he used it. Although his line of advance was very narrowly constrained, he retained at the spearhead the alternative of attacking either to the right of the rail line or to the left. As he put it in a letter from the front, he literally impaled his enemy on the "horns of a dilemma." Left flank or right, he always succeeded in deceiving.

The tenuous tradition of military deception returned to Britain from America. Lieutenant Colonel G. F. R. Henderson was Britain's most unorthodox military scholar in the nineteenth century. His classic study of the American Civil War, published in 1898, identified a whole range of strategic and tactical ruses used by the Confederates, particularly the highly unorthodox General "Stonewall" Jackson, and to which Henderson explicitly attributed their frequent attainment of surprise. Henderson received the very rare opportunity to apply his purely academic theories to war when two years later, he accompanied Lord Roberts into the hitherto—for the British—disastrous quagmire of the Boer War. As head of Roberts's intelligence service, Colonel Henderson devised the carefully coordinated plan of feint and deception that relieved Kimberly and permitted the move against Bloemfontein.

The wily British were not alone in duplicity, for not all of the lessons of deception had been forgotten by the Americans—after all they had been exposed to the Indian for generations. At the beginning of the nineteenth century, much further afield, a resourceful American commander responded to a similar irregular campaign with resourceful duplicity. The Philippine Insurrection was a protracted guerrilla rebellion led by Emilio Aguinaldo. By 1901, after two years, it had cost the lives of four thousand American soldiers, and there was no light at the end of the tunnel.

Then, on February 8, American infantry brigade commander Colonel Frederick "Scrapping Fred" Funston received intercepted dispatches from Aguinaldo ordering reassignment of several guerrilla units to his secret headquarters, located in one of the least accessible parts of the island of Luzon.

Funston took eighty-five loyal Filipino troops and disguised them as guerrillas. He and four other American officers disguised themselves as privates and simulated "prisoners," and the group started out on March 6 for the remote enemy camp. Using captured rebel stationery and forging the signature of one of Aguinaldo's most trusted commanders, Funston kept the guerrilla leader informed of the approaching "reinforcements" and received instructions as to his route. The mock army reached the headquarters village on March 24.

There, at no loss to Funston's force and with only two killed and three wounded on the rebel side, Aguinaldo was arrested. Thus did the war end by a deceptive *coup de main.*

Aguinaldo proved a good sport and gave Funston due credit, stating, "It was a bold plan, executed with skill and cleverness, in the face of difficulties which to most men would have seemed insurmountable." Funston returned to the States to receive his nation's highest award, the Medal of Honor. But his award was for an act of bravery under fire the previous year and not for the cunning deployment of his mock army.

Funston had almost singlehandedly won America's only current war, but the moralistic journalists of the time pilloried him for having won it by deceit. Turn-of-the-century Americans, it seems, accepted the motto, "It's not whether you win or lose, but how you play the game." They preferred their heroes to lose by conventional means than win by cunning. And the Americans were not alone in their affection for the heroic, the grand gesture rather than the subtle ruse. At Tanga in East Africa in 1914, Royal Navy Captain F. W. Caulfield courteously notified the off-guard Germans of the impending British landing. Only fair, you know. The British attacked. The Germans, no longer off guard, opened fire. The attack failed disastrously, the field was strewn with British bodies. Caulfield was promoted for his gentlemanly behavior. All this, mind, nearly four hundred years after the Battle of Ravenna in 1512, when combat still began with a formal chivalrous challenge.

After not hundreds but thousands of years, it appeared as if the generals had learned nothing and forgotten everything. Yet there were those endless examples for any who sought them where men won battles and wars by hiding the real, by displaying the false, by guile and cunning and duplicity—by cheating. Military men could read Machiavelli or recall the Trojan Horse or the March on Atlanta, but still, however saving of lives and successful on the battlefield deceit was, the generals clung to their big battalions and the lure of force, and soon, in World War I, the battlefields of Western Europe would absorb millions upon millions of young men sent to death guilelessly. The generals were not alone. Cheating in any field was not romantic, not proper, and most of all not understood. No one then and few even now know that in all human activity there are only a few basic categories of deception—cheating—and only one basic means to deploy the ruses of duplicity.

CHAPTER 2

The Structure of Deceit: A Theory of Cheating

♦ ♦ ♦

Oh what a tangled web we weave
When first we practice to deceive.

—SIR WALTER SCOTT, *Marmion*

SIR WALTER SCOTT implied in the lines above that cheating is not only difficult but quite complex. This is not so and especially not so if the cheater grasps the simple nature and structure of deceit. With a grasp of theory, the cheater may practice with impunity. Commenting on other matters, Lenin wrote, "Without a revolutionary theory there is no revolutionary practice." The revolutionaries' problem has always been that they have had lots of theories that have rarely worked in practice. In cheating the reverse is true, for until now there has *never* been a general theory of cheating, never even a description of the major kinds of cheating. The theoretical arena has been clouded with moral considerations: Odysseus' "unheroic" horse, Caulfield praised for warning the Germans of his attack, and Funston damned by capturing Aguinaldo by guile. Being naughty, cheating, seemed to be beneath notice. When the theorists did advocate guile, they did so on a piecemeal basis, quoting this maxim or that. Their sound pragmatic advice to military commanders often included specific elements of deception but without general theory. Flexibility was good, multiple options were useful, surprise vital, and delay often crucial to ultimate victory. But was delay a form of cheating? Or, for that matter, what is the nature of surprise? The military theorists never answered very clearly and almost no one bothered to examine guile in other aspects of human behavior.

There was a single notable exception in one arcane and unexpected area: magic. First, no "sensible" person paid much attention to mere conjurers, who were never at the center of civilization's vital interests. Second, everyone, correctly, assumed that magicians did not cheat maliciously but created effects to please the audience. Even though they had been "cheated," audiences did not feel that way, but felt confounded, surprised, delighted. Only if the illusion was exposed were they likely to feel cheated, because then the magic disappeared and with it the delight. So magicians were left alone to work out for themselves a primitive theory or model of how deception worked. Beginning with Reginald Scott's *Discouverie of Witchcraft* in 1584 and continuing into the present, there has been a steady stream of books on magic, although for obvious reasons much of the lore remains a closely guarded secret passed on only by word of mouth.

No "serious" scholar examined the magicians' world until 1894, when the father of the IQ test, Alfred Binet, published an article titled "Psychologie de la prestidigitation." In the next decade, a few early psychologists produced a half dozen scholarly studies of magic but then moved on to more "respectable" matters.

From time to time other writers noticed relationships between magic and military camouflage or between magic and theater. In 1948 Raymond Chandler noted an analogy between sleight of hand and plotting a mystery story. Actually, as early as the first century after Christ, the Roman philosopher Seneca wrote of the similarity between magicians' tricks and the art of rhetoric. Those who saw a relationship between the uses of deception in sports and in war never really got around to recognizing that deception is a universal, a branch of applied psychology that transcends time and culture. The major variants are constant, whether used in ancient Greece or medieval China. The forms of deception exist not only for wily warriors but also for husbands and lovers, novelists and thieves, and even are paralleled in the natural world. Deception is all around us and comes in six specific varieties.

THE STRUCTURE

Although cheating is a subtype of deception, the same six categories apply. Essentially, cheating, or deception is the advantageous distortion of perceived reality. The advantage falls to the cheater because the cheated person misperceives what is assumed to be the real world. A cloud of dust leads to the conclusion that the Lone Ranger is about to appear, but instead the shifty Indians swoop down. This is psychological cheating, creating a misperception; but long before there were Indians or men at all who could consciously adjust the appearance of reality to their own advantage, nature had fashioned physical distortions to the advantage of various species. The chameleon does not think about shifting colors to confound potential predators; it has been structured to do so automatically, genetically programmed cheating coming at the end of a long period of natural selection or perhaps in a single moment of mutation. In any case, the categories of physical deception are exactly the same as those of psychological deception, less interesting but just as real. It is possible to construct a taxonomy or set of standard categories that accounts for all examples of deception, whether they are by means of smoke screens, diplomatic codes, forged letters, assumed titles, the Statue of Liberty play in football, or new wine in old bottles.

Physical Cheating in Nature

Every species' environment includes its predators and its prey. Any mutation that either helps protect an organism from a predator or increases its chances of getting food or of reproducing will be passed on to the next generation. Biologists estimate that any characteristic that gives an organism as little as a 0.01 percent advantage over an organism lacking the characteristic will tend to be preserved and in 5,000 generations will spread to 50 percent of the individuals of its species. Any mutation that saves even one animal in 10,000 encounters of its species with predators will be preserved and will firmly establish itself in the species. It is these often almost imperceptible genetic advantages that explain some of the bizarre hiding and showing mutations that have been preserved and elaborated in nature.

On first consideration, the overwhelming number of nature's examples of deception, such as the polar bear or the speckled trout, appear to belong in the commonsense rubric of camouflage. Yet matters are more complex as there are two broad categories in the structure of deceit, *hiding the real* and *showing the false.* The second category cannot exist without the first, for all deception and cheating involves hiding. Level-one deception, hiding, is itself divided into three distinct parts: masking, repackaging, and dazzling. Level-two deception, showing, also has three parts: mimicking, inventing, and decoying.

HIDING

a. Masking.   Masking occurs when the real is hidden by blending with a background, integrating itself with the surroundings, or, best of all, seeking invisibility. An almost completely transparent fish becomes all but invisible and is masked from all potential enemies. An animal may blend with a generalized background, as in the case of the polar bear, whose white hair is *not* white but clear thus creating an illusion—an effect—of whiteness through the nature of reflective light that masks its presence by blending with the general background of its environment, snow. The chameleon, on the other hand, is masked by blending with different backgrounds, from twig brown to leaf green. An interesting example of very special blending is the zebra: during the day when it is least vulnerable to the big hunting cats its black and white stripes are highly visible, but at dusk, when it is most vulnerable, it becomes difficult to perceive in the high grass and is masked from the hungry lion.

b. Repackaging.   When the real is hidden by repackaging, the new package may be perceived in various ways, as dangerous or harmless or simply irrelevant. Some succulent insects repackage themselves to look like sticks: what bird wants to eat an old stick? A twig or a leaf is not always an ideal package, because when it rains the water darkens the real limb or leaf, and *voila!* the insect appears in a not very successful disguise. A very elegant adaptation in packaging is a Panamanian bark bug of the *Heteroptera* group of insects that not only looks like bark but also can change the color of its package to match the wet bark. Some insects have markings that frighten predators away, like the large eyes on each wing of the *Automeris moloneyl* moth, which frighten off hungry birds. Rockfish look like rocks and nothing eats rocks. In Kenya there is an insect colony that at rest appears to be a plant with green insects for stems, white for flowers, even pink ones for petal tips. When disturbed, the colony becomes a whirling swarm of tiny insects that as quickly as possible resettles into the "flower" package.

c. Dazzling.   All potential victims have the ultimate problem of what to do when the predator *knows* you are there. No hope of invisibility or changing the package when the wolf is at the gate. Mostly nature has worked very hard to avoid this situation by either masking or repackaging. If the first package does not work, then improvements may be devised, as in the case of the bark bug. A specific example of dazzle—confounding the pursuit—in nature occurs, when a predator attacks an octopus. The potential victim is seen and pursued. Under attack the octopus shoots out ink that dazzles the predator and masks the octopus's withdrawal to safety.

SHOWING

Showing complements hiding, and, like hiding, can be divided into three distinct parts: mimicking, inventing, and decoying.

a. Mimicking.   Animals that mimic do so not just to hide but to produce an advantageous effect—to go on the offensive. The bark bug wants to look like bark so it can go about its normal bug business undisturbed. A praying mantis, however, looks like a stick in order to lure prey close enough to seize. An anglerfish looks like a rock except for a long filament waving before its mouth; potential prey, lured close to investigate the filament, assume there is nothing down there but harmless rocks. One bird sneaking an egg into another's nest is a complex example of mimicking, the odd egg mimicking the nesting mother bird's real eggs. In Africa there are species where not only do the eggs mimic those of the host species, but on hatching the wee bird mimics the color markings of the host brood so that the impostor is both hatched and fed for free.

b. Inventing.   In general, animals rely on mimicking for safety when some form of hiding is not possible. Although there are few examples in nature of real wolves in sheep's clothing, some do exist. There is a kind of anglerfish that invents a new reality. In addition to a body like a rock and a long filament protruding from the head, on the tip of its filament this anglerfish has a simulated small swimming fish and even two pigment spots resembling a tiny fish's eyes. The anglerfish has invented an alternative reality. In Ethiopia, the bird called standard wing nightjar, appears from a distance to be a group of birds rather than one because of the placement of their feather-tip wing standards, thereby discouraging potential enemies. There is a moth, easily recognized by its prominent eyes, that also has an "eye" on its tail. A hungry bird will swoop on the moth and snatch the "eye" on the tail. The moth may make its way with part of a tail but not without its head.

c. Decoying.   Sometimes matters reach the point where it is necessary for an animal to decoy the predator away from the discovered real, for example, a nest of babies. Still you cannot win every time. When a bird fears for her brood—a brood the predator knows about—she confuses by fluttering away, seem-

ingly crippled. Under pursuit, much like a scrambling football quarterback, the bird is in effect decoying by looking left
and running right, misdirecting pursuit away from the nest.

PSYCHOLOGICAL CHEATING BY HUMANS

However much those who intend to deceive are inspired by
biological examples or are interested in applying natural phenomena, it is psychological cheating that matters to humans.
Man, unlike unthinking plants and animals, *consciously* distorts perceived reality for advantage. But when he does so,
man uses the two basic deceptive devices of nature, hiding
and showing. Humans make a philosophical assumption that
an objective reality exists, but that all life and most particularly man is deceived about its nature because of limited or
special sensory power. We see only certain light and hear only
certain sound frequencies. The pig can sense radioactivity on
its skin while man cannot. The eye actually presents visual
images upside down, but our brains adjust the image to reality and "see" right side up. Man may use his limited and
special natural sensors or his artificial ones to deceive, but
that is a matter of technique not nomenclature. There remain
only six basic ways of cheating, the three hiding variants and
the three showing ones. The basic purpose of hiding is to
screen or cloak a person, place, thing, direction, or time by a
variety of means that range from the simple to the complex.
These combined means hide by producing a *cover.* The basic
purpose of showing is consciously to display the false which,
perforce, must hide the real. In showing, the end result is to
create an EFFECT, an illusion of the false as real. All SHOW-
ING involves hiding, but HIDING almost never involves
showing.

Hiding

In *masking,* the real is hidden in a variety of ways ranging from degrees of invisibility to blending, both general and specific. An optimum type of masking would be to hide one penny among many pennies, the person placing it there being the only one to know of its "difference." In real life, an espionage mole without a control—that is, a spy assigned to take a job where contact by the secret controller might not be made for years—would be truly invisible. The mole unless revealed by the controller or himself is invisible because he is what he is except for what he *may* do later. Once he is activated under control, the purpose of his cover, his mask, changes from hiding his potential intentions to hiding his spying, but the mask remains exactly the same. Another category of invisibility is that of the needle in the haystack. In the case of the penny, the problem is to discover how this penny is unlike any other penny; in the needle-and-haystack case, the problem is to find a needle known to be present when it is masked by so much straw. Such an effective mask is the aspiration of nonmilitary commanders. Every Poseidon nuclear submarine, for example, is protected by such a mask: there may be some effort to mask the sub with a gray paint job, but the real mask is the size of the tiny, quiet needle/sub in the huge noisy haystack/ocean. Masking is, of course, the prime example of the common-sense use of the word *camouflage:* battleships painted gray to blend with the ocean or tanks painted yellow-brown to blend with the desert. Specific masking is used when antiaircraft guns are camouflaged to look like parts of real buildings. Of course, when the Mongols stirred up dust clouds to hide their movements they did not quite realize that they were employing the *theory* of masking, only that their enemies would not know their numbers.

Unlike in nature, where masking is common, in early military history simple masking was relatively rare. Soldiers rarely wore camouflage. It was generally considered more important that soldiers look like an army, dressed in gorgeous red coats or blue uniforms, in hopes that they would then act like an army. The great age of camouflage did not begin until this century: in World War One military assets could be damaged from a distance and thus had to be masked; and soldiers proved less vulnerable when they blended into the background rather than forming a mass of many splendid uniforms. Of course, charging in mass even in dirty-brown uniforms proved almost as costly during World War One as it always had been, but such passive masking of men and equipment was in some part effective.

Masking in modern military affairs is far more complex than jungle camouflage suits and dust clouds, but the principle remains the same. The evolution of the dust cloud can be seen in the development of aluminum foil to confound radar and mask attacking airplanes. In fact, a whole complicated world of electronic masking has been constructed, each advance usually leading to a new means of sophisticated discovery. Nevertheless room still remains for sheer ingenuity. In the present undersea needle-and-haystack East-West confrontation, the Soviets have a serious problem in that their submarines are sufficiently noisy so that American and Allied technicians can often track their courses. If the needle in the haystack makes noise, it will not be masked for long. In an effort to move one submarine unseen from Murmansk to Cuba, a maneuver that, if discovered, would surely have been seen in Washington as a provocation, Moscow came up with an ideal masking ruse. The submarine simply sailed the entire route directly under a harmless merchant vessel. The sound signature was masked from American listening devices—at least almost and for some time.

In the *repackaging* category, the real is hidden by a new wrapping. An armed frigate disguised as a small freighter thus becomes a Q-boat ready, when near a potential target, to discard its fake lifeboats or dummy deckhouse and become a warship. In more sporting matters a fast black horse is repackaged with paint as a slow white horse. Quite the same thing occurred in the Korean War, when the intervening Chinese downgraded their apparent strength by giving each type of unit a lower designation so that corps were renamed divisions and divisions renamed regiments and so on down to the smallest units. In the same war, and hence their direct intervention in the conflict, the Soviets gave their pilots international Nansen passports so that if they were captured they would not be seen to be Russian, and Soviet intervention in the conflict would not be revealed. Same fellows but different package. During the Sinai Campaign in October 1956, General Moshe Dayan called the opening shot, when Israeli paratroopers seized the Mitla Pass, a "reprisal" raid to delay a full-scale Egyptian counterattack.

When an object can neither blend in with the background by some form of masking nor be repackaged effectively, when, in fact, the object is known to exist within a tangible context, the qualities of the object may be changed in such a way as to confound, and this is *dazzling*. All military and diplomatic codes and ciphers are a form of dazzling: it is obvious to any eavesdropper that messages of importance are being sent, but the adjustments of the cryptographer confound. A specific example of dazzling would be the false painted wave on a ship's bow that confounds observers as to the ship's speed but not its existence. A most elegant example of dazzling occurred in 1944 when General George Patton's deception planners cloaked the Third Army's move north to relieve the German siege of Bastogne. They knew that there was no way they could prevent the Germans from realizing that Patton was moving, the volume of radio traffic if nothing else would indicate as much. So they simply sent movement orders to five different Patton "armies," only one of which was the real one. The Germans realized that the Third Army was moving but were dazzled—confounded—by instructions to five "Third Armies."

Here is a simple example of dazzling. The man knows that one end ought to be up but is confounded by multiple instructions. This is not any different, except in scale, from the five armies of Patton, only one of which was real.

Showing

In the *mimicking* category, a replica of reality is created by selecting one or more characteristics of the real in order to achieve an advantageous effect. A duck hunter uses a duck call, one single characteristic of a real duck, to create an EF-FECT for real ducks of a congenial stopping place—an economical use of mimicking. A more eager hunter may also use wooden decoys of ducks floating on the pond to persuade the ducks flying over that this particular pond is congenial and safe. The ducks thus both hear and see other contented "ducks" on the pond but not the hunter who has masked himself in his blind. The most complicated mimicking would make use of a *doppelgänger,* for example when the bright identical twin takes the place of the lazy one during an exam. On an assembly line one item mimics the next, the difference being only singularity, akin to the penny among pennies. Mimicking has regularly been used by military strategists. During World War One the Germans, although evenly matched against the Belgians before Liège in August 1914, used units from five corps, wearing their identifying patches to make up an assault force of some 20,000 men of only six brigades to mimic an overwhelming force of some 150,000. Fearing disaster, the Belgians withdrew their own 20,000-man infantry screen from the great fortress of Liège, and the Germans won without battle. Similar effects may be obtained by increasing radio traffic, scattering false unit clues, or creating a stage army that repeatedly marches up the same hill.

The following comic strip opens with Linus making the assumption that he is being *dazzled*—he knows that his teasing friends are there but is uncertain of exactly where. On whipping off the obvious packaging he is confounded to discover the wrong culprit, the bird who intensifies the EFFECT by mimicking with a "woof" as does the·dog with a "chirp."

A somewhat more bizarre case of mimicking occurred in Canada when an illiterate pensioner died in Toronto several years ago. There would no longer be a monthly check endorsed by the old man's thumbprint. His family was desolate but ingenious. They didn't inform the government that dear Dad was dead, cut off his thumb and preserved it in formaldehyde, and settled down to some years of monthly

checks endorsed as usual with his thumb print. Not until 1979 did a routine door-to-door survey of pensioners discover that his family had been the live pensioner with the dead thumb.

In the *inventing* category the false is displayed through the fashioning of an alternative reality and not simply through the mimicking of the existing reality. A false document appears real but it is not; it needn't mimic a real document—it is itself, albeit false. Rubber tanks, fake airfields, or dummy radio traffic are all invented; they are produced to show to the opponent. For example the Greeks at the siege of Syracuse in 212 BC constructed the false beach mimicking the real one; at Ragusa in 1171 the Venetians created the false fort "out of whole cloth," as did the Flemish defenders of Tournai in 1513. The Venetians and Flemish commanders thus created an EFFECT that was wholly false while the Greeks created an EFFECT that was just like the real. There was a most elegant example of inventing during World War Two: using a dead body, the British created a phantom officer who washed up on the Spanish shore carrying all sorts of false and misleading papers and documents that would make their way to the Germans. He became known in his new guise as The-Man-Who-Never-Was.

One of the most famous and long-lived examples of inventing was the Donation of Constantine, a legal document, supposedly written by Emperor Constantine, in which he entrusted Rome to the popes; in fact it was a forgery done in the early medieval period, apparently intended to bolster the papacy. For centuries it was accepted as authentic, just as are many forged art works, "new" plays by Shakespeare written in contemporary garrets, or some assumed titles and coats of arms, and the painted gunports on some warships. All are false, created by the guileful for their own advantage.

For successful mimicking or creation of the false, there is a period of time—sometimes forever, as in the case of the Donation of Constantine—during which the EFFECT must *not* be revealed as an illusion if the intended advantage is to be gained. After a certain point this may no longer matter—the money is in hand, the battle is won, or the faker is in distant parts. Yet for effect there must be hiding. What happens when the victim *knows* he is going to be dazzled when the false is presented? If the guileful person cannot hide his intention or perhaps even his invention, what then? It is clear to an observer that a certain kind of action is impending, no hiding allowed. For example, in football there must be an offensive play and in most cases it must be (or is enormously likely to be) a certain variant that can be statistically charted in advance. The book says that in this case the offensive team, this very team, this very quarterback, passes 85 percent of the time. How can this quarterback deceive? He has recourse to *decoying*—the quarterback may look left and run right. More likely and more elegantly, he may deploy his team so as to present the defense with a variety of potential directions and possibilities, hiding his real intentions by decoying with false options.

Thus the old adage "Truth is the safest lie" implies that, given a situation in which an answer must be given, the guileful will resort to the unexpected truth that will be taken as a lie. Boxing is filled with feints and decoys. Many magic tricks are based on the fact that even if the audience knows that they are to be cheated their attention is decoyed from the method. And most military attacks attempt to decoy the opposition as to the time or the direction or the place or the size of the expected battle. In the case where the battle is seen to be "impossible" at a particular time or place, much of the decoying is done by the attackers themselves, as was the case at the Battle of Quebec. A familiar event occurred at Masuria in February 1915, when the German general, Ludendorf, opened his preemptive offensive against the Russians during winter weather that the tsar's generals deemed impossibly severe for military operations.

Thus there are but six ways to cheat, three involving hiding the real by masking, repackaging, or dazzling and three involving showing the false by mimicking, inventing or decoying. The same six ways exist both in the physical world of nature and the psychological world of man. Any deception that does not fit into one of the six categories is not a true deception but rather some sort of conceit: women with purple bouffant hairdos are not cheating nor are most who use orange nail polish. A fake beauty spot, however, *may* be a case of displaying the false as real, unless it is obviously false; then it is an adornment, a conceit. Such conceits may serve a very serious purpose, as do the beards on the statues of female Pharaohs: they add legitimacy but without cheating the viewer, who is not deceived as to the actual sex represented. To find out which category any deception fits in, the first question should be whether the ruse is intended to hide or to show.

THE STRUCTURE OF DECEPTION
(with process defined)

DECEPTION
(distorting reality)

DISSIMULATION (Hiding the Real)	SIMULATION (Showing the False)
MASKING	**MIMICKING**
Conceals one's own } Charcs Matches Another's } (To Eliminate an Old Pattern or Blend It with a Background Pattern.)	Copies Another's Charcs (To Recreate an Old Pattern, Imitating It.)
REPACKAGING	**INVENTING**
Adds New } Charcs Subtracts Old } (To Modify an Old Pattern by Matching Another.)	Creates New Charcs (To Create a New Pattern.)
DAZZLING	**DECOYING**
Obscures Old } Charcs Adds Alternative } (To Blur an Old Pattern, Reducing Its Certainty.)	Creates Alternative Charcs (To Give an Additional, Alternative Pattern, Increasing Its Certainty.)

In order to be absolutely certain that the six categories are clear, it might be wise to take a brief test, the Cheating Category Exam (CCE). To which category of hiding or showing does each example belong?

CHEATING CATEGORY EXAM

1. A silencer on a pistol.
2. On 9 November 1980, New York Giant football quarter-back Simms, using slant 114 flea flicker, handed the ball to Leon Perry, the rookie fullback, who flipped the ball back to Simms, who threw it deep down the right side-line for Friede. The Dallas Cowboy cornerback Steve Wilson slipped, and Friede made a diving catch at the Dallas 7. The play led to a field goal and a rare 38–35 victory for the Giants.
3. The Trojan horse.
4. Just before the Sinai campaign in October 1956, Moshe Dayan ordered the single forward reconnaissance patrol to wear Bedouin sandals made in Hebron so that their footprints would not be different from those of ordinary Arab smugglers, in order to hide Israeli interest in Egypt.
6. Major Funston's capture of Aguinaldo by using his Filipino troops dressed like rebel Moros.
7. In 1944 the Germans used captured American B-17's to fly close to United States Eighth Air Force box formations in order to gather in-flight intelligence.
8. In 1975 the Washington, D.C., police set up a branch of the Mafia and began to purchase stolen goods in order to gather information on a wave of thefts.
9. World War Two German U-boats used rubber hull coating to reduce their sound reflection as registered on Allied sonar devices.
10. In Shakespeare's *Macbeth*, one of the unlikely predictions concerning the fate of Macbeth was that he would reign until Birnam Wood should come to Dunsinane, his castle. This in fact occurred when his opponent's approach-

ing army covered themselves with the branches of the trees of Birnam Wood.

11. The practice of maintaining normal diplomatic relations prior to an attack—the German invasion of Russia in 1941 or the Soviet invasion of Czechoslovakia in 1968.

12. Searchlights used by an attacking force at night and focused on the enemy lines.

13. At Port Laoighise prison in Ireland a woman was discovered smuggling explosives to IRA prisoners in a condom secreted within her person.

14. According to Judges 4:12, the Israelites, counseled by Deborah, lured the Canaanite legions into a marshy, narrow plain by deploying a small token force that retreated. In the marsh with its chariots inoperative, the Canaanites were ambushed by the 10,000 Israelites that then poured down the slopes of Mount Tabor.

15. The columns in classical Greek architecture appear straight but are in fact tapered slightly toward the top, which creates the usual impression of straightness.

ANSWERS

1. A silencer would be hiding-masking the sound.

2. The flea flicker is a classic example of decoying. The use of the word *razzle-dazzle* for such a play is a misnomer in terms of cheating categories, since the purpose was to show the Dallas Cowboys various options—as well as hide the Giant's ultimate intentions.

3. The Trojan horse is an example of showing-inventing: the Greeks created something that did not exist before.

4. Dayan's men were mimicking Arabs by employing a single "Arab" characteristic, sandal prints, and thus hid their existence by showing.

5. See page 65.
6. Funston was showing-inventing the "Moro" army, he and the other Americans going along as "prisoners."
7. This is an almost perfect example of showing-mimicking, for the B-17's used by the Germans *are* B-17's, *doppelgängers* except for their crews.
8. Here the police show-invent an alternative Mafia to dupe the thieves.
9. The Germans were seeking invisibility by hiding-masking their submarines with antisonar paint.
10. As long as the army under Birnam Wood remained unobserved they were hiding-masking their presence, but when they began to march toward Dunsinane, thus revealing their nature, they were hiding-dazzling Macbeth; the closer they got the less relevant the camouflage became.
11. Maintaining "normal" relations is a form of masking the actual intent to invade.
12. The attacking force is dazzling the defenders by use of the searchlights.
13. The woman was employing a means of repackaging, but the real category was masking—seeking to be invisible.
14. The Israelites had employed an invented reality—the feigned flight that led the Canaanites into a trap.
15. Here the Greeks are hiding the actual visual nature of the columns as they would be seen by the human eye by slightly repackaging them. They have hidden their real shape.

Now while there are only six *kinds* of cheating, there is only one *way* to cheat. To cheat, one chooses from one or more of the six categories one or more CHARACTERISTICS and fashions this into a RUSE that creates an ILLUSION of either COVER or EFFECT.

THE CHARACTERISTIC SPECTRUM, OR CHARCS

Once one or more of the six categories has been selected (consciously or unconsciously—to date most cheating has been done without theoretical knowledge of the six cheating categories), the planner selects one or more appropriate bits from an infinite *CHARACTERISTIC SPECTRUM*. These are the *CHARCS of cheating*. To be most cost-effective, normal practice would be to use as few charcs as possible. For example, in mimicking for military purpose, a hat on a stick to draw fire really uses only one charc to create the EFFECT of an entire soldier. At the opposite extreme, other assets—an identical twin—may allow the use of all but one characteristic or CHARC (in this case, individuality) at no additional cost.

Masking. The CHARCS may range from a few splashes of paint to the advanced technology needed to make a Poseidon "invisible" or a Stealth aircraft undetectable by Soviet radar.

Repackaging. A few bits of uniform are sufficient to repackage a person; but in Burbank, California, during World War Two, a great many CHARCS were needed to turn the Lockheed-Vega plant into an apparent suburb when seen from the air.

Dazzling. A single aspect of an object may be altered or a new aspect incorporated in order to confound. The one CHARC bow wave painted on a warship or the flashing searchlights during a night attack are cost-effective. Considerably more effort had to go into deploying CHARCS when the Americans created five of Patton's Third Army.

Mimicking. The Canadian family who used the single CHARC of the deceased man's thumb is an ideal example of the cost-effectiveness of mimicking: a cloud of dust can stand for an army or a trumpet call for a charge.

Inventing.   This category usually takes a little more effort than mimicking, since something entirely false must be created by a combination of CHARCS. Thus, during World War Two the British created a live double for General Montgomery—this was mimicking—but the invented man-who-never-was was a considerably more troublesome ruse and also more elegant. The end result, the EFFECT, of inventing has much to offer in that a fake Picasso or Corot is more likely to create the ILLUSION of the real if it does not mimic an existing painting but only a real style of painting, one characteristic of the real work.

Decoying.   Here the simple look-left-run-right option might be elaborated into an elegant military strategy of the indirect approach (which simply displays a series of options). During the various Israeli desert campaigns in the Sinai the actual option chosen often depended on last-minute selection by front-line commanders, just as in some football plays the quarterback may have preferred options at the snap of the ball but chooses another as the play unfolds. In war and football both, the options presented (and often denied) to the defense are CHARCS, characteristics of potential real offensive thrusts.

The Ruse

The RUSE is the process of choosing first the appropriate category, such as dazzling or mimicking, and then the necessary number of CHARCS to create either a COVER or an EFFECT. It must be noted again that all showing-RUSES will make use of hiding categories and CHARCS and that more than one category may be employed in any one RUSE.

There is an endless number of possible RUSES, just as one can consider an almost endless number of CHARCS (going down, if need be, to the level of subatomic particles) but each must be fashioned by the planner from one or more varieties of the six categories of cheating. The RUSE may be used by the planner for minor tactical gain (the old shell game) or for great strategic gain, as did Hitler by hiding his Operation Barbarossa invasion of Russia by continuing normal relations. RUSES, whether used to create COVER or EFFECT, themselves tend to fall into five categories:

> UNNOTICED
> BENIGN
> DESIRABLE
> UNAPPEALING
> DANGEROUS

The purpose of the CHARCS used to hide the Poseidon submarine is to fashion a RUSE that assures the ship will be UNNOTICED. The CHARCS of the apparent merchant ship that suddenly turns into a Q-boat were chosen to create a RUSE that will be BENIGN. The Trojan horse CHARCS of inventing produce a DESIRABLE RUSE. Some RUSES of war create for the planner an EFFECT seen as UN-APPEALING—two enemy armies instead of one or, for the butterfly, where nature is the planner, markings—big eyes—that are perceived by the predator as dangerous or unappealing, such as those that mimic distasteful bugs. In all five cases, the RUSE fashioned by the planner creates a COVER or an EFFECT for the potential victim who, it is hoped, will accept the ILLUSION.

The Illusion

Once the appropriate category or categories has been selected by the planner, the necessary CHARCS fashioned into a RUSE for one of the five basic purposes, either a COVER or an EFFECT—*both illusory*—exists. This is the crucial moment for the planner, for his opponent must accept the ILLUSION if he is to be cheated or deceived. Self-deception is another matter and counterdeception is an entire separate topic, but for the moment the crux of the matter is whether the EFFECT or COVER will create an effective ILLUSION. The ILLUSION may be intended to be permanent so that the deceived remains deceived, or it may be temporary, self-revealing or certain of discovery. The anonymous author of the Donation of Constantine hoped that his work would be accepted forever, while most battlefield commanders know their ILLUSIONS need only be temporary. Thus the Egyptians planning for the October War sought invisibility in that the Israelis would notice no change until it was too late. And their ILLUSION of COVER worked. Even if the COVER had begun to fray before the planned opening day of the battle, the attack still might have gone ahead. If the COVER for the Allied invasion of Normandy had collapsed a week before D-Day the attack would have to have been canceled; but, after D-Day-minus-seven, every day that the ILLUSION of COVER was accepted, this even if temporary COVER was an increasing advantage. In point of fact, the COVER lasted until the attack was already launched.

A schematic diagram of cheating using applied psychology would be:

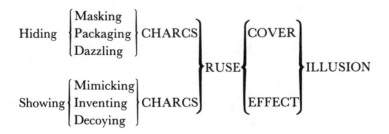

HOW TO CHEAT

Most cheating is intuitive, spontaneous, ad hoc, and seldom analyzed in retrospect. Except for magicians, deceivers have no general theory of how to cheat. This holds true even for the long tradition of military deception planning.

> GENERAL: Captain, take your men to the left and stir up some dust. Major, give him an hour and then attack on the right.

This is a clear example of mimicking by showing the false. The general would probably be taken aback if told that not only was he using one special category of cheating but also that the *way* he intended to cheat the enemy can be plotted by using Deception Loop Analysis that traces his maneuver from the CHARCS through to the final result. Even when commanders have specially designated deception planners to design and produce a series of elegant ruses, much of the cheating is done intuitively with shortcuts along the Deception Loop. Still, most commanders and skilled deception specialists, not to mention magicians, would in retrospect recognize their moves along that loop. Then, too, long after the event, historians tend to presume a far higher degree of rationality and planning than actually existed.

The complex process of cheating, that is, planning and designing the deception, can be reduced to a rather simple model, the Deception Planning Loop. The Loop is only half as complex as it appears, since the analysis and design halves are mirror images of each other. The entire cheating process may be presented as a simple linear sequence from the senior commander's strategic goal to the deception planner's goal. The general wants to surprise the enemy and win the battle as part of a grand strategy to achieve total victory. To do so he resorts to a deception stratagem that confuses the point of attack in the enemy's mind because they accept the ILLUSION of EFFECT by glimpsing in the air (CHANNEL) the false "army" created by the captain's RUSE, a cloud of dust. The dust cloud is the chosen characteristic, CHARC, from the MIMICKING category.

The General said: "Captain, take your men to the left and stir up some dust. Major, give him an hour and then attack on the right."

THE DECEPTION PLANNING LOOP

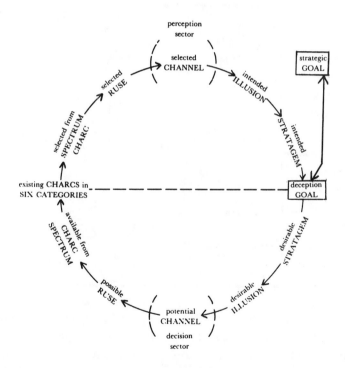

If the enemy accepts the ILLUSION, then the general's *deception goal* contributed to his *strategic goal,* winning. With rare exceptions successful deception requires a goal beyond deceit alone. Few cheat solely for the pleasure of so doing but in pursuit of some goal, and this is particularly true in military matters. Generally, cheating is a purposeful human activity that contributes to a greater ambition. And the process *always* follows the Deception Planning Loop defined by category, fashioning a RUSE from CHARCS that are projected by a selected CHANNEL as an EFFECT or COVER that, if successful, creates an ILLUSION made up of the perceived CHARCS that is, therefore, a successful STRATAGEM supporting the Deception Goal and hence the Strategic Goal. Every time.

Here we see Crazy Shirley in her strategic pursuit of Heathcliff select from the six deception categories an invention, particular books, that will lure him into position by showing him something he will want through adaptation of the existing CHARCS of the Romance Section. Here, the hiding

CHARCS are very prominent, but Shirley is essentially SHOWING—luring—by making a RUSE out of the books (CHARCS). This RUSE is then projected through Heathcliff's visual reception of the CHARCS as real, thus giving him the ILLUSION that he was safe to move close. And the Shirley STRATAGEM worked, a victory for the deception goal, and one more step in the ultimate strategic intention of subduing her elusive Heathcliff. But, as with most ILLUSIONS, the desired EFFECT was short-lived.

For Shirley and all other deception planners, the crucial moment comes as the EFFECT or COVER RUSE is transformed into an ILLUSION. This is the moment of deception, when the RUSE will be either accepted or rejected by the target audience, Heathcliff. Obviously, this acceptance or rejection of the RUSE may be partial, some CHARCS accepted and some not. Heathcliff accepted that the books were books and nothing more. He might of course have realized that they were a lure if he had heard Shirley, or he might simply have passed by the ILLUSION entirely as uninteresting or irrelevant and gone on to "spy novels." But he accepted the ILLUSION, believing what his eyes saw (CHANNEL).

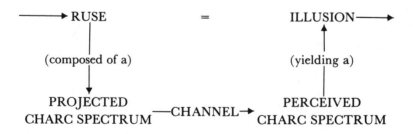

It should be remembered that Shirley and military commanders cannot *plan* ILLUSIONS and the consequent

STRATAGEM but only anticipate them in the planning process. An ILLUSION depends wholly on the external perceptions of the target audience. Thus the ILLUSION's acceptance is beyond the control of the planner. Some ILLUSIONS can almost be assured, however, because the COVER of the EFFECT is so overwhelmingly effective—the ocean is *almost* perfect COVER for a needle. The general's cloud of dust is not so certain an EFFECT and even if the opposing general accepts it as an ILLUSION, he may react in strange ways that largely ruin the stratagem. Heathcliff might simply have ignored the EFFECT and gone on to his Spy Stories, thus foiling Shirley's attempt to create an ILLUSION. Yet the possibility of projecting EFFECTS and COVERS that will be accepted as ILLUSIONS is what attracts the sly, especially military commanders, because the manipulation of such RUSES has proven so often to be cost-effective even if equally often dishonorable. And in the twentieth century the alternatives to brute force once more held an attraction to those who, during World War One, watched simplistic, straightforward commanders let their men be slaughtered by the million in return for acres of muddy real estate. It was no longer magnificent, only sordid. Without realizing the nature of the deception categories or the validity of the Deception Planning Loop, more pragmatic commanders again began to resort to guile.

CHAPTER 3

Applied Theory: Wily Warriors

♦ ♦ ♦

You can fool all of the people
some of the time.

—LINCOLN

FOR THE PURPOSES of the battlefield it is desirable for the wily
commander to fool all of his opponents, however briefly. Most
accepted ILLUSIONS are intended to be only temporary,
giving a necessary advantage of time and usually containing
an element of surprise. Few military illusions are intended to
be long-lived or permanent. Camouflage, a form of masking,
is more apparent; this particular hiding RUSE that produces
a cover was not really institutionalized until World War One.
Before then troops had indeed been hidden, as at Birnam
Wood, but uniforms still remained colorful, even when combat verged on being modern, as in the American Civil War.
Eventually the stolid World War One commanders noticed
the obvious advantage of dun-colored uniforms, mottled vehicles, and net-covered guns, although this happened very

slowly in a war notable for reliance on brute strength and not on guile. In fact, almost no war presented so few examples of cheating, even on a minor scale. Even the full impact of unexpected technological innovation was dissipated. The British introduced the tank on a small scale, the Germans gained only minor tactical advantage with poison gas, and airplane forays were little more than a spectator sport. The one major attempt to by-pass the deadlock of the trenches, the British invasion of the Dardanelles (a Winston Churchill project), came to grief as a result of inept commanders; strategic deception on a grand scale collapsed into an ignominious withdrawal that at least was made effective by the commanders' sneaking the troops off under the unsuspecting eyes of the Turkish army. By then Churchill's reputation for strategy had suffered gravely. The orthodox commanders, on the other hand, went right on sending vast numbers of troops to the battlefield for no visible gain. At least Churchill had tried—and not for the first time.

Three years before the outbreak of the Great War, Winston Churchill dreamed of a dummy fleet for the royal navy to deter the German High Seas Fleet and lure its submarines into traps. But not until two months into the war, when Churchill was first lord of the admiralty, was he able to get his plan under way. In October 1914, he wrote the following:

It is necessary to construct without delay a dummy fleet. Ten merchant vessels . . . should be selected at once. They should be distributed among various private yards not specially burdened with warship building at the present time. They are then to be mocked up to represent fast battleships of the First and Second Battle Squadrons. The actual size need not correspond exactly, as it is notoriously difficult to judge the size of vessels at sea, and frequently even destroyers are mistaken for cruisers.

We are bearing in mind particularly aerial and periscope ob-

servation where deception is much more easy. . . . Very little
metal would be required, and practically the whole work should
be executed in wood or canvas.

He explained, "Even when the enemy knows that we have
such a fleet its presence will tend to mystify and confuse his
plans, and baffle and distract the enterprise of his submarines.
He will always be in doubt as to which is the real and which
is the dummy fleet." This was to be a subtle use of mimicking
that contained elements of both decoying and dazzling—concepts unknown to Churchill, who simply possessed a naturally
inventive and devious mind. It would not matter if the Germans did discover that the phantom fleet existed because they
still would not be sure which fleet was real and which was
false, or at least not in all cases. And they would never be sure
whether or not the British were continuing to churn out
phantom battleships. At first, too, it was unlikely that the
RUSE would be denied, so that the ILLUSION would be
accepted for a time.

Ten old passenger and cargo ships were quickly selected
and reconstruction was begun that same month. Although
size was not a crucial factor, it was important that each ship's
silhouette resemble the warship it was to simulate. Accordingly, they were fitted out with broader decks, and were given
greater length, warshiplike bows and sterns, fire-control tow-
ers, turrets and guns, and the appropriate number of smoke-
stacks, ones that belched real smoke from small concealed
smoke generators. Because merchantmen without cargo ride
higher in the water than warships, each was ballasted down
with 9,000 tons of stone.

That winter the Royal Navy was supplemented with nine
dummy battleships mimicking *King George V, Centurion, Orion,
Marlborough, Ajax, Vanguard, St. Vincent, Collingwood,* and *Iron
Duke.* Although her namesake had already been lost, the tenth

dummy warship was named *Audacious* to prevent German naval intelligence from realizing that the real *Audacious* was sunk. Nine mimicked the real and one, the unreal. After these ten were "commissioned," four more liners and freighters were sent to the shipyards for similar conversion.

At first the phantom fleet anchored at the main naval base at Scapa Flow, placed in the outer roads to draw the first torpedos of any U-boats that might penetrate the well-defended base. Later they occasionally steamed out into the North Sea to lure U-boats to risk attack in the face of the very real escort warships.

Beginning in March 1915, ships of the phantom fleet were sent to the Mediterranean to support the big Allied naval effort to force their way through the Dardanelles and knock Turkey out of the war. Their role was again to act as decoys for submarines but also to draw fire from the Turkish shore batteries.

One of these vessels in the Mediterranean was the former S.S. *Merion,* a 12,000-ton liner converted to a dummy of the 30,000-ton *Tiger,* the Royal Navy's newest and largest battle cruiser. During the evening of 30 May 1915, pseudo-*Tiger* was sighted and torpedoed in the Aegean Sea by a German U-boat. The ship's captain, a seventy-year-old retired naval officer, and all but 4 of his crew of 117 managed to abandon ship successfully as the vessel, ballasted with rock, sank slowly on an even keel. The U-boat commander might have been puzzled initially by his victim's failure to heel over or plunge bow or stern first as ships normally did when torpedoed; but it must have dawned on him that he had been hoaxed when, as pseudo-*Tiger* slipped under, it shed its turrets, supposedly weighing 100 tons and left them floating off into the Aegean twilight, guns pointing to the sky.

Just as the deceiver can show strength where there is little or none, he can hide it where it is present. If the "Phantom

Fleet" was an example of sheep in wolves' clothing, the Q-boat RUSE was a wolf in sheep's clothing, the false strong mimicking the real weak.

In the fall of 1915, the British Admiralty sent three more ships, small worn-out tramp steamers, to the shipyards for conversion. This time, however, the intention was to arm them heavily for antisubmarine warfare while making them appear harmless targets to lure Q-boats. As a U-boat carried few torpedos, the hope was that its commander would waste no more than one before surfacing to finish off the "helpless" vessel with his deck gun. If the commander was suspicious, he would stay safely submerged and fire enough additional torpedoes to destroy the Q-boat and its remaining crew.

Each Q-boat was fitted with several guns. The gun positions were carefully disguised in collapsible deckhouses or lifeboats. A duplicate command post, disguised as a coil of rope on the deck, would enable the captain to remain hidden. Special steam pipes were installed that could billow out steam to make it look as though the boilers had ruptured. In case the U-boat used its deck gun, small explosive canisters were placed around the deck to confuse the gunners' aim by making near misses seem direct hits. To ensure maximum survivability, extra watertight compartments were fitted below decks and huge beams of Canadian spruce were bolted down in the hold.

On leaving port, the crews exchanged their immaculate naval uniforms for mixed sailors' garb bought secondhand from waterfront shops. Only as many crew members were allowed on deck as would be normal for a merchant ship. When the ship was attacked, the captain would remain hidden aboard with his engine room and gun crews, while the others, including one naval rating disguised as the ship's captain, would simulate panic and abandon ship.

One of these first three Q-boat conversions was the little

2,050-ton tramp steamer *Farnsborough*. She left Plymouth in
her new guise in October 1915, Captain Gordon Campbell
commanding. For six months she sailed the U-boat–infested
sea lanes off Britain's Atlantic coast. Patiently she awaited
her first attack, steaming out of port by night and returning
by day. Finally, five months later, its lookout shouted "Tor-
pedo, starboard!" The tin fish struck and its explosion tore
a 20-foot hole in the side. Captain Campbell, ordering the
"panic party" off in the lifeboats, stayed behind with his
small fighting party. While the captain and his gun crews
remained hidden, the "black gang" in the engine room, some
severely wounded, signaled that the sea was pouring in.

As the *Farnsborough* slowly settled, the cautious U-boat tra-
versed the starboard side, only its periscope showing, carefully
inspecting the damage and checking for any sign of resistance. Campbell fought the urgent temptation to open fire
from his sinking ship.

Suddenly the U-boat surfaced 300 yards off to port. Its
commander had decided to finish off his victim with his deck
gun. Campbell called off the range to his five gun crews and
ordered: "Commence firing!" As the U-boat commander
emerged from his conning tower, he was completely surprised
to see the disguise shields drop and the five 12-pounders open
fire. The sub sank instantly. Only one officer and a crewman
were saved. *Farnsborough* was eventually towed home and Captain Campbell received the Victoria Cross.

The British admiralty's adventures into deception played a
minor part in what came to be known as the Great War.
Ultimately, after years of slaughter, there would be some
large-scale attempts on the western front to engineer victories
other than by means of the dumb, direct assault on a forewarned and highly prepared enemy. There were surprise
withdrawals and sudden attacks without "proper" prepara-

tion and shifts in the axis of attack, but even then there was never the elegance to be found in many of the battle maneuvers of the American Civil War or of Napoleon's preimperial days. In fact, the only long-term use of decoying—the key major military RUSE—came, as might have been expected, away from the main center of confrontation in World War One, away from the control of the conventional.

In the Middle East, the British, suffering from the same lack of military imagination not to mention guile as in Europe, had been unable to push northeast from Egypt against the Turko-German forces under General Falkenhayn. During 1917 the main British thrust straight ahead toward Gaza had gained little but casualties. The costly failures prompted a shift in command that brought in General Allenby, who, in the words of T. E. Lawrence (Lawrence of Arabia), turned the use of deception from witty hors d'oeuvres before a battle into the main point of strategy. The third battle of Gaza would be quite unlike the first two. Still, even with Allenby and a new staff, including his main deception planner and chief intelligence officer, Major Richard Meinertzhagen, the German and Turkish commanders expected anything but innovation and imagination from the British. New commanders and old tactics had long been the book on the Allies, whether in Europe or the Middle East. They thus anticipated yet another costly and inconclusive British push from the left, seaward, straight along the coast toward Gaza.

Allenby chose to launch his attack from the right, inland flank toward Beersheba and also sought to disguise his intention through a variety of RUSES of EFFECT. Major Meinertzhagen "communicated" to German and Turkish intelligence various ingenious clues designed to focus their attention on the old familiar Gaza on the left rather than the real target of Beersheba on the right. Thus, for example, when false documents—invented for the occasion—were left in a haversack to be captured by the Turks, an alternate and advantageous reality had been created, and channeled to the enemy. Along with the haversack papers, the Germans pieced together all sorts of clues seemingly acquired by their own efforts. Realizing, that, as the British army moved toward Beersheba, the Germans and Turks would note the maneuver, Meinertzhagen leaked other clues that there *would* be an attack on Beersheba but that it would be only a small diversionary one. The Germans thus "knew" that there would be a small attack toward Beersheba on 3 January 1918, to disguise the real attack against Gaza. What they did not know was that the real British attack would come on December 31 and be toward Beersheba. On December 31, the Germans and Turks were thus caught napping—literally, for Meinertzhagen, as a final RUSE, had the Royal Flying Corps drop gift packages of cigarettes for the Turkish front-line troops, cigarettes laced with that high-potency soporific, opium. The attack surprised Falkenhayn, routed the off-guard and off-balance Turkish army, broke the stalemate, and led to the British capture of Jerusalem.

Allenby repeated the initial success the next year on September 19 at Megiddo; he used a similar feint-with-deception RUSE, only this time his line of operations was reversed and was up the coast. Coordinated with this attack were a series of feints by Major T. E. Lawrence to divert enemy attention inland to his own trans-Jordan desert front. This decoy RUSE succeeded in unbalancing the smaller and weaker Turkish-German force and precipitated their headlong flight. Seven days later all of Palestine had fallen to the British, in considerable part because the Allenby-Meinertzhagen EFFECTS were accepted as ILLUSIONS by the German and Turkish commanders.

In fact, however, in the course of World War One all too

few EFFECTS were sent or ILLUSIONS accepted. And when a few commanders did resort to guile and deception, their experience was usually forgotten. None of the nations involved had any sort of institutional memory, but a great many of those who had suffered the idiocy of brute-force generals sought less painful means to fight any future war. Some saw the airplane as the new swift strategic weapon, others sought to protect their troops by constructing deep underground fortifications along their threatened borders. Many advocated disarmament and others the virtues of armor.

But one man, British army captain B. H. Liddell Hart, produced a most influential theory on the virtues of the strategic indirect approach which he put together as a result of rummaging through military history. He found that the indirect, devious way was almost always preferable to the direct approach. Realizing that this strategy was largely a psychological approach, he quoted Lenin with approval: "The soundest strategy in war is to postpone operations until the moral disintegration of the enemy renders the delivery of the mortal blow both possible and easy."

This old-new theory was all very well for captains, but most generals tend to prepare for the next war by employing the lessons learned from the past—and, more often than not, such "lessons" prove irrelevant once the firing starts. After observing the Spanish Civil War for two years, the French "learned" to spread out their tanks rather than concentrate them in armored columns, and so the Allies were unprepared for a war of blitzkreig. In fact it appeared that they were unprepared for any war, with or without guile, so that by the autumn of 1940, with France lost and German bombers over London, the end seemed to be in sight. Hitler, however, turned east and attacked Russia. Britain got a reprieve and the war went on but this time not guilelessly.

In the Middle East the British commander, General Wa-

vell, who had learned deception under Allenby, put theory
into effective practice in his rearguard defense against the
overcautious, inept, but much larger Italian army in the western desert after the fall of France. In December 1940, he
proved the value of deception by gaining the first British strategic surprise and victory of the war. Nearly as important, he
sent his deception planning officer, Brigadier Dudley Clarke,
to London to argue the need for centralized intertheater planning and coordination of strategic deception. Wavell's revolutionary recommendation was promptly accepted because of
the fortuitous circumstance that Churchill, the old advocate
of guile in World War One, was prime minister. Churchill
avidly sought anything in those dark days of the war that
might strengthen Britain's weak hand against the Axis. And
he came with a prepared mind: to match his own inclinations
he had discussed such matters with Lawrence of Arabia and
Liddell Hart. The result was the London Controlling Section
headed by Colonel J. H. "Johnny" Bevan, coordinating small
deception planning staffs among all military echelons from
corps to theater level. The British had institutionalized military cheating, more so than any previous armed nation.

While this might seem an obvious step for the weak facing
the strong, it was still novel and by no means accepted by
Britain's allies, the Americans. As late as 1943, the United
States chief of naval operations, Admiral Ernest J. King, pen-
ciled the remark, "The element of surprise has been dissipated," on his rejection of a study recommending that
America build midget surprise-attack submarines. Surprise
for King and many Americans was the tool "of despair of
have-not nations, . . . not for us." Apparently, only a display
of naked force could avenge the wounded pride of the Pearl
Harbor "sneak" attack. Some Americans, however, were not
so inflexible. The Chairman of the Joint Chiefs of Staff, General George C. Marshall, who had been one of General John

Pershing's deception planners on the Western Front, quickly saw the wisdom of "special plans." There was still no theory, no full understanding of the various categories of cheating—but no matter, the Allies had their staff cheaters in place. And they now proceeded to cheat on a grand scale never before experienced in war. Unknowingly, they would use the Deception Loop, at no time more effectively than in planning for the invasion of Europe.

The Allied commander's strategic Goal for the real operation—OVERLORD, the invasion of Normandy—was basically to land the maximum force with the minimum resistance. From OVERLORD would flow the Battle of France and ultimate Allied victory; but the subordinate Goal of the Allied deception planners was to contribute a cluster of RUSES that would facilitate OVERLORD, specifically by inducing ILLUSIONS in the mind of the enemy, which would permit the Allies to land the maximum number of troops on and immediately after D-Day and encounter minimum resistance. Some of the RUSES were mutually exclusive and others were ignored or denied by the enemy, but some, although intended to be only temporary or self-liquidating, were in fact successfully maintained over extended periods of time. It is probably true to say that never in the history of warfare has deception planning been as extensively or skillfully deployed by commanders.

The BODYGUARD deception ("cover") plan for OVER-LORD involved more intuition than theory and relied heavily on improvisation rather than anticipation. Nevertheless, the intuitions were most often correct and the improvisations usually succeeded. In other words, BODYGUARD was, if not "scientific," certainly very sophisticated. In addition, BODY-GUARD and its various components constitute the most complex single strategic deception plan ever undertaken, deploying nearly the full array of possible types of RUSES through nearly the complete set of possible communication channels. This combination of sophistication and variety makes BODYGUARD/FORTITUDE the best real-world example of deception planning.

SPECIFIC DECEPTION GOALS

The Allied deception planners had, like all deceivers, a set of seven key variables that they could in theory manipulate as options.

General	Categories	Military Equivalents
1. Actor(s)	WHO/WHOM	Antagonists
2. Style (how)	Does WHAT	Operational methods/ technological means
3. Location	WHERE	Target/place/direction/ distance
4. Time	WHEN	Time
5. Intention	WHY	Intention
6. Consequence	With what EFFECT	Payoff
7. Size (or value or strength)	——	Strength

Although they could not hope to deceive the Germans about their main enemy (Britain, America, and Russia), they did attempt (with some success) to induce the Germans to count as highly likely the imminent entry of Turkey into the battle on the Allied side, thereby diverting some German attention to the southeast. Even less could be done to mask the Allied intention, specifically their intention to invade. A bit more was done to mask operational capabilities such as the portable Mulberry Harbours. However, the Allied deception planners deliberately and extensively (and effectively) manipulated their three remaining options: about the real time, real place, and real strength of the invasion.

Assuming (correctly) that the weight of evidence would persuade the Germans that an Anglo-American invasion of Europe—somewhere in Europe—was in the making, the initial Allied deception plans initially focused on creating uncertainty about the quarter from which the main attack would come. Then, as Normandy D-day neared, it was again assumed that the Germans would recognize that France was the main target. Conceding this, the Allied deception planners refocused on creating uncertainty about the specific beaches targeted: Britanny, Normandy, the Pas de Calais, or even Holland. The old cover targets of the Balkans, southern France, and Norway were now large but secondary threats— mere diversions.

At this point the deception planners sought to prevent the Germans from realizing that the invasion would come on June 6, on Normandy beaches, with a force of over 100,000 men on the first day. Thus the planners had to devise specific RUSES that would be accepted by the Germans as ILLUSIONS that the Allies would land, *but:*

1. At a time later than anticipated. Deception planners had to take into consideration that mutually recognized givens such as tides, weather, etc., tended to limit the plausible scope of options.
2. elsewhere along the Franco-Dutch beaches.
3. in greater strength. This would create the ILLUSION that more than one major landing was imminent.

In each of these above cases, the planners had to choose between the options of sooner or later, here or there, stronger or weaker.

It should be stressed that while many of the RUSES were somewhat contradictory, the German "buyer" was not a single individual but a collection of quarreling and uncertain observers. At times on the highest level, while Hitler did or did not buy a specific ILLUSION, some commanders and intelligence officers did accept some ILLUSIONS, and others didn't accept any. The real world of OVERLORD deception planning was typical in being uncertain, harried, intuitive, contradictory, and atheoretical. In retrospect this does not matter because, consciously or not, the planners were engaged in activities readily amenable to Loop analysis.

STRATAGEMS

The broad goals of deception led to appropriate stratagems. The overall Allied deception plan for early 1944 was Plan BODYGUARD. It coordinated British, American, and Soviet strategic diversions throughout the European theater of operations to draw the attention and military resources of Hitler and his supreme command away from Normandy.

Many separate deception plans were drawn up in support of BODYGUARD. The Soviet General Staff contributed feints in Karelia and against the Black Sea coast of Rumania and simulated an early buildup for a general offensive on the eastern front—all moves intended to keep the German units pinned in the East. Plan CASCADE was the British Middle East Command's STRATAGEM to simulate a large-scale invasion of the Balkans. Plan FORTITUDE was the Anglo-American STRATAGEM to draw attention away from Normandy as the real target of invasion and to direct attention to optional targets along the coasts of northwestern Europe. For example, FORTITUDE NORTH simulated an impending invasion of Norway.

ILLUSIONS AND RUSES

The deception planners now had to role-play the enemy, trying to visualize and anticipate the types of ILLUSIONS he could accept that would be consistent with the desired STRATAGEMS. Each ILLUSION needed one or more appropriate RUSES that the enemy could "verify."

Thus the enemy should accept the ILLUSION that a large, mobile combat force existed in the Middle East, supporting the STRATAGEM that the Allies intended an invasion of the Balkans, thereby diverting German strength far from the real scene of future action in northern France. In order to project this ILLUSION, the Army Group Mure Ruse was devised. Similarly, in France itself, the enemy should accept the ILLUSION that the main assault would come at the Pas de Calais, thereby diverting local German units away from the real landing beaches nearby in Normandy. To project this ILLUSION, the Army Group Patton Ruse was devised. To sell the ILLUSION that the time of OVERLORD D-Day was further in the future, it was decided to have the enemy believe the senior OVERLORD commanders were away from headquarters as the real D-Day approached; hence the Monty's Double, a RUSE mimicking Field Commander Montgomery. Although the latter failed to be accepted as an ILLUSION, other RUSES that were successfully sold convinced the Germans that D-Day would come later than June 6.

CHARCS

To fashion the several RUSES that made up the FORTI-
TUDE RUSE, the deception planners turned to their exclusive inventory of CHARC resources. Some of these, such as
double-cross agents and fake divisions, had been built up as
deception resources over a period of nearly two years. Others,
such as Monty's Double, were hasty improvisations.

Each CHARC is the smallest object or act of deception
that can be recognized as incorporating elements of either
hiding or showing. The following list gives an example
of each of the six types of CHARCS, the three hiding types
and the three showing ones, used by the FORTITUDE
PLANNERS.

EXAMPLES OF FORTITUDE ARTIFICES USED
IN PLAN FORTITUDE

A. Hiding
  1. Masking
     A controlled enemy agent (CEA)
  2. Repackaging
     A wooden-framed canvas covering over a real tank
  3. Dazzling
     Photo-recon flights over the cover targets in addition
     to the "real" flights over Normandy
B. Showing
  1. Mimicking
     An actor disguised as General Montgomery
  2. Inventing
     An inflatable-rubber dummy "tank"
  3. Decoying
     A feint attack

The FORTITUDE deception planners had completed the anticipatory pause of their deception planning Loop and were now ready to begin the design phase.

From their existing inventory of CHARCS the planners selected those most appropriate for their intended RUSES. The CHARCS were henceforth viewed by the planners as the building blocks of their whole illusory edifice. One of the most complex and effective RUSES was the Army Group Patton Ruse.

THE ARMY GROUP PATTON (FUSAG) RUSE

The linchpin of Plan FORTITUDE was the FUSAG ruse, the large-scale effort to simulate a complete army group, the First U.S. Army Group, or FUSAG, positioned in East Anglia opposite the Pas de Calais and commanded by General Patton; Allied Intelligence knew the German Command expected FUSAG to spearhead the main Allied invasion of Hitler's "Fortress Europe." The immediate purpose of the FUSAG Ruse was to induce the Germans to perceive the ILLUSION of a powerful Allied force in East Anglia, commanded by the feared Patton and poised to strike, and to persuade them that the main D-Day landing would be at the Pas de Calais. The ultimate goal of this RUSE was to make the German military divert much of its meager resources to the useless defense of this irrelevant cover target.

The following figure shows how the FUSAG Ruse was in fact constructed out of several CHARCS and communicated to the enemy through specific CHANNELS. It also shows the victim's perceptions and the ILLUSION achieved. (The square brackets in this and the last two figures indicate the CHARCS that failed to be "sold.")

THE ARMY GROUP PATTON (FUSAG) RUSE

PURPOSE: To simulate a (notional) First U.S. Army Group (FUSAG) in East Anglia capable of invading the Pas de Calais.

RUSE	CHARCS PROJECTED	CHANNELS	VICTIM'S PERCEIVED CHARCS	ILLUSION
	1. Real General Patton in (notional) command of FUSAG.	1a. Press leaks via pro-Axis neutrals to military intelligence.	1. General Patton commands FUSAG.	
		1b. Rumors planted on military intelligence agents in Portugal.		
		1c. Controlled agents via radio to military intelligence case officers.		
	2. Signal traffic mimics radio communications not of a complete army group.	2. FUSAG military radio codes read by German army radio intercept team.	2. FUSAG radio net is real.	

FUSAG	3. Signals traffic actually broadcast from East Anglia.	3. FUSAG radio traffic triangulated by German army radio direction finders.	3. FUSAG transmitters located in East Anglia.	FUSAG targeted on Pas de Calais
	4. Dummy landing craft, tank parks, and aircraft displayed in East Anglia.	4a. Controlled agents to German military intelligence officers.	4a. FUSAG confirmed in East Anglia.	
		4b. Visual display.	4b. Luftwaffe neglects to overfly East Anglia.	

The Allied invasion of France, Operation OVERLORD, represented a high point in military deception, but the practice is still with us: as witness the Communist "surprise" invasion of South Korea, General MacArthur's "impossible" landing at Inchon, the "unforeseen" Chinese intervention, the various examples of the Israelis taking recourse to Liddell Hart's indirect approach and to all six categories of cheating just before the 1967 Six-day War, as well as the Egyptians' masking efforts before the 1973 October War.

After World War Two, however, the most serious military problems related to cheating focused increasingly on nuclear strategy, the ultimate level of potential violence. On the hiding level, the problem for Russia and the United States (less so for the other nuclear powers with limited arsenals) has been to ensure that they possess sufficient delivery systems to mount a second strike: This capability would, in theory, dissuade an enemy from making a first strike. There is no advantage in a "surprise" first strike that provokes a catastrophic response. In fact, it is important that both sides have a second-strike capacity; this (in theory) assures a stable balance of terror. An enormous body of strategic analysis of these problems and possibilities has built up in universities, government bureaus, and so-called think tanks. For a time, deception was involved in the problem in only two technical ways: masking delivery systems (especially nuclear submarines) or discovering delivery systems (mostly missile sites) through photography or other information recorded by spy planes or satellites. This was largely a zero-sum game for the involved—to discover the location of an enemy system was an absolute benefit with no advantage to the other side. Then came the limitations embodied in the Strategic Arms Limitation Talks (SALT) and the agreed necessity to verify the presence of those systems.

SALT introduced not only the element of agreed verification (how can we be assured that hence "we" will not be hit?) but also of cheating (how could "they" violate the agreed limitations and hide the fact?). Almost as soon as SALT I was signed, the skeptical in America—and presumably in Russia—assumed that cheating was underway: larger missiles were being made to look like old missiles (the Wolf-in-Sheep's-Clothing-RUSE), new restrictions were being fudged, and goodness knows what. Actually, large-scale cheating was difficult because of the accuracy of the satellite spy cameras (they can read newspaper headlines), although they are hampered by bad weather and unfavorable light conditions, and they cannot penetrate absolute masking. Nevertheless, the cynics were unconvinced. A way would have to be found to deploy the proposed new American missile system, the MX mobile missile, without undercutting the verification features of SALT. How to show and then swiftly hide? A wide variety of schemes were suggested, several based on a misunderstanding of the old shell game. Experts suggested moving the missiles around to various decoy silos, or placing them on railway cars moving along covered ditches that could be shown openly, or putting 200 MX missiles in a field of 4,000 identical shelters, or keeping them in aircraft that could take off at any sign of Soviet attack. Everyone agreed on one factor: whatever option was chosen would be enormously costly. Everyone ignored the fact that in the *real* shell game, there is never a pea under *any* of the shells.

The ingenious American military actually appeared to have come up with the invisible pea when it was revealed that a Stealth bomber was being developed, which would not show up on Soviet radar. For military purposes this meant that the plane was invisible: by the time it could be detected it would be too late. Art Buchwald, no mean strategist he, explored the implications of total masking represented ɔy the Stealth—since no one can see it. It could be presented (inventing) as a false reality to the Soviets, who will waste vast sums countering the threat. When they find they have been cheated, we announce an invisible submarine; finally, when the Soviets, cunning chaps, no longer respond to the threat of invisible weapons systems, the United States will be truly ready.

The Americans will leak that they have decided to build an invisible aircraft carrier. The Soviets will think this is more "disinformation" being put out by our side and will do nothing about it. But this time we'll go ahead with the plans, and the Soviets will wake up one morning and see hundreds of invisible aircraft carriers off their shores.

"If they're invisible, how will they see them?

Because we will deny they are there."

CHAPTER 4

Deceivers and Dupes: Profiles

♦ ♦ ♦

There's a sucker born every minute.

—MICHAEL CASSIUS MCDONALD, 1873

SINCE THERE ARE ONLY six categories of cheating and only one way of cheating (by using the Deception Loop), it is hardly surprising that there are relatively few types of persons who cheat or who are cheated. It is possible to find out the cheater potential of almost anyone. And, as Lincoln pointed out, it is possible to cheat *all* the people *some* of the time, so while some may not be promising deceivers, everyone is a potential dupe—although some are more promising dupes than others. Some people are natural deceivers, even if they lead absolutely blameless lives totally within the accepted canons, never aware of their potential for guile. Others with the most limited natural talent in such matters plod steadfastly through life earning a modest living by cheating. Simply because the waiting pool of dupes is so enormous, even a poor cheater can put together a crude RUSE that will produce a modest EFFECT—note that the shell game and three-card monte are still with us on urban street corners. More interesting by far are the naturally talented cheaters who consciously employ their talents to fashion far more elegant RUSES. In fact, some cheaters are so enormously talented and, as we all are, surrounded with eager potential dupes that they work almost intuitively, often even denying to themselves that they cheat at all.

No one is quite sure what makes the ideal cheater, but the ideal dupe obviously accepts all EFFECTS and COVERS as ILLUSIONS every time. Some experts assume that the deceiver thinks in a different manner from the rest of us, has what one magician called a "trick brain." Another magician called it "double think" or "lateral thinking" and from a quite different profession the pioneering American cryptanalyst (decoding specialist), Major Herbert O. Yardley, referred to people who have the ability to think up ruses as "cipher brains." Dr. B. Stewart Whaley, theorist of deception, contends that this devious or indirect mind is possessed by all deceivers, whether they are magicians, psychics, con artists, mystery writers, comedians, practical jokers, card sharks, counterespionage officers, or military deception planners. Yet everyone, with few exceptions, cheats; it is simply that the types of cheaters on Whaley's list earn their living by cheating and thus must be assumed to have a "trick brain," while those they deceive do not. It is possible to construct, bit by bit, a more universal profile of the cheater, beginning with the inclination to be manipulative and ending with the more or less conscious fashioning of a RUSE.

Fortunately for the student of cheating, social scientists have begun a rigorous examination of those who would practice deceit naturally. In 1954 Dr. Richard Christie, a professor of social psychology at Columbia University, began guilelessly what was to become a career-long study of the Machiavellian personality. Initially, he thought he could separate the deceivers from the dupes by means of a simple test. In 1873 Chicago gambling impresario Mike McDonald (not P. T. Barnum) first uttered the immortal sentence, "There's a sucker born every minute." Christie hypothesized that if he asked his students whether this statement was true or false, on the basis of their answers he would be able to discriminate nicely between persons who were highly manipulative and would agree and those who were not and would not. The experiment failed because none of the students agreed with the statement (and some of them *must* have been Machiavellian). When questioned, the guileless, as expected, disagreed, on technical grounds; but the guileful disagreed with the question as phrased because, as they said, "There's *at least* one sucker born every minute."

Christie and his students and colleagues went back to the drawing board. They have now produced over forty experimental studies of the psychological and social characteristics of persons who expect and use guile, deceit, and opportunism in their personal relationships. Their basic test instrument is, appropriately, called the Machiavellian (Mach) Scale, for the test questions are based mainly on Machiavelli's own aphorisms about human nature and winning tactics. In fact, you can rate your Cheater's potential here and now in a slimmed-down version of the Christie test—but ONLY if you do not cheat. Do you agree with the following statements?

CHEATERS TEST

Agree *Disagree*

1. The best way to handle people is to tell them what they want to hear. ____ ____

	Agree	*Disagree*
2. When you ask someone to do something for you it is best to give your real reasons for wanting it rather than giving reasons that might carry more weight.	___	___
3. Anyone who completely trusts anyone else is asking for trouble.	___	___
4. It is hard to get ahead without cutting corners here and there.	___	___
5. Honesty is the best policy in all cases.	___	___
6. It is safest to assume that all people have a vicious streak and that it will come out when they are given a chance.	___	___
7. Never tell anyone the real reasons you did something unless it is useful to do so.	___	___
8. One should take action only when sure it is morally right.	___	___
9. It is wise to flatter important people.	___	___
10. All in all, it is better to be humble and honest than important and dishonest.	___	___
11. Barnum was very wrong when he said there's a sucker born every minute.	___	___
12. People suffering from incurable diseases should have the choice of being put painlessly to death.	___	___
13. It is possible to be good in all respects.	___	___
14. Most people are basically good and kind.	___	___
15. There is no excuse for lying to someone else.	___	___
16. Most men forget more easily the death of their father than the loss of their property.	___	___

	Agree	*Disagree*
17. Most people who get ahead in the world lead clean, moral lives.	____	____
18. Generally speaking, men won't work hard unless they're forced to do so.	____	____
19. The biggest difference between most criminals and other people is that criminals are stupid enough to get caught.	____	____
20. Most men are brave.	____	____

This is one of those rare and splendid tests that not only have no "correct" answers but also, in this case, no answers at all; for it should be obvious in every case which would be the Machiavellian answer.* Obviously the more answers that are based on cynicism and pragmatism and the fewer on ethics and morality, the higher the Cheater rating. This Cheater rating is cheating potential: one may in fact believe that few people get ahead by leading clean, moral lives but still act as if you didn't believe it. For those with high-Cheater ratings this view may be comforting, but is an illusion.

Perhaps the most important of Christie's many findings is that his Machiavellians ("high Mach's") are not merely believers in the gullibility of others, not only themselves willing to practice guile, but they are, in fact, generally rather successful at manipulating others either for personal gain in competitive situations or to take control in cooperative groups. To attain these goals they are willing to bluff, cheat, and deceive, they are alert to possibilities for such manipulation, are innovative in devising ruses, are willing to take risks *if* these seem

---

* For those who would feel cheated without their real Cheaters-test score, these statements are to be rated from "strongly agree" (5 points) to "strongly disagree" (1 point).

to have payoffs, are willing to seize the initiative, but are cooperative when mutual gain is apparent. In other words, if you are a high-Mach it is very likely that you will base your actions on Machiavellian principles, wittingly or unwittingly. You stand with the deceivers.

Yet even a moment's thought will indicate that there are different kinds of deceivers, even if each has a high-Mach rating. Some people cheat on their income tax with great skill, annually confounding the Internal Revenue Service with their cunningly planned returns, while others seemingly spontaneously walk out on their bar bill. Some believe themselves when they say, "The check is in the mail," while others plot endless delays through intermittent correspondence with their creditors. Thus, while all potential deceivers have high-Mach, they can be quickly categorized as either the highly spontaneous or the highly structured.

There is another division closely related to the spontaneous/structured split: the differences in *why* cheaters cheat that in part determine *how* they cheat. The values prohibiting cheating are culturally bound: they are absorbed largely automatically without necessarily being taught—they are reinforced through practically all existing institutions. Thus, for example, the Ten Commandments are goal, guide, and goad. Honesty, we are told again and again, is the best policy, the *only* policy. This may or may not be true, but according to society it *should* be true. The reason all such moral values are taught with such care is that the major purpose of a society is to maintain its existence. Institutions must be sanctified, behavior controlled, the future structured to the past's shape. Society's values are enormously conservative, intended to prevent change.

There are two groups who resist the imposition of public values. The first group comprise those less favored in existing society. For them, the "values" prevent them from achieving what they deserve and are denied. Thus Karl Marx insisted that religion was the opiate of the people, a "value" imposed by the powerful, by threatened haves to control the weak but dangerous have-nots. When conservative values are not inculcated or are rejected society has a rebel. When we focus solely on the individual who is denied we have a rebel-deceiver.

The second group is composed of those who are more favored in existing society. They do not fear the have-nots, for there appears to be plenty for all and thus they have no interest in maintaining the old values. They are not attempting to seize the necessary but to spend an excess. They have no religion and they drift on a wave of personal values. They simply do not accept society's values, they are the Rogues, playing grasshopper to the Rebel ants. They deceive just as consciously as the Rebels but in a very different manner. It is also possible to determine a person's Rogue/Rebel potential, which exists not only for the high Mach's but for almost all low Mach's as well.

REBEL/ROGUE TEST

1. Would you rather address a joint session of Congress on a topic of your choice or spend a rainy evening talking to a lonely, attractive someone?
2. Do you prefer red or blue?
3. Do you believe it helps to convince a doubter if you touch the person as well as talk to him or her?
4. When you say "The check is in the mail," is it or should it be?
5. Is "I'll think about that tomorrow" often a shrewd strategy?
6. Have you ever made lists of books to read?

7. Have you ever been lonely in a crowd?
8. Are you basically cuddly?
9. Would you prefer a cat or a dog?
10. Do you wear your hair a bit too long?
11. Would you rather read the book or see the play?
12. Is something bound to work out somehow even if you do not take matters in hand?
13. Would you rather go to a party where you knew everyone or no one?
14. Was President Carter's problem his style or his lack of vision?
15. Would you rather be considered sincere or competent?
16. Did you bother to take this test?

Regardless of high- or low-Mach ratings, everyone is going to be more or less like a Rogue or more or less like a Rebel. People will fall in the big middle of the bell curve, as happens most with the spontaneous structured cheating chart.

The Rogue Persona

Impulsive, charming, intuitive. Often spontaneous, exudes warmth. Mediterranean, not Scandinavian. Enthusiastic, no matter what the obstacle. Often criminally optimistic. At times holds only a slender grasp on objective reality. Makes a good but unfaithful friend. Irrepressible. Red over Blue. Cuddly, likes romping dogs. Popular, flexible, erratic, apparently naive. Touches while talking. Convinces by personal conversation. Irresistible close up. Unconcerned with lists and tests and the rigors of reading. Eager to meet and convince the strange. Seductive in manner. Incapable of introspection or isolation. Always, always convinced that this time is the right time. Eager to be open, sincere, and so believes, for style is all. Anger—fire—lava.

The Rebel Persona

Analytical, argumentative. Dedicated, determined, cool, ever cool. Devout. A cat person with plans and programs. Life is a list, love an illusion. Reality is structured by the system. Vision is an agenda. Time is valuable and people merely pieces to move. A bad and unforgiving enemy. Introspective. A blue person, often arrogant, always rigid, admirable but distant, a master or mistress of sophisticated rationalizations. Convinces through public oratory. Cleanliness before good fellowship. Ice—angst—ire.

Thus, in daily life the Rogue depends on intuition, the grasshopper leap of the moment, the need to seduce every woman, convince every man (or the reverse), to impose his persona through tender, loving concern. The Rebel remains analytical, woos with structured wisdom, brings a model to problems, maximizes options, thinks upon tomorrow today. If the Rebel shows cunning, it is not the Rogue's low cunning; if the Rebel is loving, the act is discriminating, not undiscriminating. The Rogue seeks to manipulate those he can touch, fondle, charm. The Rebel moves history, classes, exercising power by manipulation.

President	*Type*
Ronald Reagan	Rogue
Jimmy Carter	Rebel
Gerald Ford	Rogue
Richard Nixon	Rebel
Lyndon Johnson	Rogue
John Kennedy	Rogue
Dwight Eisenhower	Rogue
Harry Truman	Rebel
Franklin Roosevelt	Rogue

President	Type
Herbert Hoover	Rebel
Calvin Coolidge	Rebel
Warren Harding	Rogue
Woodrow Wilson	Rebel
William Taft	Rebel
Theodore Roosevelt	Rogue

For the Optimum Impact on men and mores:

1. A Rebel employing a Rogue's facade
2. A Rogue employing a Rebel's means

For the Worst-Case results:

1. A Rebel without a cause
2. A Rogue without friends

While each person will tend toward either Rogue or Rebel, toward a high- or low-Mach rating, be more structured or more spontaneous, it is likely that a high-Mach with nearly all the characteristics of *either* a Rogue or a Rebel will indicate massive cheating potential. Having the inclination to deceive, perceiving the wisdom and advantage of guile, and possessed of a persona that makes manipulation simultaneously possible and attractive (doing what comes naturally), the cheater-candidate stands at the threshold of the act.

All the cheater-candidate needs in order to act at this point is legitimation. The Rogue arrives at his rationalizations without great thought while the Rebel has a manifesto in mind. Rationalizations are necessary for the potential cheater, for whether Rogue or Rebel, his actions are directed by inner criteria. If he is to be a cheater, he is not interested in others' opinions and values, unless these can be manipulated to advantage. He has looked into his heart and discovered his own path. Not for him or her the sanctions imposed by a traditional society, the laws of the tribe, but those he has fashioned for himself. Not for him the clumsy consensus of the crowd. He is beyond that: Fences for fools! Limits for the greedy or obsolete! He has his own limits, his own rules, shaped to his needs, not those of others.

Since the condemnation of cheating is a cultural value, the potential cheater must add to his own internalized and unstated assumptions a comforting set of rationalizations. There are but four:

1. I NEED IT.
2. THEY DESERVE IT.
3. IT WON'T MATTER ANYWAY.
4. NO ONE WILL KNOW ANYHOW.

So he rationalizes. "I had a bad year at the shop (not to mention the races) and the kids need shoes and the rent is due and the IRS is crooked and besides, what's a few thou when the government has billions and what they don't know won't hurt me."

"Although constructing a fake horse may violate some small Hellenic honor code, it is no longer tolerable to maintain a siege because of the stupid Trojan persistence; after victory no one will care or even remember except that we won."

"Since the invasion of France is an enormous risk, every precaution must be taken to save Allied lives and confound the enemy, and, of course, cheating for the state is commendable, in this case honorable, and a triumph in Normandy is the main consideration."

There are two sets of legitimation. First, those rationalizations by Rebels who intend to destroy unfair systems and those by Rogues seeking to enjoy denied privileges. These are the ILLICIT CHEATS. The second set comprises those deceptions by Rebels who intend to destroy the enemy by (perhaps) unfair means, and by Rogues who snatch an opportune chance for victory. These are the AUTHORIZED CHEATS. Remember that even the latter, especially at times when the public and governmental Mach level is low, have their problems with others who feel the construction of a fake horse unworthy of the nation. In any case, once the potential cheater moves down the slippery slope of legitimate rationalizations, once his internal fail-safe devices falter, his concern shifts from his own needs to those of his target.

Everyone, anyone, can be a dupe and is likely at some point to be duped. Lincoln was profoundly accurate when he pointed out that *all* the people could be fooled *some* of the time. And at the very least it must be accepted that all human beings are regularly and irretrievably deceived by the nature of nature. Our perception of "reality" is determined in part by our physiology and in part by psychological adjustment, most of which takes place early on. Thus, raw data flow from the real world to our sense organs. Light waves are seen by our eyes, sound waves heard in our ears, solidity is felt by touch, pressure by yet other specialized nerves. And much is not sensed at all, waves too fine or pressures too light. All this vast and unending stream of sensory data is then transmitted to the brain—pulses, pings, surges of current. Only after these data are processed by the brain do they become perceptions. Such perceptions may bear little relation to objective reality but nonetheless seem real. For example, the "stars" one sees after a jolt on the head are mistaken sensations of light produced by cells in the retina, optic nerve, or brain that have been mechanically disturbed. These nerve cells release weak chemical-electrical impulses that travel along the nerve to the area of the brain that processes visual information. The brain misinterprets these impulses as light flashes and the jolted see stars.

A thoroughly naive brain does not perceive distinctions between those various sensory signals, its perceptions are on a timeless, infinitely rich "undifferentiated aesthetic continuum," as the philosopher F. S. C. Northrup characterized it. No brain is absolutely naive, but relatively naive perception is common in young children. In adults it apparently occurs only while they are undergoing a so-called mystical experience. Most people, however, cope with the flood of sensory data in order to pursue conventional lives. They tune out or off, readjust, interpret, and shape. For example, the lens of the eye reverses everything, both upside down and left-as-right. A naive brain naturally perceives the same. Babies soon learn by touch to orient the objective reality with the reversed picture of it in their heads and thereby to "correct" this optical illusion. Adults take this correction for granted and are no longer capable of noticing that our whole view of the external world is literally upside down. We know better than to accept the direct evidence of our senses. We are no longer deceived by the nature of our nature.

In some cases, the nature of human biology is such that it is impossible not to be deceived by, for example, "the evidence of our eyes." Even though we know that a stick appears crooked in water because of the laws of refraction, our eyes cannot make it straight. The world is filled with optical illusion. Some can be denied by an act of will.

Most of these physical illusions such as after-images appear where no flag might be or mirages representing water or sanctuary or landscapes where none exist are mostly curiosities. There are, however, a few exceptions in films, art, magic, and commerce.

The apparent movement perceived by audiences viewing films or television is an illusion. What in fact is projected and what the eye senses on the movie screen is a cascade of still pictures interspersed with blanks. Every second our retinas accurately detect a series of sixteen frames of silent film or twenty-four of sound film interrupted by an equal number of blanks that make up 30 percent of the viewing time. The false perception of motion takes place not in our eyes, which do not deceive us, but in our brain, which does. The persistence of image that gives the illusion of continuous movement is due to the brain's inability to sort out the separate images transmitted from the retina of the eye fast enough. "The appearance of continuity," cinema Professor Thorold Dickinson remarked, "is maintained mentally in accord with the creative ability of the film-maker, like a conjurer, to keep the ball of illusion airborne."

The film itself is, of course, also often faked; the French magician, Georges Méliès, first introduced trick cinema photography in 1898 among other effects, he made his head appear to leave his shoulders, rise into the air, and then multiply into several heads.

The recorded sound track, introduced commercially in 1926, is also an illusion, the recordings being only a mechanical or electronic simulation of the voices of the actors. Moreover, studio "dubbing," the technique of making subsequent additions to the sound track, which was introduced by 1932, allows artificial sounds to replace the original ones present during filming. For example, almost all Italian movies produced since 1944 substitute the voices of readers for those of most of the on-film actors. To hear as well as see Gina Lollobrigida or Sophia Loren, you must catch them in their Hollywood-made films.

Some perceptions of "reality" have commercial value because people "taste" in mysterious ways. Food technologists add orange color to synthetic orange drinks because without the color people think the drink does not taste orangey. In one test when the correct colors for specific flavors, such as lemon for yellow and purple for grape, were scrambled, only 22 percent of the tasters could guess the correct flavor. The ultimate example is that most people prefer the taste of canned tomato juice to the real article, which they think tastes "funny"—so much so that aluminum can makers are contemplating adding the tinny taste to their tomato juice so that it will then taste more "natural."

If learned perceptions can trick the taste and the very nature of the eye makes possible "moving pictures," then a combination of learned perceptions and the nature of the eye determine not how but what most people see in art. One recondite school of art criticism has suggested that great art is often the result of ophthalmological problems: Renoir was nearsighted, Rembrandt farsighted, Van Gogh may have had glaucoma, and El Greco astigmatism, while cataracts afflicted a number of artists from Titian to Turner. None apparently was color-blind. And a few natural illusions in the hands of magicians can be manipulated to advantage or rather to assist in the achievement of surprise EFFECTS and the audience's ILLUSIONS. Even a magician's use of physical aspects of deception plays but a small part in a heritage of psychological guile, cheating in the same six categories, employing the Deception Loop, to bring delight to generation after generation of deceived audiences, who gladly pay for the privilege. Tinny tomato juice may come and go, but the now-you-see-it-now-you-don't Cups-and-Balls trick is ageless. It should be noted that *all* magician's tricks employ one of the forms of showing (although, obviously, as always, showing involves one or more of the CHARCS of hiding) and, if the magician is to stay in business, all his tricks must remain permanent ILLUSIONS. To tell how the illusion was achieved would cheat the audience.

The magician's main problem and that of most cheaters is that the potential dupe must not have an absolutely simple mind: a naive brain, unable to distinguish and control raw data, is unable to fashion perceptions from "reality," so too must the dupe be able to follow the decoy. To be misled, a dupe must be bright enough to be led. The late American comedian, Joe Penner, hit upon this paradoxical truth when he said, "You can't fool me; I'm too ignorant." People who are too dull, too inattentive, too uninformed, too naive, or too literal are hard to cheat. They are the bane of the liar, the cheat, the magician, no help to the comedian, and they are dangerous opponents on the playing field or the battlefield. The simpleminded child will not be decoyed by the magician's misdirection and patter, won't recognize when a trick is supposed to begin or end or why he should look either left or right. What the cheat wants in a dupe is not innocence but another cheat—who is not only fair game but often an even better dupe than the honest man. "The most distrustful persons," cunning Cardinal de Retz noted in the seventeenth century, "are often the biggest dupes."

Matters have hardly changed since the seventeeth century. Con artists feast on those with larceny in their hearts and devious counterspies prey on cheating spies. The more guileful they are the more gullible they can become. It is thus inordinately difficult for a cheat to realize that he can be cheated, for after all, as a high Mach he tends to think of the world as "them," the dupes, and "me," the deceiver, thus missing the thrust of Lincoln's axiom. Being a dupe in most cases has small significance, the loss of marginal funds or a slice of pride. But in a few cases the powers of the dupe are such that the very world shifts.

By June 1941, Joseph Stalin, one of the great Rogues of all time, had become the undisputed master of the Soviet Union, one-eighth of the world. By supreme cunning and utter ruthlessness he crushed all opposition in the general populace as well as specifically in the Communist Party, the government, the Red Army, and the secret police, sending millions to their deaths or into forced labor. Moreover, his two major international enemies, capitalist Britain and fascist Germany, were locked in a struggle to the death. Admittedly, he was concerned about the future when, as seemed likely, Germany would crush Britain; but he believed that his purge-shattered Red Army would regain sufficient strength by the next year to repel any attack and perhaps even make a preemptive strike, itself invading and destroying a war-weary Germany.

Then, on the morning of 22 June 1941, Stalin's illusion of safety was rudely shattered when the Nazi blitzkrieg swept into Russia. He was completely surprised. Indeed, initially thinking that this was only some kind of local "provocation," Stalin withheld the order for an all-out counterattack until that afternoon when he first accepted the fact that Hitler had indeed launched an all-out invasion. How was it possible for Stalin to be so thoroughly surprised and deceived?

Stalin was aware through his several intelligence sources that Hitler had moved the bulk of his army to within striking distance of the Soviet frontier, but he assumed this was for the purpose, initially, of training for the forthcoming invasion of Britain and, later, for bluffing him into making various economic and territorial concessions to Germany. Stalin was also aware that Hitler intended to attack Bolshevik Russia sometime in the future, but he assumed Hitler would not attempt this until he had brought Britain to her knees. Even at the last moment, when Stalin realized that Hitler had both the capability to invade and just might not wait until Britain collapsed, he still expected that Hitler would issue an ultimatum before attacking. Specifically, as June 22 dawned, Stalin was nervously but eagerly awaiting a set of German demands for economic and territorial concessions. Then, Stalin thought, he would have three options: negotiating for time, conceding or negotiating to gain time, or at worst, launching a preemptive strike. All these perceived options were illusions. In fact, Hitler was fully decided to invade, and invade without terms, negotiations, or ultimata. The elaborate, sophisticated, and carefully orchestrated German deception plan had simply fed a mass of false clues pointing to these several assumptions into the Soviet intelligence network. And Stalin had bought it all.

In sum, Stalin was too certain of his command of the threads of diplomatic-political-military intrigue. He arrogantly assumed his 1939 nonaggression pact with Hitler had bought, if not a permanent truce, at least enough time to rebuild the Red Army to the state of unassailability from which he had himself reduced it by the Great Purges. Unwilling to abandon entirely his preconceived policy of appeasement, Stalin was largely deafened to the authentic signals of approaching doom and preferred listening to the soothing misinformation and disinformation that allowed him a false sense of mastery over the flow of events.

Stalin, that most distrustful of persons, had become one of the century's biggest dupes. Knowing how the game of guile was played, he had allowed himself to be cheated by Hitler by insisting on following the devices and desires of his own heart. He accepted the pattern of events he wanted to find. He was guilty of violating what might be called the Von Moltke Principle.

The nineteenth-century chief of the Prussian General Staff Helmuth von Moltke the Elder once instructed his officers, "Gentlemen, I notice that there are always three courses open to the enemy, and that he usually takes the fourth." The operation of this Von Moltke Principle is often simply the result of incomplete information or of self-deception, but it is also a prime goal of all the better deceivers. They will try to hide their own intentions so their victims will more easily misperceive the most likely shape of things to come. In essence, the deceiver tries to manipulate the perceptions of the deceived to bias him or her toward developing an hypothesis about the situation that is firm but wrong, and wrong in a way that is advantageous to the deceiver. Stalin was duped into accepting *his* desired pattern just as Montcalm on the Plain of Abraham accepted *his* seized battlefield and Goliath *his* rules for single combat. A dupe sees not only what is guilefully offered, the false, but also what he wants to see, often equally false. The problem is the pattern.

A former United States Air Force colonel recently devised an interesting slide show to illustrate the problem of pattern recognition. His lecture began with a discussion of a major problem the British RAF photo interpretation team at Medmenham faced in World War Two: recognizing and counting enemy aircraft on airfields photographed from overflying RAF Mosquito photoreconnaissance planes.

It was obvious from his slides that clear-weather photographs at low altitude posed no problem—each enemy aircraft stood out in sufficient detail to identify its specific type. Medium-altitude photos were grainier, but bombers could still be easily distinguished from, say, fighters. But high-altitude shots by the Mosquitos at their maximum elevation were very grainy; often only the number of planes could be counted. He would then ask his audience to identify a series of blow-ups. The first was too grainy to show any pattern. Number two began to show some vague dark/light contrast. With number three these contrasts became a dark horizontal strip and a slightly longer dark vertical one. At number four, someone spoke up to announce "one aircraft." With picture number five, most of the others agreed. At six, another said "single-engined aircraft." At seven, most agreed to that. Then came eight, nine, and ten in rapid order and we suddenly realized that we had been looking all the time at a familiar picture of Christ on the cross.

As a lesson in applied psychology, this slide show was an example of misdirection at its best and also showed the devious brain at work. The audience had been conditioned to expect to see one or more airplanes. The emerging vertical and horizontal lines were consistent with the hypothesis "airplane." As the image came into sharper focus the lack of any forward protrusions from the "wings" suggested a single-engined aircraft, a fighter rather than a multiengined plane, which would probably be identified as a bomber. When the final slides appeared, the audience was surprised because they had been led, by misdirection, to follow a false trail of expectation. Instead of a plane the last slide showed the Crucifiction.

Even, *especially,* the most cunning assume patterns that conform to expected reality. One of the most celebrated magicians of his era was Harry Houdini, who by 1899 had added escapes to his magic show to become the king of handcuffs and monarch of leg shackles. Appearing at the Orpheum Theatre in Kansas City that year he added his later famous jail-break challenge in which, stripped naked and manacled at wrists and ankles, he escaped his bonds in under eight minutes. He now added "Champion Jail Breaker" to his advertisements, but he neglected to mention an embarrassing event that had occurred at the same time.

In the lobby of Kansas City's Savoy Hotel, Houdini had stepped into a booth to place a telephone call. Mr. E. P.

Williams, a traveling salesman, recognized the magician and decided on a bit of fun at the master escapologist's expense. Borrowing the key to the phone booth from the desk clerk, the prankster locked the door. When Houdini finished his call and tried to open the door, he found he could not, kicking, battering, and yelling until a crowd gathered. At that point Williams ostentatiously unlocked the door. Henceforth, Houdini never entered a telephone booth without keeping one foot firmly set between the door and the frame. Houdini had been made to realize that the whole world was a stage for him. In fact, Houdini eventually used the audience's assumption of the nature of the stage—the size of the magician's world—to display one of magic's greatest ILLUSIONS.

The great English magic inventor, P. T. Selbit, introduced his "Walking-Through-a-Wall" illusion in 1914, the effect of which was that the magician seemed to pass through a solid wall. Within a month Houdini had purchased the American performing rights and introduced the feat as a sensation in New York City.

Volunteers were invited to the stage, where they inspected a large canvas sheet to verify that it was whole. It was spread upon the floor and a thick brick wall, 12 feet long and 8 feet high was pushed on stage on rollers and lowered onto the center of the canvas, with the end to the audience. The volunteers would verify that the wall was indeed solid and had no secret panels or loose bricks. Next, two large three-paneled screens were carried on, examined, and then placed at the center of the wall, one on each side, directly opposite one another. In Houdini's version, the magician then entered, went behind the left-side screen, and closed it. The volunteers and audience could see both sides and both ends of the wall and all of its top, yet when the left-hand screen was opened, Houdini had disappeared, only to reappear instantly from behind the screen on the other side. The volunteers were again allowed to examine the wall, sheet, and screens to satisfy themselves that there were no secret openings.

Although this trick fooled almost all who saw it, the method was, as usual in magic, simplicity itself. When the canvas was being examined, the magician explained that it was used to "prove that trapdoors do not play in this mystery." Indeed, there were no gimmicks in the wall, the screens, or the canvas; all were just what they seemed. The setup seemingly excluded the effective use of any trapdoor in the stage, even if there were one. Yet that is how the trick is worked. After Houdini entered the first screen, he lay down flat on the canvas while an offstage assistant released a large trapdoor directly beneath the magician. The weight of his body stretched the canvas just enough for Houdini to wriggle under the wall.

The audience has been misled into limiting its speculation to the area above stage when, in fact, the secret lies below it, completely outside the space they are trying to build their hypotheses on. The choice of the real method is dissimulated by the magician and his audience is left with a set of incomplete or irrelevant scraps of evidence from which they will be unable to construct a viable hypothesis about how the effect would have been obtained.

An audience at a magic show naturally expects to be duped, has even paid money for the privilege. Most dupes, however, find the exposed ILLUSION painful, none more so than those who, like Stalin, had assumed to the bitter, disillusioned end that they controlled the game, knew the limits of the stage, the rules of play, that they were the cunning ones. And the more cunning they have been in the past, the more painful their loss of innocence will be.

By 1869 Jay Gould, an archetypical Rogue, was already a

multimillionaire at the age of thirty-three. As one of New York's most famous financiers and leading impresarios of America's rapidly expanding railroads, Gould was ruthless in a cutthroat market, astute, cunning, distrustful, a man of high-Mach. Nevertheless his self-assurance and greed soon made him the public victim of a major financial hoax.

Gould invested heavily in the Erie Railroad when it was discovered that the market was flooded with several hundred thousand dollars' worth of counterfeit Erie Railroad stock certificates. Not only did Gould stand to lose much of his investment with Erie, but his reputation slipped in the face of the embarrassing newspaper gossip.

At this point Gould's money and reputation were saved by the fortuitous intervention of Lord John Gordon-Gordon, a Scottish peer and newcomer to the ranks of America's railway barons. Lord Gordon-Gordon proved through handwriting experts that the counterfeiting was the work of several of the railroad's own top executives, who sought to supplement their already generous salaries by this fraud.

The Scottish lord then came from his Minneapolis head-quarters to New York, where he arranged to meet Gould through the famous newspaper publisher, Horace "Go West Young Man" Greeley. Gordon-Gordon suggested that Greeley and Gould join him in buying up a controlling inter-est in the troubled Erie Railroad. Gould and his friend Greeley agreed, and their joint venture prospered. It proved more prosperous for Gordon-Gordon, though, than it did for Gould, who over the next three years lent his cash-poor associ-ate and now intimate friend nearly a million dollars to buy up stock certificates. Gould later recalled, "When I requested a receipt, he refused to do this or accept the money. He said that his integrity and honor were sufficient and that his word was as binding as his signature." Fearing he would lose both a valuable business associate and personal friend, Gould agreed to lend the money without legal proof.

Gould soon came to regret his own greed-driven generosity when in 1873 Gordon-Gordon suddenly dumped his million dollars' worth of stock, thereby also lowering the value of Gould's own stock. Gould, realizing he had been swindled, sued Gordon-Gordon. Gordon-Gordon made such a fine impression during the trial that once when he was being viciously cross-examined by the famous Elihu Root, the judge interrupted, declaring that a royalist should not be persecuted like a commoner.

At this point Gould's old cunning reasserted itself; he took a simple step that any prudent man would have taken when Lord Gordon-Gordon first came into his life. Gould made up a list of all the noble relatives and celebrated friends that the Scotsman claimed to have in Britain and wrote to them. All denied any knowledge of the man. Confronted with this evidence of his imposture and stripped of his name, the Rogue Scot fled to Canada. Subsequent investigation showed that he was, in fact, one John Crowningsfield, the illegitimate issue of a merchant seaman and a London barmaid, who had made his original nest egg in Scotland working as a con artist.

The impostor disappeared with Gould's cool million, Horace Greeley went on to become an unsuccessful presidential candidate, and Jay Gould spent his last two decades going from one financial success to another—but with less gullibility.

In the case of Gould and Lord Gordon-Gordon or Hitler and Stalin, the relationship of deceiver and dupe was between two cunning Rogues, one employing his cherished means to cheat the other. At times the relationship may be between guile and absolute innocence, between evil and good. In his tragic play, *Othello,* Shakespeare, pits Iago, a Rogue-deceiver at his most cunning, against Othello, a dupe at his most foolish. Iago is devious, scheming, cunning, and evil. Othello is straightforward, open, and inherently good. Yet the evil villian destroys the good hero in large part because Othello is not absolutely good and hence is not beyond Iago's wiles. If he were perfect he would be beyond betrayal, but Iago discovers he can be made jealous.

There are deceiver-dupe relationships that are neither Rogue-Rogue nor Rebel-Rebel, such as the Iago-Othello relationship. This is particularly true in military deception, where rational, authorized cheating is afoot or may be presumed to be. Allied military deception planning in World War Two was largely in the hands of amateurs, civilians in uniform— some Rogues but mostly Rebels. A businessman-turned-colonel was the British coordinator of deception. A best-selling writer of thrillers was his principal aide. A magician was one of Britain's leading innovators of camouflage. Politician and future Senator Harold Stassen was Admiral Halsey's deception officer in the Pacific. James Bond creater Ian Fleming's older brother, Peter, an explorer-adventurer, ran deception operations for Mountbatten in India/Burma. World-famous movie star Douglas Fairbanks, Jr., ran the United States Navy deception in the Mediterranean. And a civilian scientist who remained in civvies designed most of the innovative deceptions for the RAF Bomber Command. All of these men and others did adequate to fine jobs in an unfamiliar setting. Relatively few professional soldiers were assigned to deception planning. But one plain soldier, a Rebel with high, if authorized, Mach, was perhaps the best of all.

Dudley Wrangel Clarke was born in the South Africa Transvaal in 1899 on the eve of the Boer War. Raised in Britain, he was in uniform by age sixteen and remained a professional soldier all his life. Throughout his career he was the ideal staff officer, never holding or seeking command and, despite his efforts, never in combat—the perfect military Jeeves. His values were those of a Victorian gentleman, and although he was a handsome man with an eye for the ladies he somehow always lost them to others. Yet such seemingly unpromising material concealed one of the most innovatively deceptive minds in history.

Clarke was, as his 1974 obituary in *The Times* stated, "no ordinary man." And Field Marshall Alexander, his wartime boss, declared that Clarke had "done as much to win the war as any other officer." Clarke was above all clear thinking, blunt, respectful of authority but never in awe of it. He had a deep appreciation of the flaws and foibles of himself and of others. He was the consummate realist. His friends and colleagues testify to his "puckish sense of humour" and an endearing character "containing a boundless sense of the ridiculous." These were the qualities he brought to General Wavell of World War One deception fame when, in the late 1930's, Clarke served as his aide for two years in Palestine. And it was from Wavell that he learned about military deception.

After the outbreak of World War Two, Clarke was back in London where, in June 1940, he first proved his ability to do the unusual by founding a group he called the Commandos, a name he took from his childhood memories of the maruading Boer commandos. Then, later that year, Wavell, tiring of having to act as his own deception planner, summoned Colonel Clarke to Cairo to serve in that capacity.

For the duration of the war, Clarke ran the "A" Force, the senior deception coordinating staff in the Middle East, which churned out a succession of largely successful deception operations that baffled the Italians and Germans. He ran the first British "double agents" and with greater skill than was the

case later when this was done out of London. He devised the
idea of entire dummy military units, including whole divisions, corps, and armies. He coined the term *notional* for
dummy or bogus units, a term still used by military deception
specialists.

A superb example of Clarke's devious thinking occurred in
Cairo around the end of 1942, when Major Oliver Thynne
discovered that the Germans had learned to distinguish the
dummy British aircraft from the real ones because the flimsy
dummies were supported by struts under their wings. At that
time Major Thynne was a novice planner with Clarke's "A"
Force. When Major Thynne reported this interesting intelligence to his boss, Brigadier Dudley Clarke, the "master of
deception" fired back:

"Well, what have you done about it?"

"Done about it, Dudley? What could I do about it?"

"Tell them to put struts under the wings of all the real
ones, of course!"

Of course? Hardly. The straightforward mind, having recognized a flaw in the dummies, would have ordered the camouflage department to correct it. But Clarke's devious mind
immediately saw a way to capitalize on the flaw. By putting
dummy struts on the real planes while grounded, enemy pilots would avoid them as targets for strafing and bombing.
Moreover, it would cause the German photointerpreters to
underestimate and mislocate the real RAF planes.

If Clarke is an ideal example of an authorized deceiver
cheating his opponent dupes, a splendid example of an absolute Rogue cheating dupes with trained but unprepared
minds can be found in the adventures of the "psychic" Uri
Geller, Israel's gift to the Rogue's gallery of deceivers. Geller
claimed not to be a performer of cunning tricks but to have
the power to work real miracles by supernatural means. He

claimed to be the genuine article, and his spoon-bending trick was a perfect example of the devious brain winning over the straight one. It is a particularly useful trick in a situation where you have to work impromptu, without a chance to prepare a spoon in advance, without a confederate to "put in the work" as one goes along, without wires and mirrors. Here, you are alone and verily performing a miracle.

Call for two identical spoons. Stack them one inside the other to show they are alike. Explain that one will serve as the "standard" for later comparison and set it aside or hand it to a sucker. Tell another sucker to pick up the "test" spoon and announce you will now "try" (keep it modest) to make it bend.

Begin to rub the handle of the spoon very delicately with just the tip of your index finger. Ask the dupe if he/she doesn't feel the spoon getting warmer (as it will when the room temperature metal warms in the hand). Take the usual several minutes (to show how *very* difficult miracles are) and ask if the spoon isn't getting just a bit tingly (which the *hand* probably will if held in an awkward position for so long). Then announce modestly that you "feel the experiment may have worked this time" (covering for possible future failures). Have the first sucker bring forward the "standard" spoon and when the two are stacked, lo! there is a visible bend. If you feel really audacious you can try this at least one more time and sure enough the bend will be greater each time.

The audience will swear you never held the "test" spoon and, for once, they are right. Their error was in failing to notice that the "experiment" did not begin and end during the period covered in the previous paragraph but *two* paragraphs above. You did not even have to hold the "test" spoon at that point in the trick because while setting the seemingly irrelevant and therefore innocent "standard" spoon aside is when you bent *it:* the one-ahead maneuver.

Matters might have been different if Geller's audience had been composed of children, for they tend to make poor dupes. Being quite naive in their perceptions, they pose a particular problem for magicians or "psychics." It is not just, as most persons say, a problem of children's relatively short attention span; it is more a question of how to work misdirection on minds that are indiscriminate, taking in almost everything. The misdirection must be very strong and specially geared to the limited kinds of objects that even the youngest have already been taught to perceive as salient—balloons, candy, large bright balls, dolls, live animals. Children are better than adults at catching the old one-ahead maneuver; not yet "educated" to recognize when one event "ends" and the next "begins," they sometimes notice the overlap—but adults almost never do.

It is far, far better to attempt to cheat the distrustful, trained mind. These, the scientists, intelligence analysts, policemen, researchers, engineers, and journalists are highly trained in logical thinking, even more so if they are high Mach and have a strong Rebel or Rogue personality. Rigorous training tends to lead to straight thinking. Prideful of their abilities in observation and deductive reasoning, they do not realize that this straight-line approach is totally inappropriate, even dysfunctional, when used to detect deception. Thus Uri Geller was more than willing to bend spoons in Professor Taylor's laboratory at London University or in the research areas of Drs. Targ and Puthoff at Stanford Research Institute. There, under controlled conditions, Geller confounded the scientists, who did not suspect that it was Geller who was controlling the experimental conditions. They did not recognize that the "observers" were often confederates. They invariably failed to detect the one-ahead maneuvers, because they were professionally conditioned to think in terms of series of disconnected experiments, so they could not perceive when the routine consisted of overlapping events. Their reliance on their proven system proved misguided and Geller successfully deceived them.

There seems to be little hope of detecting deception. The trained and innocent are duped. The cunning and prepared are duped. Everybody can be fooled some of the time. Anyone can be a dupe. There is no apparent defense against trickery, any more than the human eye can turn a movie into frozen frames or make the stick in the water look straight. Stalin was fooled by the German invasion and Hitler by the Allied one. Gould was cheated by Gordon-Gordon just as the learned doctors were by Geller and Houdini by Mr. Williams. At least if you *know* the quarterback may look left and throw right, there is hope for a successful counterdeception. And at least in cne area, magic, everyone seeks to be a dupe, cheated time and time again. Buying ILLUSION after ILLUSION, bemused in all seasons, deceived with elegance. In a world of cheaters there is one safe place in the very eye of the storm, but beyond the magician's stage lurk the seven less savory arenas of the eightfold way.

PART II

CHEATING—THE EIGHTFOLD WAY

CHAPTER 5

Magic

♦ ♦ ♦

The fundamental principle of the
magician's art is misdirection.

—Blackstone the Magician, 1958

New York magazine's theater critic, John Simon, in reviewing the 1980 Broadway musical production of *Blackstone!*, wrote that "going to magic shows is surely a form of intellectual masochism: the idea is to be duped, had, irredeemably bamboozled, and left with the unpleasant gnawing suspicion that there may be something to the supernatural after all." The humorless Mr. Simon felt cheated, for he had missed the point. Audiences go seeking the pleasure of receiving a benign surprise, they seek to be cheated, duped, bamboozled, deceived, gulled . . . beguiled.

Unique among all cheaters, the magician proclaims before all those he is about to deceive that he is going to do so. The audience knows he will try to trick them. For the time they are in his presence, they can give their entire attention to the magician's efforts and try to detect the method by which he achieves his ILLUSIONS. No other act of deception is so concentrated in time or so free of extraneous distractions. Yet magicians are the most consistently successful of all deceivers.

Every magician must plan and practice deception for each trick, for without cheating there would be no magic, no surprise. Cheating is the essential part of the profession. This is not true of other professions. For example, while most successful military commanders use deception, other commanders need not, getting by on a sheer superiority of force that permits the luxurious squandering of men and materiel. Consequently, a close look at the ancient art of magic can tell us more than war about the nature of deception and deception planning. Indeed, we probably can learn more about cheating by examining magic and magicians than by studying any other single field that practices it.

What is magic? The late Harry Blackstone said, "Magic is nothing but pure psychology—applied in the right place." And, he explained, its fundamental principle is "misdirection." And misdirection, showing the false, is simply decoying, one of the six ways to cheat.

Misdirection is the magician's word for deception or cheating. It implies the twofold essence of deception, the play between alternatives where the real is dissimulated or hidden while the false is simulated or shown. All magic, like much cheating, comes down to this simple interplay. And, like all great theories, this one is simple. It is only the execution that demands skill.

Misdirection in magic—decoying—was explained as early as 1634 by the pseudonymous British magician, Hocus Pokus Junior, in his classic book, *The Anatomie of Legerdemain or The Art of Juggling*. He wrote that the conjurer uses "such gestures of body as may lead away the spectator's eyes from a strict and diligent beholding of his manner of conveyance." As this is one of the earliest known books on magic, the author's clear statement of the principle of misdirection suggests that magicians were probably consciously aware of this fundamental principle of their art even earlier.

Showing and hiding, as noted, are the two opposite components or modes of deception. Both are simultaneously present in every EFFECT created by a magician. These two modes exist in their simplest form in magical apparatus. "Apparatus" is the magician's term for "gimmicked" paraphernalia, as distinguished from ordinary articles that may be used such as real coins, cups, or cards. The late American magician John Mulholland made a further useful distinction between a "gimmick," which he defines as a secret device or bit of apparatus masked and so never seen by the audience, and a "fake," which is a piece of apparatus packaged so that the audience sees but does not understand. Thus a "gimmick" is masked, while a "fake" is repackaged.

"Conjurers," wrote magician Henry Hay, "live in a half world, divided into out front (which is magical) and back stage (where the wires are)." The first is what is portrayed; it is the "effect" the audience perceives. The latter is what is concealed; it is the hidden method or routine by which the effect is obtained. The effect is shown and the method is hidden at the same time. It was magicians who first reduced these two facts to a theoretical principle.

The principle is relatively easy to grasp. What the greedy want to know is the method that cheated them. In this chapter they will be cheated, for with few exceptions this analysis of magic concerns the underlying principles and the general techniques—the ways and means—rather than an array of specific tricks.

To begin with, in stage magic the conjurer often uses "assistants." These are of two types, overt or covert. Both illustrate the simplest type of magical misdirection. Overt assistants are openly part of the act, clearly identified as such by special costumes or by their announced role in a trick. While the audience perceives them as merely part of the pageantry they are repackaged confederates; for example a "dumb blonde" who hands the masterful magician a prop will often be the one actually doing the necessary "loads" or "steals"—the magician merely subsequently revealing *her* trick to the audience while claiming it as his own. At such deceptive moments the two roles are unexpectedly switched, the magician only simulating his usual role while the assistant dissimulates her secret role as the real magician. The covert type of assistant is called a *confederate,* or *plant.* Confederates pretend to be members of the audience and thereby hide their secret connection with the performer. The main role of the confederate is to act as a spy in the audience who "signals" secret information to the magician.

In addition to confederates, the magician uses signaling, accomplished either by physical means (radio, pulled cords, knee knocks, etc.) or by visual-verbal means that use any of a number of secret two-person codes. As every card cheat who works "double-o" with a confederate knows, there are two basic types of signaling codes, gesture and voice. For example, when Uri Geller first performed in Israel, his confederates used an unnecessarily complicated gesture code to enable the self-styled psychic to reveal "telepathically" a three-digit number written down out of his sight: 1 = touch left eye, 2 = touch right eye, 3 = scratch nose, and so on.

The public has long marveled over animals that can count or otherwise "think." Magicians know that these animal stunts are usually performed by charlatans and con artists who bilk credulous suckers. The first promoter of a "clever" animal hoax may have been no less a personage than Sir Walter Raleigh, who exhibited the sensational horse, Morocco, and his trainer, a man named Banks, almost 400 years ago. The white steed would stamp his hoof the number of times shown by the spots on a large pair of thrown dice, the total number of coins in a customer's pocket, or the age of anyone who whispered it to his trainer. This nonsense fooled almost everyone, including Shakespeare and Ben Jonson, until exposed by an anonymous British magician in 1612 in his book, *The Art of Juggling.* All the dumb beast could do was respond to visual cues from his trainer. The horse had been trained to keep its eyes "always upon his master." Whenever Banks stood stock still, the horse would start to paw the ground. As soon as Morocco had made the correct number of pawings, Banks would shrug his shoulders and move about a bit and the beast took that as his signal to stop pawing.

Magicians have many methods for gaining secret information from their audiences. They can use confederates as spies. In addition they may simply peek, in one of three different ways: by direct line of sight, indirectly by mirrors, or by surreptitious opening of "sealed" containers. The first two methods are also used by card cheats, and all three methods are used by psychics.

Line-of-sight peeking, blatant as it is, is nevertheless often practiced by magicians and psychics in mind-reading acts. A quick sideways glance often suffices. Blindfolds seldom pose a problem, as "psychics" know three method for seeing through them and magicians know not only those three methods but a fourth as well.

Mirrors or other reflecting surfaces permit unsuspected peeking. Magicians and psychics use them surreptitiously to observe the actions of their audiences. Tiny mirrors or reflectors, called "shiners" by both magicians and card cheats, are used to glimpse a bottom card or a card being dealt. For example, workable card shiners can be improvised by a dealer who applies a drop of water to a table surface or applies nail lacquer to the first joint of his left forefinger.

Joaquín María Argamasilla ran a profitable scam during the first quarter of this century by claiming to be able to see through metal. His talent was even vouched for by the French Nobel prize-winning physiologist Richet. He was "The Spaniard with X-ray Eyes." Then, in 1924 he was put out of business when the great Houdini exposed him as a peeker. Argamasilla used a special metal box with hinges and a padlock-hasp built with just enough play to permit him to lever it open a crack and get a quick look at the dice or one-word message in the seemingly sealed box when he held it to his forehead.

Even more basic than these cheating means is the magician's one-ahead-principle, which is the most effective way by far for achieving misdirection because it induces the victim to misperceive the entire pattern of the operation, whether it is a magic routine, a con game, a practical joke, a political initiative, or a military campaign. Faced with a one-ahead situation, even such highly skilled observers as scientists, reporters, or intelligence analysts invariably fail to report, much less grasp, the significance of *all* relevant details. And they always overlook the one crucial step in the deception, because the cheater is one step ahead. Magicians also apply this principle to several multistep tricks such as cups-and-balls and even to an entire routine or set of ostensibly separate tricks, which are carefully planned to make a maximum use of the one-ahead principle.

Uri Geller, for example, takes full advantage of his pose of being nervously uncertain about his "powers" to work ahead on more than one trick at a time. Being "nervous" and "spontaneous," he frequently jumps up and down, moves around the room, goes to the men's room, charges off to another room entirely with his audience trailing behind, or "passes" on one stunt and turns to another. All very "natural" and disarmingly impromptu, yet these apparently random and therefore seemingly irrevelant actions permit him to set up the next trick, or even the one after that, *before* he finishes the first one. He uses these opportunities to palm or pocket a spoon or other object that requires "work" such as bending or is to be found later to have been "teleported" to a part of the room or building in which Geller, all will swear, had never been. Of course he, or sometimes a confederate, had been there, but several minutes before and as part of a different and therefore apparently unrelated trick.

Thus, by working ahead, the magician can use one trick to set up future ones until a whole routine or major part of an entire performance flows from one trick into the next. Being ignorant of the one-ahead principle, the audience members, particularly scientists and reporters, try to analyze each trick separately, unaware that its solution lies in the unperceived interface between it and one or more previous tricks or, for that matter, nontricks.

Almost all magicians work one ahead, and all good ones do so frequently, as do many mystery writers, some comedians, and a few card sharks. This is not true of other types of deceivers. Most con artists, practical jokers, counterespionage case officers, politicians, and military deception planners apply the one-ahead principle rarely, if at all. The reason for this difference between magic and other deception/cheating fields is simply that only magicians recognize and teach "one ahead" as a principle; but it could be as effective, or nearly as effective, and commonly applied in all the other fields.

Most magicians can fool all of their audience most of the time. Cups-and-balls has deceived over two hundred generations of audiences, yet it is still part of the conjurer's standard

repertoire. Most magicians are content to keep to proven successes that delight and amaze their naive audiences. But it is a
very different story when magicians gather in private. A visit
to a magician's club like Ced Clute's much missed Magic
Cellar in San Francisco will find several magicians gathered
at the bar or around the cocktail tables, eagerly showing each
other the latest gimmicks or new variations on old sleight-of-
hand routines. They delight in these innovations, often even
more than a lay audience will, because as experts they recognize they are seeing something new, however slight the variation. Also, many of these new variations are too complicated
or too slow moving or too subtle to be adapted for public
performance; they remain confined to the circle of the broth-
erhood of magicians.

A few magicians—perhaps a dozen in any one generation—
are major innovators. These are the men who invent entirely
new tricks to advance the art of magic. And these tricks will
usually fool most of their colleagues when first performed.
Only the best magicians, those with deep understanding of
the principles of their art, will be able to detect the nature of
these deceptions.

The truly great innovators, those who discover a completely new principle of magic, are very rare indeed—at most
one or two each generation. When they unveil an invention,
even the best among their colleagues will be unable to detect
the secret. Just a decade ago the ancient art of conjuring was
treated to just such a new principle. It was developed by the
greatest living inventor, the Canadian Mr. Dai Vernon. It is
an application of the modern mathematical field of topology,
which is breeding a whole new set of magic tricks.

Topological cards have now become a major new field for
innovation. The deft Mr. Jeff Busby places a packet of three
cards face up on the table. Without picking them up, he fans

them out to show their sequence: red-black-red. He squares the packet and rotates the two top cards 180 degrees. He fans the cards again but lo! the sequence is now red-red-black, the black middle card having apparently slipped to the bottom.

How is this simple effect accomplished? Watching fellow magicians immediately rule out any sleight of hand. For, although Busby is a master manipulator, by keeping the cards flat on the table he has made it impossible to work any sleight that could alter their sequence. The magicians conclude that the cards have been gimmicked—the two concealed cards must be printed or cut and pasted to be red at one end, black at the other. At this point Busby picks up the packet for the first time, rips it across, and casually passes the six halves out for inspection. The other magicians compare the ragged halves and realize that Busby had used regular cards all along. They are baffled.

This seemingly simple trick is interesting because, while no professional magician has been able to guess the secret, nearly all topologists immediately recognize the underlying mathematical principle and quickly deduce the necessary and simple method.

In their never-ending search for new effects to baffle and delight easily jaded audiences, magicians have always been quick to borrow the latest inventions and principles of science, particularly those developed by physicists, engineers, chemists, and mathematicians. Indeed, many magician-inventors themselves received early training in laboratories and machine shops.

The ancient Roman engineers were masters of hydraulic and pneumatic engineering; they invented elaborate water and sound devices that were used by the priests to convince the gullible public of the priests' supernatural powers.

The Romans' mechanical engineering was also quite advanced; by the thirteenth century substantial progress had been made in this field in Western Europe. In the middle of that century a French mechanical engineer, Guillaume Boucher, while working in Zagreb (then one of the most advanced cities of Europe), was captured during a Mongol raid into Croatia and carried off as a slave to Mongolia to impress the Great Khan's guest with his seemingly miraculous automata. But this was charlatanism. The British magician Isaac Fawkes was perhaps the first to introduce mechanical automata into a magic act, when, beginning in 1722, he began displaying a series of increasingly elaborate mechanical devices designed and built by a famous London clockmaker, Christopher Pinchbeck. In 1769 Baron von Kempelen, counselor on mechanics to Empress Maria Theresa, produced the most famous automaton of all time, his mysterious chess-playing Turk. And magic continued to keep pace with technology:

1. In 1772 an American magician, Jacob Philadelphia, was using the magic lantern, the primitive prototype of the slide projector, to project spectral figures onto a screen of smoke.

2. In 1784 the Italian physicist-turned-magician, Professor Giovanni Pinetti, borrowed from chemistry to use self-igniting phosphorus in a striking trick, only a few years after the Prussian scientist-magician Gustavus Katterfelto had invented the phosphorus match.

3. In 1787 an Italian magician, Signor Falconi, used a concealed magnet to stop watches and attract small objects made of or containing iron.

4. The still popular Bullet-Catching trick was already old when demonstrated in New York City in 1787 by an

Irish conjurer, John Brenon, who apparently caught a pistol-fired bullet in his handkerchief. The use of these gimmicked firearms is, however, truly dangerous, as proven by the deaths onstage of at least two performers, the most recent in 1918.

5. In 1839 the brilliant French magician, Jean Eugène Robert-Houdin, used his skill as a professional clock-maker to exhibit a transparent clock gimmicked so that the hands seemed to move without machinery.

6. In 1840 an Austrian engraver-turned-magician, Ludwig Döbler, first applied electricity to magic, opening his act in spectacular fashion by using concealed wires to ignite simultaneously the turpentine-soaked wicks of the 100 candles that lit his stage. Around 1849, Robert-Houdin repaid technology by inventing the world's first electrically operated burglar alarm system.

7. In 1845 Robert-Houdin introduced the electromagnet to magic. He gimmicked an empty trunk with an iron plate concealed in the bottom so that when electricity was switched on to activate a powerful electromagnet beneath the stage, even a very strong volunteer could not lift the trunk.

8. The English physics laboratory mechanic Thomas W. Tobin had built equipment for lectures on optics at the Royal Polytechnic Institute in the early 1860's. In 1865 he modified one of the laboratory mirror demonstrations to enable magician Alfred Stodare to premiere "The Sphinx" illusion, the first seemingly disembodied yet obviously live talking head.

9. In 1868 English conjurer Robert Heller used the telegraph to signal his assistant in a mind-reading act.

10. In 1898 French magician Georges Méliès created the first trick effects in motion picture film. At the same time Méliès created the first film studio sets, bringing the illusion of outdoor "scenery" to the cinema.

11. The gyroscope was adapted in 1912 by the English magician, P. T. Selbit, when he introduced his comical act, "The Wrestling Cheese." When he concealed the gyroscope in a large wheel of cheese, six strong volunteers could not handle it.

12. In 1916 British magician David Devant first used the semitransparent mirror, adapting it to his stunning illusion, "The Magic Mirror." Depending on the direction and intensity of the stage lighting, a large mirrored pane would become alternately a mirror or clear glass. With this clever device Devant successively concealed, produced, and vanished three different persons.

13. Wireless radio was adapted by an anonymous British magician as part of his mind-reading act in 1916. The rather large receiver of the time was concealed in the medium's ample turban.

14. While the trick film had been introduced by Méliès as a marvel in itself, Polish-American magician Horace Goldin first used moving pictures as part of a major effect in 1920 in his "Film to Life" illusion. Three years later he adapted the phonograph as well and premiered a talking-picture mentalist act called "The Girl with the Celluloid Mind," in which a prerecorded voice was synchronized with the filmed lip movements.

15. The invention of sponge rubber led to its adaptation around 1930 to various sleights, where its compressibility

was useful. Ironically, some magicians soon found they preferred natural sponges and substituted them in their acts.

16. In 1974 Uri Geller brought magic into the atomic age when he apparently smuggled a slightly radioactive substance into a London University laboratory. This unsuspected beta-particle source was sufficient to trigger a Geiger counter, to the amazement of the observer-physicists present, Professors John Hasted and John Taylor and Dr. Jack Sarfatti. When later asked why they had not searched Geller's clothing or body, Dr. Sarfatti found the suggestion "surprising and ingenious."

17. Chemistry laboratories have been raided to yield up flash paper and luminous paint and a few specific effects, including two of the several methods for turning water into wine.

18. Mathematics has been raided to produce several effects. Straight arithmetic gives several "self-working" counting tricks; geometry yields some unusual card effects; statistics gives a few useful ways to "force" numbers; and topology provides magicians with some new card, box, and paper effects. For example, the topologist's familiar Möbius Strip, discovered in 1858, soon emerged as the conjurer's mysterious Afghan Bands, cloth loops that are torn lengthwise to yield first the expected two separate loops and then, surprisingly, two interlocked loops, and finally a single double-length loop.

Thus do magicians freely take the developments of science and technology and exploit them for their art. Few if any magicians, however, deceive themselves that these innovations do anything more than refresh a tired repertoire of effects. They add nothing to the ancient psychological principles of deception and cheating.

Soldiers and others in fields that employ deception often presume that innovations in science and technology fundamentally change or "modernize" the nature of deception; but magicians know that deception is a facet of psychology, as old as the minds of humans. At most, technological innovation—however revolutionary it may prove in its economic or military consequences—affects deception only by expanding or concentrating the range of alternative methods that can be used to achieve a particular effect. This is the principle of multiple causation.

One effect can be brought about in more than one way. All effects of magicians can be produced in multiple ways. In other words, there is usually more than one way to do a trick; yet the observed result will be the same. To begin with, the effect of every sleight of hand can, in theory, be simulated by a gimmick, although the reverse is not necessarily true. Moreover most effects can be achieved by either more than one type of sleight of hand or more than one type of gimmick. There is no known effect and possibly no potential effect that cannot be achieved by at least two entirely different methods.

Thus, there are two distinctly differently ways to work both the Cups-and-Balls trick (sleight of hand or gimmicks) and the Chinese Wands (counterweights or wind-up springs). There are three ways to Saw a Woman in Half. The Clock-Dial trick is also worked by three different basic techniques (pulleys, magnetism, or electricity). Bullet catching is done in three different ways. There are at least three methods for performing levitation. There are four ways to see through a blindfold. "Psychic" reproduction of drawings can be done by five separate methods. Many coin and card tricks can be done by alternative means, like the beautiful Diminishing Cards trick, for which five entirely different approaches can be used. Forcing is done by at least six basic methods with well over 200 minor variations. The Rising-Card trick, invented around 1574 by Italian mechanical engineer Abram Colorni, is now performed by three methods (threads, clockwork, or sleights) in over 400 variations.

The possibility of multiple causation gives rise to one of the most delightful and most important types of tricks, the Sucker Gag or Sucker Effect. It is the magician's version of the Double Bluff.

Johnny Carson, who started in show business doing club dates as a conjurer, enjoys inviting fellow magicians to perform on his nighttime TV show. One of his favorites is Tony Slydini. One evening, the unblinking camera eye let us look directly down at Slydini's hands in tight close-up. All we see is those two hands resting on a green felt cloth. As Slydini's disembodied voice patters on, the hands begin to manipulate a half dollar, vanishing it from one hand and making it reappear in the other. He ends his skilled display of prestidigitation by explaining how he had done that trick, showing the operation again but in slightly slowed motion. Yes, we can all see how the transfer has been made. "Now," Slydini announces, "one last time, *very* slow!" Oops! Nothing happens! And then, as both hands open, we realize we have been well and truly had. The coin has already been transferred right before our eyes by yet another but seemingly impossible means.

Recently, young street magician Gregg Mackler was performing outside Nathan's grand saloon in Georgetown. He included a common but neat Sucker Gag for his enthusiastic evening audience of tourists and Washingtonians.

First he showed a small, bright red sponge-ball in his left

hand. A quick pass and it was in his right—a bit obviously though, as the audience easily guessed. Once again into the left hand and a slow pass back into the right. This time we could all just make out the telltale flash of red in his right hand as he closed it into a fist. "Which hand do you think the ball's in now," he asks a young woman. "In your right!", we all cry. To this he casually announces "No," opening his hand to reveal a huge bright red *square*.

OK, we think, so he had *two* red sponges. "Yes," he anticipates with a broad smile that congratulates us for having found him out, "the red ball is still in my left hand," which he opens to reveal . . . a *black* ball.

Cheers and laughter all around, for we wanted this fine fellow to fool us. Within a minute, before our very eyes and without a gimmick (well, *maybe* one), he had made three secret moves: a "load," a "switch," and a "steal."

The academic theorist of deception, B. Stewart Whaley, relates that in 1976 he invented a magic effect that uses a basic technique that falls in a rare and important category. Never publicly performed, the PK swindle, "PK" for *psychokinetic,* is described here for the first time.

> I place a fresh pack of cards faceup on the table and spread it to display the original pattern of suits, each in its king-through-ace sequence. Explaining (truthfully) that I will demonstrate how important the cut is and why many professional gamblers make three cuts to better mix the cards, I begin a series of simple cuts. Spreading out the upturned cards again shows them now rather thoroughly shuffled. (They are.) I square the deck and turn it facedown.
>
> Taking a pair of dice, I announce (lying) that I can control the throw psychokinetically so that [the dice] will come up with a number I choose. The proof of this is that the number of cuts dictated by the dice will still enable me to predict the first five

cards after the cuts. I predict these cards, throw the dice, cut the number of times specified by the dice, and turn up in order the first five cards showing that they are indeed the ones predicted and in the order specified.

Loaded dice? No, and to prove this I hand the dice to a member of the audience for inspection and then have one of them throw. This time I predict the bottom five cards, cut the decreed number of times, and lo! deal them off the bottom.

Sleight of hand? No, and to prove this I hand over the cards as well. I now predict the 6th through 10th and the other person throws the dice *and* cuts the cards *and* turns over the 6th through 10th cards. Again, prediction fulfilled, yet I have touched neither the cards nor the dice. I compliment my audience on their ability as magicians. My compliment is quite sincere, for they have indeed learned well.

What is the explanation of the PK Swindle? It used no sleight nor gimmick much less any "psi" ability. The cards were honest playing cards, the dice were fair dice, and I didn't peek. Therefore it was, in magician's jargon, a "swindle." A swindle is not itself a trick. *Nothing* happens but the audience thinks it does. By repetition, I even taught them how to do it—but not why. Their minds had been conditioned so they accepted my interpretation of the non-event. Because they have been convinced they "shuffled" the cards even when they cut them *in the facedown position,* they cannot understand that their throwing the dice is irrelevant. They discard one hypothesis after another in their effort to explain the trick until they are left with . . . none.*

As pure psychology, the Swindle is the most elegant of all types of magic. It is a perfect case of "Much Ado About Nothing." Its simplest form, as used by card manipulators, is the "false shuffle" or "false cut." The basis of this PK Swindle, in fact, is a most remarkable false cut invented by Dai Vernon

* Whaley, *Unpublished bar and pub conversations,* 1981.

about ten years ago. Vernon's false cut is unique in that it involves no sleight of hand, depending entirely on a geometrical oddity that audiences remain unaware of.

"Forcing" is the other main type of Swindle. Forcing is used by magicians (and others) to give the victim the illusion of having a free choice. There are at least six different basic methods for forcing—ambiguous instructions, sleight of hand, self-working false options, culture-bound predispositions, loaded choice, and suggestion.

1. The first type of "force" involves giving ambiguous instructions to the victim. It is called conjurer's choice, or *equivoque* (from the French word meaning "ambiguity"). Its oldest form is the "right-or-left" force in which the close-up magician stands before his audience with two objects on his table. He asks them to "choose the right or the left one." Fair enough? No, see what happens. If the audience says "left" and that is not the one the conjurer wants to force, he arbitrarily picks up the other object in *his* left hand while audaciously declaring (and thereby redefining) it to be the "left" one.

   A later version of this type of conjurer's choice is the "take-it-or-leave-it" force. Here the magician asks the spectator to "touch either one." If the spectator touches the object to be forced, the conjurer simply straightforwardly picks it up and uses it. However, if the spectator touches the other one, the magician casually but deviously states, "OK, we'll put that one aside."

   Although the conjurer's choice is logically as obvious as the old "Heads I win, tails you lose" joke, audiences seldom realize that they had no real choice. The magician simply manipulates the verbal ambiguity he has built into his instructions to the victim to his own advantage, the "choice" remaining his alone.

2. The second basic type of "force" uses sleight of hand. There are over 200 known variations, most involving card tricks; the classic version is the Fan Force. Here the magician fans the deck facedown in his hand and invites the spectator to choose one. Then, as the victim's fingers reach toward the fanned cards, the magician deftly shifts it to bring the forcecard directly before the victim's fingers and then feeds it into them. Magician Henry Hay points out, "An atmosphere of total indifference is best calculated to bring success to the fan force. If the spectator thinks you don't care, he won't bother being choosy."

3. The third basic type is the self-working force. It is the magician's sure-thing equivalent of the con artist's "proposition bet." These are really in the nature of mathematical puzzles. For example, if you want to force the number 9, have the spectator write down any six-digit number, add two zeros, subtract the first number, and add up the digits of the answer. The result at this point will always be either 18, 27, or 36. Have him then add the two digits of whichever of those three answers he got and the final total will always be 9, well and truly. To force the number 14, have a spectator shake a pair of dice in a flat-bottomed glass tumbler, add the two uppermost numbers, raise the glass to see the bottom faces, and add those two numbers to the first pair. The total will be 14 because the opposite faces of each honest die always total 7.

4. The fourth type of force relies on certain common cultural or physiological predispositions. Because they are only tendencies, they are never a sure thing but often useful,

particularly for "psychics" who are allowed frequent "misses." For example, most persons when standing at one end of a row of five objects will choose the second one from their end. Similarly, most persons will tend to choose the number 7 when offered numbers from 5 to 10 and will pick 15 when offered 10 to 20.

5. The fifth type of force gives the victim a psychologically loaded choice, literally tempting him without his knowing. This is designed around the deceiver's knowledge of the victim's preferences or system of values. The victim is offered a set of two or more choices carefully tailored to fit higher-lower values or bad-better-best preferences. In its most primitive form this is the story of foxy grandpa who offers a child the choice of a dime or a nickel and the child, mistaking size for value, chooses the larger but less valuable coin. It has been said that Kissinger used to present Nixon with three options, each carefully weighted so that one was clearly bad, another was obviously better, and the third—the one Kissinger wanted all along—was likely to be perceived by the President as best.

6. The sixth type of force is the layman's familiar "power of suggestion" and is closely related to the previous type. The magician weaves the subject to be forced into his patter, thereby subtly predisposing the volunteer's mind to work in desired directions. Uri Geller is a master of this. You too, like Geller, can usually force suckers to draw a circle inside a triangle by instructing them, "Draw a simple figure, like a square," and they will usually draw a triangle. Then tell them, "Draw a different geometrical figure inside the first," and they will tend to put in a circle. After all, how many "simple" geometrical figures are there, and besides you have biased their choice.

DECEIVING THE SENSES

All the senses can be deceived. That is, all the identifying characteristics (CHARCS) of objects or events that our senses detect can be both simulated and dissimulated. Some of these illusions are natural, depending on physical principles such as a mirage or the bent-stick-in-water. Others are physiological, such as those optical illusions that prey upon the brain's inability to process effectively conflicting cues. But most illusions are psychological in origin. Magicians are aware of all three types and occasionally use the first two, but it is the psychologically induced illusion of which they are the masters.

Visual Deception

Most magic tricks involve visual deception. The magician cleverly manipulates the various cues and clues upon which the eye depends to help the brain form perceptions. Magicians are acutely concerned with the need to conceal the secret moves and methods of their tricks from the audience. Consequently they have evolved a series of principles and methods of visual masking.

Friar Roger Bacon, the thirteenth-century English philosopher, was perhaps the first in a long line of naive observers to perpetuate the most common false theory of magic when he wrote of "persons who create illusions by the rapidity of the movements of their hands." *New York* magazine's drama critic John Simon became a more recent dupe when he declared in 1980 that "the hand is still quicker than the eye."

This widely held belief that the hand is quicker than the eye is the very opposite of the truth. The human eye perceives visual data extremely quickly, and the brain processes it into perceptions at speeds of up to a hundred meters per second, all far faster than any hand movement. Indeed, if you know what a sleight-of-hand expert is doing, you see that many of his key moves are deliberately slow, to avoid being noticed as would any unnaturally rapid movement. There are a few magic tricks that do depend for their effect on actions faster than visual perception; however, all these require mechanical gimmicks.

How dull this grand manual art would be if it depended merely on a natural physiological gap in our ability to perceive. In fact, sleight of hand, like all magic, works only because it short-circuits our conventional wisdom by deception. It is the brain, not the eye, that is fooled. But rather than accept magic as a revelation of the labyrinthine processes of the mind, uneasy people prefer a less disturbing, less subversive explanation, literally deceiving themselves with a comforting pseudoscientific myth.

Concerned with the need to conceal their secret moves and mechanisms from the view of the audience, magicians are quite aware of the problem of lines of sight and angles of view; so much so that they call them simply "angles." The Angle Principle defines the limits of visibility and invisibility in which the magician must operate.

Because of the angle principle, even some of the biggest illusions of all, such as Levitation or Walking-Through-a-Wall, are among the easiest to achieve. They are played upon the traditional deep stage, which gives the audience a largely head-on view with perhaps no more than a 45-degree angle view in from each side. All the secret moves and mechanisms can easily hide within the remaining 90-degree or so arc of invisibility.

So-called close-up magic, with the magician behind a small

table, imposes intrinsically more severe limitations on the angles he can work within. Even then, the close-up worker will place his table in a corner so that he is surrounded on only three sides, giving him a slim margin to work behind his hands or underneath the table. The few tricks that can be worked when fully surrounded are called "angleproof."

"It's all done with mirrors," is another of those myths about their art that magicians welcome because it further baffles their audiences. On some occasions, however, when the audience least suspects it, mirrors are indeed used as the gimmick. In those cases the magician depends on the principle of optics that states, "The angle of reflection is equal to the angle of incidence." In other words, an observer at point A in the following figure looking toward a mirror tilted at a 45-degree angle will see the reflection at point D of whatever object lies along the line BC. This is the gimmick in many pieces of apparatus such as the Mirror Glass, which hides small objects in a seemingly empty water glass.

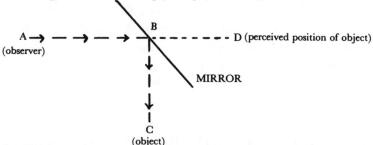

If two mirrors at right angles to each other are placed before an audience at a 45-degree angle, the observers mistake the reflection of the side walls for the back wall. This gimmick can be applied to a small box, a large cabinet or cage, or even the entire stage, to vanish or produce objects of any desired size from an egg to an elephant. This type of illusion was borrowed from the optics laboratory and adapted to magic by

"Colonel" Alfred Stodare when he first presented it on a London stage in 1865. Because of the somewhat complicated mathematics of the angles, we are easily baffled by the results even when we know we are in the presence of mirrors.

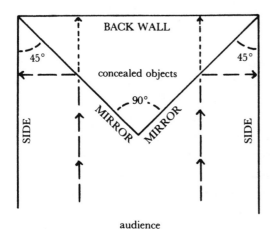

When two mirrors are arranged as at left, the viewer mistakes the side walls for the back wall and perceives an empty box, when in fact at least one quarter of the stage's area falls behind the invisible mirrors.

Then there is "Black Art." This magician's principle states that a dead black object against a dead black background is invisible because it blends into that background and casts no telltale shadow. This principle was discovered by accident by the mid-nineteenth century German magician Max Auzinger while he was watching a play in a Berlin theater. He noticed that the white teeth of a black actor in a darkened dungeon set seemed disembodied and flashed on and off as the actor opened and closed his mouth. Black Art became a standard part of the magician's repertoire when William Ellsworth Robinson introduced it in America in 1873 and Bautier De Kolta brought it to England fifteen years later.

Black Art was the basis of several major illusions. It was also used by some early mediums to create the illusion of the Dancing Handkerchiefs. A few magicians such as the late Harry Blackstone excelled at it. Today, however, it is seldom seen in magic performances, although traces are preserved in the use of "invisible" black thread and the small Black Art Table, and French mime Marcel Marceau recently included in his act an amusing Black Art magic scene.

Acoustical Deception

The ear is easier to deceive than the eye. Indeed, of all the senses, hearing is the one most vulnerable to deception; as Gideon's trumpeters learned, the ear's recognition ability is easily misled by sound effects. Magicians make only occasional use of acoustical deception, but when they do, it is most effective. Here are three examples, one used by sleight-of-hand dice cheats, another by con artists, the last by coin manipulators. The "spirit rappings" of spiritualists is also discussed.

The familiar rattling of dice being shaken seemingly assures the other players of "a fair shake." However, a dice "mechanic" who plans to give this reassurance to a sucker can simulate this characteristic sound before making any of his several "controlled shots." The mechanic picks up the pair of dice in the Lock Grip, in which the dice are boxed in a loose fist by the two middle fingers on one side and the pinkie, forefinger, and thumb on the other three sides. This box is just large enough so the mechanic can make the dice "cackle" realistically, yet small enough to keep them from rotating and making him lose control. Although the two middle fingers protrude a bit unnaturally, this hold is hard to spot when the hand is seemingly shaking the dice.

The Rattle Bars are the basis of a perfectly legitimate magic trick and can, therefore, be bought from any magic shop. They are also the basis of an interesting con game and probably originated as such. Indeed, it is really just a sound version of the shell game. The con artist displays three small metal tubes, each about three inches long. One contains a sliding metal slug that rattles when the tube is shaken back and forth; the other two are mute. The suckers are bet they can't keep track of the bar that rattles. Although the trickster moves them about on the table just slow enough that the suckers are sure they have followed the rattling bar, when they point to it, the con artist "proves" it mute by picking up one of the others and making it seem to rattle. The secret is that the trickster has palmed a second rattling bar which, when he picks up and shakes either of the mute bars in the same hand, makes them simulate a rattler.

Because people expect coins to be noisy, clinking together or "talking" when handled, magicians who specialize in coin manipulation take advantage of this expectation to simulate the sound in various passes such as the Downs Click Pass. This pass enhances the illusion of coins passing from one hand to the other or into a container.

Coin manipulators have a special and very serious problem suppressing unwanted sound. To avoid the telltale "talk" of two or more concealed coins clinking against one another requires special handling and much practice. Similarly, most card manipulators learn to avoid the distinctive "talk" that normally accompanies covert dealing of the bottom card.

Glass tumblers or other resonating objects can be made to give off sound mysteriously. Tuning forks can do this at a distance by sympathetic vibration. Other methods (including use of an ordinary string) can set objects vibrating and producing sound by direct but unnoticed contact.

Not only does the ear easily mistake one sound for another, but its weak stereophonic and directional sense is also easily fooled by false cues. This directional limitation makes the illusion of ventriloquism possible.

Until well into the nineteenth century, ventriloquism was popularly thought to be a form of black magic whose performers were feared and sometimes persecuted. Many conjurers of the time included ventriloquism in their repertoire, and John Rannie, a Scot who came to America in 1801, was one. He conversed with horses about the weather and with dogs about politics. A month-old baby held by Rannie in Portland, Maine, predicted the town would be destroyed by earthquake in three days and credulous families fled.

Today, ventriloquism is recognized as pure entertainment, but most audiences still think the performer somehow "throws his voice." This is physically impossible. Actually, the ventriloquist, like the conjurer, relies entirely on misdirection. He speaks in a false voice with minimum lip movement while acting as if the sound comes from another direction. This is why a semiskilled ventriloquist and super performer like Edgar Bergen, who was also an amateur magician, was just as effective with "Charlie McCarthy" on the movie or TV screen with their monophonic sound as he was live on stage.

Tactile Deception

Our so-called sense of touch (actually comprising separate sensors for feeling, temperature, pain, pressure, and weight) is also subject to deception. Outright physiological misperception is rare in that there are far fewer tactile than optical illusions. The best known example is Aristotle's Illusion: cross your fingers, rub the tips down the ridge of your nose, and you feel two noses. There are also physiological illusions involving the sense of pain—trauma in one part of the body sensed as pain in another ("referred pain") and the tingling felt by amputees who continue to feel a tingling that seems to come from the limb that has in fact been amputated. A curious weight illusion results from the interplay of expectation and physiology. Because experience teaches us that large objects are generally heavier than small ones, our brain anticipates the need for greater power to lift large objects and adjusts our muscles accordingly. Consequently, if two objects, say, tin cans of equal weight but different size are picked up simultaneously in each hand, the larger one will feel lighter because the arm picking it up will have overadjusted.

The main use that magicians make of touch is to have the spectator "verify" the continued presence of an object ("You *do* feel the coin under the handkerchief?") that has already been replaced by a different but similarly shaped object. Thus spiritualists in a séance can link a ring of hands held under the table in a lightless room by a dummy hand so as to leave one of the medium's hands free.

Several coins lie on a table. They are identical except for their dates. Turning his back, the magician instructs a spectator to choose one and memorize its date. After the spectator returns it to the table, the performer quickly examines each coin in turn and announces the chosen one. The coin picked up by the spectator will be slightly warmer than the others.

Another touch trick involving temperature sense is to place metal foil in the hand of a volunteer and announce that it is getting warm, warmer, so warm that it is literally too hot to handle; the volunteer drops the foil with a scream. The foil has been treated in advance with a special chemical that reacts exothermically with the volunteer's skin, causing it to burn. This is one trick that should be exposed, because the chemical is highly poisonous and can cause crippling and even death, particularly to any performer who handles it regularly. Uri Geller dropped this from his bag of tricks when he came to the United States in 1972.

Our sense of pressure is also easily deceived—much more so than most people realize, so they are that much more readily taken by surprise. For example, if the magician places two rather than only one sponge-ball in your hand and closes your fingers over into a fist, you will be unable to detect the second one even though the combined pressure is twice as great as with only one sponge-ball. Both feel and pressure are simultaneously deceived if the magician presses a small hard object such as a coin into your palm and then immediately steals it back while he folds your fingers over into a fist. For a second or two before the pressure wears off, your empty fist will signal your brain that you are still holding the coin.

Muscle fatigue often goes unnoticed, frequently with surprising results. Test this on yourself with the following old parlor trick. Stand parallel to a wall at slightly more than arm's length. Put one arm straight out and lean hard against the wall, palm flat and supporting your weight. Hold this pose for a minute or two and then stand up straight and let your arm hang stiffly at your side. Within seconds the arm will slowly begin to rise straight out, seemingly of its own volition. This odd consequence of unperceived muscle fatigue is the basis of several other parlor tricks as well as some of the effects used by mediums in their séances, providing the motive power for the moving planchette on the Ouija board as well as for table tilting. Incidentally this last trick was first exposed by the great nineteenth-century British physicist, Michael Faraday.

Altogether there are relatively few touch tricks. Even such an innovative magician as the late "Jean Huggard" (John Boyce) added no touch tricks to the repertoire, even though he continued to invent many tricks after he went blind in his later years. The mainline tradition of magic concentrates on visual effects. Magicians make surprisingly little use of sound and less of touch.

Smell and Taste

The two remaining senses, smell and taste, are seldom used deceptively by magicians—they leave those largely to perfumers and food processers. As early as 1650, however, French water conjurer Floram Marchand was able to spew out from his mouth streams of fluid, each with different but strong aromas of his choice. This trick was probably accomplished by vials of essences concealed in his mouth which he could crush one by one, mixing each with the plain water he regurgitated. Messy, but effective.

The only magic trick that combines both smell and taste is the Inexhaustible Bottle. Its original version, first reported in 1635, was a keg with a single spigot from which the conjurer could produce any of three alcoholic beverages requested by his most appreciative taste-test volunteers. This trick was accomplished by three secret compartments controlled by air holes to the outside. By 1848 Robert-Houdin had substituted an opaque bottle—actually a simulated one made of tin—able to dispense five different fluids from as many compartments. Modern performers like Think-a-Drink Hoffman have increased the number of drinks available by having one compartment dispense flavorless vodka into glasses, each of which conceals a drop or two of various flavoring essences.

Cheating the senses is simply one aspect of magic, but the cheated, like the drama critic Simon, suspect that *real* magic is involved rather than simply skill. In fact, those who claim that they are capable of tapping the supernatural on call are the bane of most magicians' lives: mind readers, seers, psychics, the lot, cheaters all. And no magician hesitates to reveal *those* tricks, thereby cheating the cheaters of their EFFECTS, destroying the gullibles' ILLUSION.

Mind reading, or "mentalism," as it is sometimes called, existed as a set of separate tricks at least as early as the second century, when the Greek mystic, Alexander the Paphlagonian, simulated clairvoyance. It has been a standard addition to magicians' bags of tricks ever since the elegant Italian conjurer, Pinetti, premiered the first full mentalist act before King George III at Windsor Castle in 1784. It is baffling, amusing, and perhaps a bit unsettling; but ethical performers make only a jest of their "psychic" abilities, particularly when offstage.

Spiritualism began in 1848, when the young Fox sisters, Margaret and Katie, publicized their "Spirit Rappings" in upstate New York. Within five years, an estimated 30,000 Americans were practicing mediums. Spiritualism has remained a profitable business, despite Margaret Fox's eventual confession and demonstration of her lifelong fraud. The Spirit Rappings that fooled thousands were done by simply snapping the toes.

There is further connection, an antagonistic one, between magicians and psychics. Since 1851, when John Henry Anderson, The Great Wizard of the North, exposed the spiritualist tricks of the Fox sisters, calling them "conjurers in disguise," magicians have placed themselves in the forefront of trying to enlighten the public about psychic charlatans. Beginning in 1865, the soon-to-be-famous English conjurer, John Nevil Maskelyne, exposed the spiritualism of the American Davenport brothers, who were then touring British stages. Houdini made this task a virtual crusade in the 1920's, but was unable to dissuade his close friend, Sir Arthur Conan Doyle, from his spiritualist beliefs. Most recently, the Amazing Randi and Martin Gardner have been among the more effective in exposing the audacious frauds of the popular "psychic" Uri Geller. Yet, because an exposé is so prosaic compared with the seductive frauds they reveal, it is small wonder that many retain a touching belief in the supernatural, *real* magic.

Two major recent popular American entertainers, the late Joseph Dunninger and The Amazing Kreskin, openly encouraged gullibility by pretending to have "real" telepathic powers. Their false claims make them fair game for an exposé. One of their major effects was pirated by Kreskin from Dunninger, much to the annoyance of the older man. The master mentalist seats himself in a chair onstage, takes up pad and pen, theatrically dons his impressive horn-rimmed glasses, and starts to doodle. The doodles, he explains help focus the mind. His assistant passes among the TV studio audience, selects one of the several celebrities present to allay any suspicion of collusion, and asks her to whisper some secret. The mentalist scribbles a bit on his pad, "tuning in" on the celebrity's mind. Then he slowly zeros in until he announces the secret. The studio audience and home viewers alike are amazed.

The mentalist had literally tuned in, not by ESP but by radio. Pad and pencil are pure misdirection to justify the glasses worn by Dunninger and Kreskin. The heavy sidebars of the glasses conceal a miniature radio receiver and tiny ear speaker. The transmitter on the assistant catches the whispered secret. The only amazing thing about this trick is that millions of persons are still fooled by the Radio Cue Prompter, although it has been widely used ever since 1916 when it was first introduced.

Another facet of "supernatural" power is revealed as mere "Muscle Reading." The magician or mentalist has his subject hide an object, takes his hand, and asks him to direct the magician's search by giving unvoiced mental instructions such as "go this way," "reach higher," or "stop." With little hesitation, the magician leads the subject to the object and finds it.

This curious trick depends on the physiological fact that people's muscles reflexively respond to their mind's unspoken directional clues. All the magician need do is feel the subject's slight restraining tug if he starts in a wrong direction. The subject need only concentrate intensely and his muscle reflexes do the rest. He is the unwitting confederate of the magician.

Muscle reading, then called "mind reading," was invented around 1870 by the American pseudoclairvoyant, Washington Irving Bishop, who even used it to complete horse-and-buggy rides blindfolded. Modern muscle readers take to blindfolded automobile driving. In this case, the wise mentalist (like Bishop) supplements his muscle-reading skill with a see-through blindfold. When Dunninger introduced the blind auto drive in Hartford in 1917 he pretended he wasn't cheating; but when Randi did it spectacularly on the Mike Douglas TV show in 1974 it was only to expose Uri Geller's own clumsy blindfolded driving.

The notorious Geller, the fading superstar of the psychics, was born in Tel Aviv in 1946. After dropping out of high school and failing officers' training in the Israeli Army, he was a fashion model briefly and then in 1967 a camp counselor. In camp, one of his young charges was "Shipi" Shtrang, and when Geller introduced him to a conjuring textbook they began a lifelong collaboration in magic, Uri as the glamorous performer, Shipi as his not too obtrusive confederate.

Beginning in 1968, they performed a mentalist act at private parties and night clubs but were soon ordered by an Israeli court to desist from using the words *ESP, parapsychology,* or *psychokinesis* in their advertising. The court was satisfied their act was only straight conjuring. Geller's popularity in Israel declined further in 1971, when local newspapers disclosed that a widely publicized photograph of Geller with Sophia Loren had been faked by him. At that low point, Dr. Andrija Puharich, M.D., an American parapsychology buff, "discovered" the handsome, personable young Israeli and brought him to the United States.

After his arrival in the United States in 1972, Geller quickly gained international celebrity status, making frequent well-paid public demonstrations, particularly at university campuses. Throughout 1973 he made several major TV appearances, fooling Mike Douglas, Barbara Walters, and, in England, Richard Dimbleby. And he easily deceived the few gullible scientists whom he let carry him and his entourage of confederates off to their laboratories in America and Britain.

Geller is a skilled magician, but his skill lies more in misdirection, of which he is a master, than in manual dexterity. His palming and other sleights are fumbling, though audacious. His blindfolded automobile driving is clumsy, although he has been practicing since 1970. He is ineffective with hypnosis. His pencil reading, one way to "telepathically" reproduce another's drawing, is weak. Even his latest stunt, levitation, is just an old parlor game. Nevertheless, Geller will try anything he thinks he might get away with. He lies easily. He says he was born on Cyprus, yet he really moved there with his mother at the age of twelve. Other times he introduces Shtrang as his younger brother although Geller is an only son. And once he claimed he piloted an Israeli Air Force Phantom jet by psychic means; a word from the Israeli government and he dropped this claim. His first manager, Baruch Cotni, has reported catching Shtrang signaling to Geller. His former chauffeur admits working extra duty as a confederate. His longtime lover, Hannah Shtrang, Shipi's sister, openly admits helping in the secret signaling. A later ex-manager, Danny Pelz, not only admitted filling in as a confederate but also gave detailed accounts of how Geller worked his other tricks. He has been caught out by American and British magicians as well as by a BBC-TV technician, and even on the video frames of a Mike Douglas TV show. Challenged concerning such evidence, Geller once dismissed it by saying, "Oh, sure, there's always someone who says they saw me cheating."

Geller does make highly effective use of confederates. He uses them to observe "secrets" and signal these to him, to smuggle in prepared objects, and to create some of the miraculous events that "always seem to happen" when scientists and reporters are watching him.

Dr. John Taylor, British physicist and mathematician at London University, was convinced in 1973–74 that Geller could fix "broken" watches. "He never touches them," Professor Taylor recalls, for once accurately, "but asks someone else to take them while he holds his hands over theirs." Taylor also notes correctly that "this method is not a hundred-percent effective, nor does the watch always keep going." The scientist gullibly attributes this "remarkable phenomenon" to the magician's "supermind."

Phone up your friends and neighbors and ask them to bring their old broken watches over for after-dinner coffee. Have them check that their watches are stopped even though wound. Have them close their fists over the watches so you "won't be able to touch them," then wave your hands over their fists, and after sixty seconds say "Abracadabra." Command them to open their hands and lo! most of the watches will have started. True, as Dr. Taylor says, they won't keep going more than a few minutes or hours, so have your friends take their semistarters to a watch maker and tell him, "This watch needs cleaning." And that is, indeed, all it needs, because the lubricating oil in most watches gradually thickens to the point that the works stick. The only "remarkable" thing about this trick is that a physicist like Dr. Taylor would forget that thick oil is temporarily thinned by warmth, such as the warmth of a hand.

Geller's big smash-hit trick is bending spoons, nails, and keys. He does the actual bending the same way anyone does, by leverage. The only trick is that Geller uses his considerable skills at misdirection to make his audience believe otherwise. There are over a dozen ways to bend these objects surreptitiously and Geller uses most of them.

In one case when Geller finds himself in a situation that is informal and chaotic—and he is expert at creating chaos—he can do the following version of spoon bending. Let's say he starts out with a straight spoon, although he or one of his confederates can usually manage to smuggle in a prebent one. He strokes it a while and then, announcing he has given up, turns to another trick. This distracts his audience's attention so that while discarding the spoon he can manage to put a small bend in it. Later, say after ten minutes, when he returns to the spoon trick, he has already gotten it prepared. The spoon is bent! He can sometimes repeat this flimflam so that "it keeps on bending!" Finally, as the performance is ending, he often gets an unobserved chance to bend it almost double and leave it behind some furniture where his amazed host will later find it and assume it had kept on bending through the night. This is the magician's principle of "working one ahead."

The magician, while of course eager to expose the fraud's use of **real** magic, tricks and deceptions, is even more eager to hide his own methods and the principles that make possible the audience's illusion. His effects are trade secrets, for where would he be without a surprised audience, delightfully cheated again. While every magic trick ends in a surprise, none leave unambiguous or telltale clues to how the trick was done. This is an extraordinary constraint, yet all magicians accept it. They take it for granted and few, if any, realize it is their unique ability to overcome this hurdle that places them first among all other kinds of deception planners.

The joke writer and the art illusionist *must* reveal all; they cannot even try to hide their methods. The military deception planner and the con artist will *usually* reveal their methods at the moment of surprise; seldom do they even attempt to mask their means. Only magicians—and their dishonest imitators, the psychics and gambling sharks—plan *all* deceptions in such a way that the "how" is never revealed, not only during the trick but even by retrospective analysis. Magicians have five lines of defense against disclosure:

1. A key part of magicians' misdirection consists of encouraging the public to accept myths of how magic is done. It's up his sleeve? Not when you think it is. Then it's all done with mirrors? Well, sometimes—but just try to spot when! The hand is quicker than the eye? Never, but this is, as noted, the most persistent popular explanation for sleight of hand.

    Thirteen-year-old Henry Hay spent three memorable

days in 1924 studying sleights with fifty-six-year-old Thomas Nelson Downs, then America's finest all-round sleight-of-hand artist. Downs' upstairs neighbor watched the talented young boy do some tricks and remarked, "You're pretty good, but you're not as fast as Tommy yet," to which the boy replied, "You know, the real reason he's so great is because he's slow, not fast." After the neighbor left, Downs cautioned his pupil, saying, "You don't ever want to tell 'em that about being slow, let 'em think you're fast."

Such myths about techniques and principles are the first line of defense against disclosure for magicians, psychics, and some gambling sharks. As the young Hay learned from Downs, if the performer uses sleights and the audience correctly assumes he does, they will still be unable to detect the slow moves if they are looking for fast ones.

2. The deceiver's second line of defense is Dazzle. If you distract and confuse your victim with irrelevancies or "noise," he is less likely to notice the essential moves and gimmicks. Skimpily clad female or dwarf assistants, colorful and strange paraphernalia, and moving quickly from one trick to another, all aid in distraction. Better magicians make only sparing and carefully selected use of such dazzle, howevever, because it can too easily create such chaos and confusion that even the intended effect gets lost.

3. The deceiver's third line of defense against disclosure is never to tell the audience *exactly* what he is about to do. Not only does this assure that the finale, being unexpected, will come as a surprise; but it sets the audience off on one or more false trails in their effort to detect the method. Moreover, because the audience does not know

just what the trick is to be, they don't know what to look for. This spreads their attention so thin that almost no one ever remembers the key moves, thereby making them incapable of figuring out the method. It is precisely for this reason that magicians usually decline to repeat a trick—unless they are setting up their audience for a Sucker Gag.

4. The fourth line of defense is the one-ahead principle, which prevents the audience from perceiving the true beginning of a trick, the part where certain key moves may have to be done in plain view. If used effectively, particularly when combined with the never-tell principle, the audience fails to see that these moves are connected with the trick. Being one step ahead is probably the single most effective line of defense, but it is not always possible to use.

5. The fifth and last-ditch line of defense occurs during the publicly perceived part of the trick. Even if used alone it is sufficient to deter all but the most penetrating analysis of a trick. Moreover, it is always available to the magician. It might be called the Options Game. This is pure deception in which the magician either simulates an alternative but notional method or dissimulates the one actually used. And for maximum effect the magician uses both at the same time. This procedure leads to a contest of wits between the audience which tries to evolve an hypothesis about how the effect was done and the magician who must divert them from settling on the correct hypothesis. This game is possible because of the principle of multiple causation.

Dr. Max Dessoir, an early psychologist, pointed out in 1897, "What makes prestidigitation the art of deception is not the technical outward appearance, but the psychological kernel." Like the football quarterback, the magician is faced every time with the problem of decoying the expectant viewers. He must always hide some of his real apparatus and activities while simultaneously showing the false to decoy the audience into accepting his EFFECT as an ILLUSION.

It might be appropriate to end with another of B. Stewart Whaley's barroom adventures concerning his capacity, like Uri Geller, to make watches seemingly run faster . . . or slower, if he so wills it. This ILLUSION inevitably baffles the audience, too often willing to accept the supernatural explanation than admire the magician's skill, even the skill of an amateur like Whaley.

> One 1975 weekend evening at the Magic Cellar I was approached by an attractive and beautifully dressed young woman who cheerily announced she was doing her Ph.D. in comparative religion at some unheard-of local university and had just popped in for a bit of field research on her dissertation on magic. I explained that I was not myself a magician but introduced her to my friends who were. It soon transpired [that] she thought she was interviewing a circle of *real* magicians and our combined efforts to dissuade her met a closed mind. For her, *real* magicians included the ubiquitous Uri Geller, and she cited his ability to make watches run faster. Out of growing boredom, I suddenly proclaimed my conviction that *she* also had mind-over-matter powers.
>
> It was her turn to deny any talent for *real* magic, but I said a simple test would show that she too could make a watch run faster. I asked her to remove her own wristwatch, using it for the test "to prevent the possibility of a trick watch," I lied. I held it up so "everyone can synchronize their watches." Placing the watch in her open hand, I commanded her to close her fist and concentrate hard on making it run faster as I, Gellerlike, stroked the back of her closed hand. "Harder," I ordered, as she furrowed her brow in mighty mental effort. After two minutes of this hum-

bug, I declared my belief in her success and told her to check the time. Lo! it was twelve minutes ahead of itself! Mass hallucination? Had fourteen minutes merely *seemed* like two during the tense ordeal? No! The other watches verified that only her's had gained.

The young scholar was amazed but modestly attributed the "Miracle" to *my* powers. To undo some of the psychic nonsense I caused, I admitted that she was probably right and, anyway, could prove the necessity of my "help" if she were unable to repeat the effect in the privacy of her own room. With that she wandered wonderingly out into the gentler magic of a San Francisco evening.

Mine, like Geller's, was a cruel trick but at least I hadn't sent my victim away with the delusion that she had powers she didn't. Accelerated time was, of course, all my own doing. I had noticed she wore a stem winder. On the pretext of 'verifying' the time, I got momentary possession of it. Then, while handing it back to her, I flicked out the stem with my thumbnail and rotated it clockwise with my thumb to advance the time, distracting her eyes by fixing them with mine and uttering some prattle. If my victim is no more observant than the average trained scientific observer she probably swears I "never touched the watch." A final relevant point! This was the first and last time in my life I have practiced sleight of hand. I rehearsed this trick on the spot and entirely in my mind, knowing only the theory of misdirection.*

As Blackstone pointed out, misdirection is everything—as Dessoir noted, there must be a psychological core to cheat the audience. Skill in hiding, whether a knowledge of mirrors or skill of hand, is the physical basis for all misdirection—decoying the viewer away from the real and toward the false. Whaley, intuitively using the Deception Loop, planned his

* B. Stewart Whaley, *Bar and Pub Conversations*, (unpublished), 1980.

trick to begin before the young lady realized that the "experiment" had already begun. At that point, he decoyed her eyes away from her watch hand, in fact, her realization that he had even touched the watch. After that all was golden, for the EFFECT was completed before the subject knew it had been fashioned. All that remained was the lead-in to the certain ILLUSION, a watch that, unaided except by *real* magic, ran fast. Alas, for such young ladies and others, there is no *real* magic; cheating is cheating and forewarned is forearmed, for beyond the arena of the magician's stage, those who cheat for gain lie in wait—perhaps for your loss in the world of the eightfold way minus magic.

CHAPTER 6

Games and Sports

♦ ♦ ♦

MAN: Say, is that a game of chance?
W. C. FIELDS: Not the way I play it.

An ounce of deception is worth a
240-pound tackle.
—Attributed to Jake McCandless,
Princeton football coach

GAMES AND SPORTS are rather different matters despite the fact
that both are played. In games it is rare that the player would
bother if money were not involved, while in sports, the player,
whether amateur or professional, is prohibited from wagering
on the outcome. In sports one must play the game, regardless
of the odds or the motivation—pleasure, a scholarship, an outrageous paycheck—but *fairly*. In games of chance, as in sports,
one may resort to deception, bluff, pretense, and false signals,
but the bottom line is winning money, not points. Then, too,
while games require various skills, physical agility is rarely a

major factor. In any case, both may, indeed usually do, involve *fair* deception and, alack, both have and will involve unfair deception—not playing the game, but *cheating*.

How could it be otherwise? There is so much money involved in gambling on outcomes. Gambling is, of course, a worldwide activity and has been so since ancient times. Britons alone wager some $5 billion (£2 thousand million) on games and sports each year, losing about one-tenth or $500 million dollars of it. Americans wager the astronomical sum of nearly $500 billion annually and also lose approximately ten percent or $50 billion. With that kind of money floating around, cheating abounds. In the United States, perhaps as much as $5 billion goes to crooked politicians and cops as protection money, "ice" for the illegal gambling that makes up nearly 90 percent of the business. Many casinos and the few private winners cheat the Internal Revenue Service by "skimming," failure to report income from winnings. Many gambling joints cheat their customers, many thousands of card and dice sharks cheat their friends and acquaintances, and some basketball players adjust the point spread to personal advantage.

GAMES OF CHANCE

House and Home

Even as the first dollar is wagered at the corner bookie joint or across the casino blackjack table, the gambler has been legally "cheated" by his host. Under the profound there-is-no-free-lunch principle, the customer must pay to play and in playing is assured of losing—sooner or later, more or less. Enter the *Vigorish*.

Assuming they are not being actually cheated, players at casinos, fairgrounds, charitable lotteries, and racetracks must still buck the vigorish. This is the house take or "edge," the percentage (or "PC") of all bets that the establishment charges for letting the bettors use its facilities. (For some games, such as Poker and Skin, the house only charges a straight fee.) Unless you know the PC at least approximately, you don't have to worry about whether the house cheats because you will already be cheating yourself. To help you avoid this, the more popular of these games are listed in the following table, together with the usual house percentages for each. If you don't like the odds, get wise and get out.

Despite the intrinsic interest and value of such a table, this is the first time one has been published. Operators of gambling establishments, from the shadiest "numbers" man up through the posh casino at Monte Carlo to the state government itself in New York's Off-Track Betting (OTB) parlors, have a vested interest in keeping secret their PC on any given game. They do not believe in truth-in-advertising because an informed bettor might take his business elsewhere. For example, on the horses alone, how many suckers would continue to patronize New York's legal OTB parlors if they knew the state government was ripping them off a whopping 24 percent of all bets when they can go either out to the track or just around the corner to a small illegal bookie, where in both places they will get charged only 18 percent. Better yet, go to a big bookie, who will charge as little as 5 percent.

VIGORISH TEST

When one gambles against the "house" at casinos, fairgrounds, carnivals, race tracks, public club houses, with bookies, or at charity bazaars, one must pay the edge. The player never gets an even break. In some cases the odds against a decent return for the gambler would break a camel's back. First, it is most unwise to play a game of chance simply because you *like* the game, unless, of course, you accept the fact that you have little or no chance of winning. Some people would play the slots if they never got a nickel back just to watch the spinning tumblers, hear the clinks and clanks, just to *be* in the Golden Nugget or Caesar's. Others might like a little more chance of winning factored into their games. You can take the Vigorish Test to find out what your sucker quotient is. Estimate the house percentage of the game of your choice. Just check the popular games listed below that you enjoy in their various settings.

[*In alphabetical order*]

_____ Ace-Deuce-Jack (cards)

_____ Baccarat (in U.S.)

_____ Baccarat (in Europe or Latin America)

_____ Bank Craps (dice)

_____ Barbudi (Dice; Even-up Craps)

_____ Baseball (bookies)

_____ Baseball Pool Cards

_____ Basketball (bookies)

_____ Beat the Shaker (1 die; High Dice, Beat the Banker)

_____ Beat the Shaker (2 dice)

_____ Bingo (New York licensed)

_____ Bingo (elsewhere)

_____ Blackjack (Twenty-One, cards; in U.S.)

_____ Blackjack (in England)

_____ Boule (in Europe)

_____ Card Craps (3-percent "book" charge; cards)

_____ Card Craps (5-percent "book" charge)

_____ Chemin de Fer (in U.S.; Shimmy)

_____ Chemin de Fer (in Europe)

_____ Chuck-a-Luck (Bird Cage)

_____ Crown and Anchor (dice)

_____ Dogs, The (on-track pari-mutuel)

_____ Faro (cards)

_____ Four-Five-Six (dice)

_____ Football (bookies)

_____ Football Pools

_____ Harness Racing

_____ Hazard (dice)

_____ Horses (on-track pari-mutuel)

_____ Horses (OTB in New York)

_____ Horses (OTB in Puerto Rico)

_____ Horses (unlicensed bookies)

_____ Horses (Latin American tracks)

_____ Irish Sweepstakes

_____ Keno (cards)

_____ Klondike (dice)

_____ Money Craps (dice)

_____ Monte (cards)

_____ Mouse Game (a mouse; at carnivals)

_____ New York Craps (dice)

_____ Numbers

_____ One-ball (ball; carnivals)

_____ Penny Pitch (pennies; at carnivals)

_____ Penny Tossing (Two Up)

_____ Punchboard

_____ Quarter-horse racing (on track)

_____ Raffles

_____ Roulette (in U.S.)

_____ Roulette (in Europe and Latin America)

_____ Shell Game

_____ Skarney Baccarat

_____ Slot Machines

_____ Stuss (cards)

_____ Three-Card Monte (cards)

_____ Trente et Quarante (Rouge et Noir; cards)

_____ Twenty-Six (Dice)

_____ Under and Over Seven (dice)

_____ Wheel of Fortune (carnivals)

_____ Wheel of Fortune (casinos)

_____ Ziginette (cards)

To learn your score for the games checked, find their value in the following table of House Percentages. Ignore the high figure, ignore the fraction, ignore the plus marks, simply choose the lowest number in the Percent Range.

HOUSE PERCENTAGES

Game	Percent Range
Money Craps	* 0⅘–4¾
Bank Craps	* 0⅘–17
Baccarat (in U.S.)	* 1⅕–1⅓
Chemin de Fer (in U.S.)	* 1⅕–1⅓
Roulette (in Europe and Latin America)	* 1⅓–2⅔
Trente et Quarante (in Europe)	1½
Card Craps (3-percent "book" charge)	* 1½–3
Scarney Baccarat	* 2–2½
Blackjack (in U.S.)	* 2–6⅓
Faro	2 +

Game	Percent Range
Four-Five-Six	2½
Barbudi	2½
Card Craps (5-percent "book" charge)	* 2½–4¾
New York Craps	* 2½–4¾
Monte	3
Hazard	* 3–30
Blackjack (in England)	* 3½–5
Blackjack ("Counting" systems)	4
Baseball (bookies)	* 4½–8⅓
Basketball (bookies)	* 4½–8⅓
Football (bookies)	* 4½–8⅓
Penny Tossing	4¾
Baccarat (in Europe and Latin America)	5
Chemin de Fer (in Europe)	5
Horse Racing (illegal bookies, the bigger the cheaper)	5–18
Klondike (dice)	* 5⅕–11
Roulette (in USA)	* 5¼–8
Stuss	6
Chuck-a-Luck	8
Crown and Anchor	8
Ziginette	10
Bingo (outside New York State)	10 +
Ace-Deuce-Jack	10½
Beat the Shaker (with 2 dice)	11
Boule	11
Quarter-Horse Racing (on-track)	13–18
Harness Racing (on-track)	13–20
Wheel of Fortune (casinos)	15–30 +
Beat the Shaker (with 1 die)	17
Under and Over Seven	17

Game	Percent Range
Horse Racing (on-track)	18
Keno	* 19–26
Twenty-Six	20
Dog Racing (on-track in Florida)	20
Horse Racing (on-track in Latin America)	22–43
Horse Racing (OTB in New York)	24
Slot Machines (rarely only 5–15 percent)	25–50
Bingo (New York licensed)	29
Wheel of Fortune (carnivals)	40
Mouse Game (carnivals)	40–50
Horse Racing (OTB in Puerto Rico)	43
Raffles	45–90
One Ball (carnivals)	49
Punchboard	50–60
The Numbers	51–61
Irish Sweepstakes	about 60
Football Pools	60
Baseball Pool Cards	to 80
Penny Pitch (carnivals)	about 80
Three-Card Monte	100
Shell Game	100

* Payoffs depend on player's choice of strategy.

Source: The dean of American gambling authorities, John Scarne, has complained for years about the vast amount of misinformation given (often deliberately) in books, articles, and by word-of-mouth about the house take. This table, the first of its kind, in almost all cases used his figures, almost all others having proven to be inaccurate, often underestimating the true percentages by as much as a quarter to a half.

If you have checked only one game, its percentage is your score. If you have checked two or more games, add the separate scores and divide by the number of games. For example, if you checked both Roulette in the United States (5 percent) and Slot Machines (25 percent), then your score is 15:

$$5 + 25 = 30 \div 2 = 15$$

This means that in the VIGORISH TEST your sucker quotient is 15 percent.

COMPARATIVE SUCKER SCORES

Score

1–4	Cautious Gambler (Dull Dog)
5–7	Average Gambler (Sly Dog)
8–24	Average Sucker (Most Dogs)
25–90	Easy Mark (Dumb Dog)
90–100	Damn Fool (Dog without a Day)

It will be apparent why modern casinos are reluctant to offer their customers the grand, traditional, but low-profit casino games of Faro and Monte and why American casinos add a second "house" zero to their roulette wheels. It is also clear why casinos keep regular customers at the comfortable 4- to 6-percent take range of games like Blackjack. And the various forms of Craps do well because most players are too ignorant of the low-percentage strategies that would hold the operators to those less than 1-percent minimum profits. Those games where the house take is 10 percent and above are real dogs, strictly for suckers. Needless to say, Three-Card Monte and the Shell Game—where the house take is 100 percent unless the shark lets you win as a come-on—aren't games of chance but sheer swindles.

ON THE PREVALENCE OF CHEATING

Experts rightly caution that cheating at card games is very common, even among friends in private homes for small stakes. John "the Professor" Scarne, goes further, asserting that "more cheating takes place at private or so-called friendly card games than at all other forms of gambling combined." He reasons that this is because it is so easy to get away with in a group of amateurs and estimates that one out of every ten men and women in such games are cheats. If more *total* cheating occurs in "friendly" games, Scarne finds the highest *proportion* in "big-time money games patronized by men and women who know little about cheating techniques." He estimates that at least one card-shark will be present and "working" in two thirds of these games held mainly in anonymous hotel rooms and private homes. Contrary to popular myth, licensed casinos at least offer generally honest games: why should they risk getting a bad reputation when their legal take already favors them by around 5 percent of all wagers for the most popular games.

Cheating is moderately common in "friendly" bridge games, and it is a very serious, if delicate, issue in professional tournaments. Although little money is at stake, most of the more than one thousand annual bridge tournaments in the United States hear at least one rumor of some team having cheated, usually by illegal signaling. Formal accusations of cheating are, however, rare, because most bridge players prefer to ignore the problem.

Blackjack offers many fine opportunities for the card cheat, possibly more than any other single game except Gin Rummy. Scarne goes so far as to assert that "more cheating takes place at the Blackjack tables than in any other casino banking game." One of the charms of Blackjack is that everyone has a chance to cheat: the house can cheat the player while the player and even the dealer cheat the house.

Investigating cheating among American G.I.'s in World

War Two, Scarne observed some two hundred games of Craps and detected loaded dice in one out of five. Although loaded dice are used less often now, as players have gradually wised up, Scarne still detected them in one out of ten games of Private Craps as recently as ten years ago.

There are only four games that by their very nature offer substantial protection against any cheating. The first two are the board games Chess and Checkers, where about the only things a cheat can do is move or remove a piece and desperately hope his opponent is too drunk, too high, or too forgetful to notice. The other two are the dice games of Aces and Barbudi, where the dice pass too quickly for either sleights or gaffed "percentage" dice to be very effective. These four are the only games in which an amateur can be almost sure of getting an even break. They might also be good games in which to meet relatively honest folk to join you in Poker or Bridge. Cheating is also rare in the card games of Hearts, Pinochle, and Bingo.

The more ephemeral the setting or the more transient the players, the more likely it is that cheating will occur. The conventioners' hotel, the cruise ship, long-distance trains— these provide ideal circumstances for the gambling cheat. The naive patron is a prime target of opportunity, a "fish" that few "sharks" will let pass. "Cheat 'em while the cheatin's good," they say; and it is never more tempting than where the shark can be long gone before the sucker thinks to complain.

LEGAL HIDING, LYING, AND BLUFFING

Simple legal hiding of cards occurs in almost all card games. The few exceptions include the Italian game of Ziginette and some of the solitaire games such as Pyramid and Monte

Carlo. Several games such as Dominos, Scrabble, and Stratego depend on the successful concealment of one or more counters.

A few games require outright lying, in which case the lying is both legal and ethical. This is true in the two children's card games of Cheat and I Doubt It. Popular bar games are Liar's Dice and Liar's Poker. The recent board games of Diplomacy and Junta stress both lying and secret collusion to set up a double cross. In all games in which lying is an integral part of the game, the lie is in fact merely a bid or declaration that must be either challenged or accepted before play can continue. These games require lying.

There are many other games in which lies are permitted but not required. Thus players of Rummy, Poker, and Chess may use verbal or body language to convey false impressions of strength or weakness, fatigue or alertness, knowledge or ignorance, luck or lack of it. These ruses are called "coffee-housing" and have become a fine art in the hands of chess masters from Bishop Ruy Lopez to Bobby Fischer. Although of dubious ethicality, such ploys are tolerated in all games except bridge, where they can too easily be the vehicle for secret, illegal signaling.

The most sophisticated form of legal, ethical, and integral lying is bluffing. It is truly deceptive because it is part of the strategy of play in those few games in which it is allowed. Bluffing is legal deception, and games that include it become games of skill and not mere games of chance. Despite the popularity of bluffing games, for some reason very few of the hundreds of card, dice, and board games incorporate the element of bluff. The only current ones that do so are the card games of American Poker and Skarney, English Brag, German *Pochspiel,* and the recent American parlor card game of

Rat Fink. The "lie" in Liar's Dice (played with dice) and the similar Liar's Poker (played with serial numbers on dollar bills) is in effect a bluff, as demonstrated by the fact that Liar's Dice is also called Bluffing Dice. So too with the legal "miscall" in the Match Game (played with matches). A bluff does not change the chances of getting any particular hand. Bluffing does, however, change the chances of winning more of the larger pots than the bluffer's cards deserve.

Persia is the source of what was possibly the world's first card game involving bluff. This was Ās-Nās, invented in the fourteenth century. It was played with a deck of twenty cards divided equally among five values: lions, kings, ladies, soldiers, and dancing girls. These were shuffled and dealt out among four players. Because the deck was exhausted in the deal, there was no draw. The hand was simply bet and shown. It was its element of bluff that quickly caught on in the New World five centuries later, when in the early 1820's sailors brought the game from Persia to New Orleans. There it was adapted to local custom and the hybrid became Poker. It quickly underwent several modifications: values immediately became aces, kings, queens, jacks, and tens; the fifty-two–card deck came in around 1837, the draw and the ranking of flushes during the Civil War, straights were ranked in the early 1860's, and stud and jackpots were introduced around 1870. At that point Poker became the game it has remained to this day.

The first theory of Poker was developed in a classic work, *Theory of Games and Economic Behavior,* published in 1944 by the brilliant mathematicians John von Neumann and Oskar Morgenstern. They wrote, "Of the two possible motives for bluffing, the first is to give an impression of strength in weakness; the second is the desire to give an impression of weakness in strength. Both are instances of inverted signaling, i.e., of misleading the opposition." Von Neumann and Morgenstern clearly saw the twofold nature of all deception, hiding and showing. The two made a further mathematical analysis of Poker that proved the experts' intuition right all along in their claim that successful Poker depends not merely on randomly intermixing bluffs with straight play, but that it is essential occasionally to try to bluff weak hands, even though these are likely to be called, in order to make the high hands pay. All other things being equal, the best situations for bluffing in Poker occur in the following circumstances:

1. Any time the ratio of the price of being called is high compared to the value of the pot
2. Whenever all the "loose," that is, reckless players (particularly novices), have folded and all but one or two "tight," that is, conservative, players, remain in the game
3. In high stake games, because these are more likely a) to yield situation number 1 above and b) to discourage "loose" players from calling just "to keep you honest"
4. Whenever you have evidence that the other players still in the pot perceive you as playing "tight"
5. If, holding a strong hand early in the game, you check and then reraise
6. When you hold a fair defensive hand such as two pairs
7. When you are sitting last

Any bluffing game such as Poker played between compulsive truth tellers would be very dull. Its outcome would depend only on how well each player had memorized the probabilities of receiving and improving hands. If all players had equal knowledge of the probabilities, each would have a statistically equal chance of winning and the game would cease to be one of skill and would be one of only information. This is why chess, being a game of "perfect information," lends itself to computerization and partly explains why fundamentally "stupid" computers have been programmed to play at the "master" level. But computerized Poker will remain a child's game until bluffing strategies are programmed into it.

CHEATING AT CARDS

All the sleights used by card cheats are also used by magicians. Consequently, few magicians ever gamble for money. As Houdini explained, "If I win I am accused of cheating; if I lose they think I am a lousy magician." When Scarne plays cards with friends, he accepts the condition that he never touch the cards, except to use one hand to lift the edges to see his own.

Sleight-of-hand card cheats, of course, take great care to hide their mastery of magician's manipulative skills. They avoid the eye-catching theatrical card flourishes, like "fanning" and "springing," that the magician flaunts to advertise his skill.

Of the 150,000,000 decks of cards sold each year in America, Scarne estimates that 1 percent get marked at some point. Yet, as he discovered in his 1972 gambling survey, only 2 percent of average players have any idea of how to detect these "readers."

Although gambling cheats use many of the sleights and a few of the gimmicks used by magicians, they are not magicians. They share neither the jargon of magicians nor their highly developed theory. Moreover, while each magician will have an extensive repertoire of tricks, the cheat will tend to perfect and use only one or two. Consequently it is not surprising that cheats do not even have special jargon to identify some of the types of things they do. For example, as seen earlier, one of the most potent tools of the magician is the One-Ahead Principle. When some cheats occasionally use this, they do so without recognizing or further using the underlying principle.

Arnold "The Brain" Rothstein was New York City's biggest gambler during the Roaring Twenties; he was the man who had bankrolled the 1919 World Series fix. In 1928 he lost $340,000 at a hotel-room game of high-spade cut but refused to pay because he claimed he had been cheated with a gaffed deck—his own. Having a suspicious nature, Rothstein had brought along his own deck, one he had purchased at the cigar stand in the hotel lobby. If he is to be believed, he was the victim of that lovely one-ahead scam of planting doctored decks with the local source of supply. In any case, Rothstein died for his story when, a few weeks later, on leaving Lindy's Restaurant on Broadway, he was gunned down with a single 38-caliber gut shot.

Rothstein had fallen for an oldie. Nearly a century earlier, bartenders working in collusion with gamblers on Mississippi riverboats would make sure that the "fresh cards" called for by other players would all be marked to the cheat's specifications. Only about fifteen years before Rothstein's blunder, Western Europe had been flooded with American-made De Land playing cards, all marked so that the card mob only need look for games using those distinctive decks. More recently, during the racing season at Saratoga, a card mob sneaked into the local supplier's warehouse and substituted their own cases of marked cards. For weeks, most games in that big gambling town were using the gang's cards. It is still a widely used scam at hotel newsstands, neighborhood shops, private clubs, and lodges, where the unsuspecting management can be tempted by a "salesperson" selling cards at bargain prices. And if they suspect the truth, a little bribery will often suffice.

Signaling

Signaling is how one person illegally tells his partner what cards he or a sucker holds. Professional gambling cheats call signals "signs" or "offices" or "the wire." By whatever name, they give decisive advantage in Partnership games such as Bridge and Partnership Pinochle as well as in such loner's games as Poker, Hearts, and Gin Rummy.

Mechanical devices by which a confederate can signal his cards (or those of the sucker) are almost as old as cards themselves. Cards, invented in China in the tenth century, reached Europe by the end of the thirteenth. Sixteenth-century mathematician-physician Geronimo Cardano, in *Liber de Luda Aleae ("Book of Games of Chance")*, described the *Organum* ("organ"), a loose floorboard with a string attached. The dishonest host sat himself with one foot on the loose board while his confederate would make appropriate tugs on the concealed string to signal his own cards. Today, some partners mechanically signal each other by a string ending in small hooks attached under the table to each other's clothing or simply by kneeing or foot-tapping.

The Victorian novelist William Makepeace Thackeray was a close observer of professional gamblers and card cheats. In *The Memoirs of Barry Lyndon, Esq.,* Thackeray's hero-scoundrel recounts his acting as confederate to his wealthy uncle in their cutthroat games of Écarté. Disguised as a valet, Barry would signal the situation. "If, for instance, I wiped the dust off the chair with my napkin, it was to show that the enemy was strong in diamonds; if I pushed it, he had ace, king; if I said 'Punch or wine, my lord?' hearts was meant; if 'Wine or punch?' clubs. If I blew my nose, it was to indicate that there was another confederate employed by the adversary; and *then*, I warrant you, some pretty trials of skill would take place."

Radio in the form of the so-called Radio Cue Prompter is also used to pass signals to a partner-player from a confederate peeking at the cards from a hole in the ceiling, through a two-way mirror, or by just kibitzing inside the game room itself. This innovation came into use in 1916 among magicians and mediums. But the lack of thick eyeglasses concealing the receiver, as used by Dunninger or Kreskin, is no proof of innocence, because in the gamblers' version the receiver is strapped to a leg and delivers a series of coded dot-and-dash electrical shocks.

The Radio Cue Prompter was adapted to card cheating at least as early as 1949, when Scarne uncovered its use in a posh southern California bridge club run by Las Vegas gamblers. Using ten tables, each monitored by the club staff through as many ceiling holes, this one casino and its ex-movie star host managed to bilk several million dollars a year from Hollywood celebrities. Although Scarne's investigation closed down this particular "peek joint," suckers seemingly never learn. Only two decades later, another group of Las Vegas gamblers set up a peek joint in the Los Angeles area and bilked another group of Hollywood celebrities out of hundreds of thousands of bucks in Bridge and Gin Rummy.

Nor are even private, "friendly" games immune to the Radio Cue Prompter. The late Nick "The Greek" Dandolos,

America's most famous gambler of the midcentury, was once taken by a Radio Cue Prompter for a cool half million dollars in a private two-week poolside session of Gin Rummy at the Flamingo Hotel casino in Las Vegas. These devices are not only readily available through gambling supply house catalogues but are in fact sold in surprisingly large numbers. In 1960 alone, a single electronics company sold several hundred Radio Cue Prompters.

More illegal signaling probably takes place in the ostensibly genteel game of Bridge than in any other game. After all, Bridge depends on legal signaling ("Bidding"), so it is an obvious temptation even among amateurs to work out private codes with their partners. This can go to comic extremes, as in Roald Dahl's story, *My Lady Love, My Dove.* Dahl's fictional couple worked up from simple codes to increasingly elaborate ones, using finger positions, combinations of phrasing, and vocal intonations until they were finally using some 500 signals—to a point where they could no longer remember the codes and promptly lost all their ill-gotten winnings.

The first major international Bridge scandal occurred in the 1965 world championship match at Buenos Aires, when two members of the British team were publicly accused of using illegal finger signals; they were found guilty and banished from play for three years by the World Bridge Federation. A more recent scandal erupted at the Bermuda Bowl championship in 1975, when two partners on the Italian team were accused of and reprimanded for exchanging foot signals under the table.

There is one and only one system of signals that absolutely defies detection, although no book on cheating at cards or mind reading in magic mentions it. It is published here for the first time. Until now it was a system known only to cryptologists and readers of their books; consequently, only professional or amateur cryptologists could have applied it to cheating, and then only after 1918, when the method was first discovered.

The unbreakable ("holocryptic") code is called the "one-time" system. It was worked out in 1918 by Major Joseph O. Mauborgne, a brilliant thirty-six-year-old U.S. Army Signal Corps cryptologist. He was the first to recognize that the only codes and ciphers that can never be solved are those whose "key" contains no systematic pattern, no repetition. The only way this condition, one demanded by statistical theory, can be met is by a key that is purely random.

Consequently, all you and your unscrupulous partner at Bridge or secret confederate at Poker need do to avoid the possibility of detection is agree on a private set of signals that are keyed to a sequence of random numbers. Moreover this system is elegantly simple, more so than the elaborate ones used by Barry Lyndon or Uri Geller. For example, in Gin Rummy all that you need know from your confederate is whether the opponent holds a high count or a low count in unmatched cards. Thus the only signals needed are for "high" and "low." These can even be indicated by such normally suspiciously obvious "natural" gestures as coughing, sneezing, throat clearing, head scratching, or nose picking. Your signaler will be quickly cleared of suspicion when no pattern of meaning can be deduced from his gestures. To do this you and your confederate develop your one-time key. Toss a coin and record the sequence of heads and tails, say HHTHT and so on. If heads equals the number one and tails two, that gives you a random key of 11212, and so on. List it in one column and decide that, say, coughing and sneezing are your two signals. In the keyed sequence, the coughs and sneezes take on the following set of meanings:

Sequence	Key	Signal	Meaning	Signal	Meaning
1	1	cough	high	sneeze	low
2	1	cough	high	sneeze	low
3	2	cough	low	sneeze	high
4	1	cough	high	sneeze	low
5	2	cough	low	sneeze	high

Thus you have made a random binary code in which the first and second signals given mean high if the signal is a cough and low if a sneeze, but the third signal means the reverse, and so on for as many of these as both you and your confederate can memorize in advance of play. A similar method can be used to develop one-time codes indicating the four suits or the ten points or the various crucial types of hands covering all card games.

Admittedly, the one-time system of signaling is, while simple in principle, difficult in practice. A new random key must be prepared and perfectly memorized for each game; and it requires alertness, otherwise you may lose your place in the sequence. Many cheats and mind readers already go to such lengths to memorize codes that can be easily broken. But if you use the one-time system, even a very keen card detective who hears those coughs and sees those finger movements and suspects one-time signaling, there is no way he can prove it. For this is exactly the same one-time system by which the world's major intelligence services and multinational corporations shield their most secret communications.

Cheating at Poker

Poker is *the* game for deceivers—legal and illegal. It is the only card game that positively encourages deception, from first card to last call. Even honest games are "honest" only because the rules permit the deceitful bluffing that is the heart and soul of Poker. Just play the odds right, you say, and trust to luck? Not if you want at least an even chance against players who bluff. And remember the expression "poker face," that careful dissimulation of any emotion that might betray one's cards. And beyond bluffing, beyond the odds, await opportunities for the *true* cheat.

The first recorded Poker game is, appropriately, a story of cheating. It was observed by English actor Joe Cowell while he was on a theatrical tour down the Mississippi from Louisville to New Orleans by steamboat in December 1829.

The deal had passed to a man wearing green spectacles and a diamond stickpin. At that point the riverboat ran aground in the fog and in the confusion everyone rushed outside to see what had happened. Everyone, that is, except Green Spectacles, who loitered at the table, casually shuffling and cutting the deck as if bemused. When play resumed, he dealt out four hands while Cowell and others kibitzed. The man on Specs's left (holding four queens and an ace, the second highest possible hand by the rules of the time) cautiously bet only ten bucks, hoping to avoid scaring the other out. The second player, a greenhorn lawyer and son of the mayor of Pittsburgh foolishly only matched the bet, not recognizing the true power of his hand. The next player (holding four jacks and an ace) confidently matched and raised five hundred dollars. Now it was Specs's turn.

"I must see that," said Green Spectacles, who now took up his hand (for the first time) with "I am sure to win" trembling at his fingertips, for you couldn't see his eyes through his glasses. He paused a moment in disappointed astonishment and sighed, "I pass," and threw his cards upon the table.

The first player met and raised another thousand. The pot now held over two thousand dollars.

The young lawyer had had time to calculate the power of his hand—four kings with an ace. It could not be beat, but he still hesitated at the impossibility, as if he thought it could. He looked at the money staked and then at his hand again and, lingeringly, put his wallet on the table and called.

Specs had, it seems, been a bit confused himself by the boat accident. He had tried to stack the deck for a killing but got the sequence wrong in his haste. Consequently he had dealt the young man the winning hand intended for himself and had given himself only four tens and an ace. Fortunately for Specs's continued good health, the other players did not question such an unlikely set of hands, much less why, with the fourth best-possible cards, Specs had folded. In any case, Specs had the presence to say, "Did you ever see the likes on't?", as he pushed the rich pot to the still startled lawyer.

Joe Cowell kept his mouth shut that night but later wrote of Poker, "In that pursuit, as in all others, even among the players, some black-sheep and black-legs will creep in." His *some* was a gross understatement, for by the next year over eight hundred professional gamblers were plying their shady trade on the river, welcome by the riverboat captains, officers, and barmen who served as willing accomplices in this lucrative game. Cheating was common, as the pros mastered marked cards, reflectors, stacked decks, and false shuffles. And few were as clumsy as Green Spectacles.

CHEATING AT DICE

Dice is one of the world's oldest and most widespread gambling games. Dice have been found in prehistoric tombs in the Near East, in Iron Age sites in Northern Europe, and in both North and South America. And cheating at dice is almost as old. The Natural History Museum in Chicago has several pairs of bone and soapstone dice from ancient Egyptian tombs that are loaded to throw twos and fives. The 2,000-year-old Sanskrit epic of India, the *Mahābhārata,* describes how "Dorjooden, having made a false [loaded] set of dice, challenged Judishter, the commander of troops he was fighting, to play, which being accepted by him, he, in a short time, lost all his wealth and kingdoms." The Greeks and the Romans after them used loads as well as dice cups with built-in crossbars to prevent cheats from "sliding" otherwise honest Dice. The Roman emperor Caligula reportedly cheated at dice, and it is known that Roman Dice sharks used misspotted dice, which require sleight of hand to get them in and out of play without being detected.

The direct ancestor of modern Craps is the once popular English Dice game, Hazard. Writing of that early game in 1674 in *The Compleat Gamester,* Charles Cotton covered the vast array of cheating techniques already in use in his day. He describes gaffed (rigged) cups and dice, the latter comprising loads, tops, files, rounds, and the pin gaff. He describes the pivot test for loads. He even describes three sleight-of-hand techniques: palming, the whip shot, and the drop shot. All of these foregoing techniques, except the recently outmoded Pin Gaff, are still in use. Moreover, they cover most types of Dice cheating except for a few oldies and the modern "electric" (electromagnetic) dice.

In Liar's Dice the ways of cheating are quite different from those in Craps. Slider cups, gaffed dice, and sleights give little if any advantage. The reason is that winning does not depend on having the higher hand but on figuring out when the opponent is bluffing. The only significant way to gain unfair advantage is by changing the value of one's dice just before the final call. This is accomplished when the hustler, grasping the cup in both hands, tilts it up to look at his own hand. At this moment, he can surreptitiously slip a pinkie under the cup and flip one or more dice to give him a new set of winning values.

The only two other effective ways of cheating are a consequence of the fact that Liar's Dice, unlike Craps, depends on keeping secret the value of one's hand under the cup. Consequently, as in card games, a confederate who signals the opponent's hand gives a perfect edge. And even a confederate who signals only his own hand will give a marginal advantage.

THE MECHANICS OF CHEATING

Every single type of equipment used in gambling games can and has been gaffed (fixed, tampered with). All gaffed items are examples of simulative camouflage in which the fake is disguised to look like the real. Most, including many tired items that only a semiinformed "catalogue man" would invest in, are available by mail or express order from certain catalogue houses specializing in gambling equipment and so-called magic gear. You can find these dealers through the advertisements in the sleazier men's magazines.

Gaffed equipment includes the usual variety of marked cards, "stripper" decks with some cards shaved to abet the "mechanic," loaded dice, misspotted dice, double-headed coins to cheat at Penny Tossing and Heads-or-Tails, and roulette wheels wired to favor certain numbers. In addition there are some rather bizarre items such as a Chuck-a-Luck cage with a built-in magnet and set of iron-loaded dice; a complete electromagnetic Craps table; gaffed slot machines; a recently invented fingertip bingo card that works mechanically "Two-way" to come up with winning numbers every time; a card-dealing box ("Shoe") that deals preselected cards in Blackjack, Baccarat, and Shimmy; Put-and-Take tops with edges shaved to always land "put" when the sucker spins it clockwise, as most players will, but always falls "take" when the cheat spins it counterclockwise; punchboards and pushcards sold with instructions listing the winning holes; a set of marked dominos; and even loaded tiddlywinks.

In addition to all this camouflaged equipment, you can also buy or improvise a whole range of special cheating tools. A tiny mirror ("shiner") under a fingernail is a big help to peekers. A small metal spring clip ("the bug") can be attached to the underside of a card table to stash an ace or two. A bit of lead under a fingernail can be used to mark cards during play. And so forth. By 1949, radio had been adapted in the form of the "Radio Cue Prompter" by means of which a confederate can signal to the cheater. All these devices must, of course, be completely concealed (dissimulatively camouflaged) because they are dead giveaways if spotted.

Crooked gambling dens ("Bust-Out Joints") and crooked carnivals ("Flat Stores") still use gaffed equipment because they have enough musclemen handy to protect themselves if caught by a player. However, no smart cheat working alone today will risk being caught with such telltale gadgets. They much prefer to depend on sleight of hand, peeking, dropped cards, or miscounts, all of which can be excused as one-time "accidents" with at least enough plausibility to get them banished with nothing worse than a profitless game. Peeking, for example, is a fine art with some cheats. Many women peekers ("glimpsers," "Glim Workers") place a highly polished object such as a silver cigarette case or lighter on the table to help them see the bottoms of the cards they are dealing. Peeking works fine in such card games as Poker, Bridge, Gin Rummy, Canasta, and Red Dog, where secret knowledge of the whereabouts of even one card gives an edge.

Unless you enjoy spending your money on obsolete equipment and getting hurt when caught using it, don't buy any of the following three types of gear. Strictly sucker items, they are expensive and not, as they say in the gambling cheat's trade, "lumpproof."

Holdout Machines

The "Kepplinger," one of the masterpieces of nineteenth-century mechanical engineering, was a phenomenal success when introduced to San Francisco's Barbary Coast in 1888 by its inventor, P. J. "Lucky Dutchman" Kepplinger. This was a marvelous Rube Goldberg–like contraption of wires, cords, pulleys, an adjustable tube, a metal plate, a hook, a false sleeve cuff, and a hold-out slide, all connected from the right cuff up the arm and across the shoulder down to the knees. By spreading or closing his knees, the cards Kepplinger wanted were delivered and his extras plucked back up his sleeve. The gadget worked fine until the inventor was caught in play by three gamblers and forced to make copies for each of them. "Kepplingers" were popular with some poker sharks for a few decades but were gradually abandoned as word got out to the general playing public. No smart cheat would risk being caught with one up his sleeve today, although some gambling catalogues still offer various "improved" models for several hundred dollars.

Luminous Readers

Mark a red-backed deck with green ink or pencil and the marks will show up clearly if viewed through red-tinted glasses or an old-fashioned transparent red eyeshade. Although this is *very* old-fashioned, the supply houses still try to push this junk. In a pathetic effort to update their technology, they have even offered red-tinted contact lenses since the 1950's. You can buy these premarked cards for about twenty dollars and the contact lenses for over $200—if you really don't mind being seen with ruby-colored pupils.

Concealed Blackjack Computer

This latest and most expensive item comes complete with traveling case and preprogramed minicomputer, wired shoes, electronic light-up glasses, and training lessons for a mere $5,000. Keith Taft, a devout Baptist and self-taught computer engineer, with partner Harvard Business School ex-stockbroker Ken Uston, invented this widely proclaimed money maker. In 1977 Taft and Uston and their gang of five two-man teams cleaned up $130,000 in Las Vegas in twenty-two days. That's almost $600 per day per player, so you might figure recovering the cost of the computer in nine grueling days at the casinos.

As W. C. Fields indicated, a great many games of chance leave very little to chance. The house takes quite legal vigorish, often an outrageous amount, even before the play begins. The chap across the table, the friendly opponent in poker or bridge, is encouraged, nay all but required, to lie about his cards or intentions. Worse, the hacking cough or the fluttering fingers may indicate not quite so legal deception underway. The cards may not fall nor the dice bounce as nature intended. The unwrapped deck may be stacked and the glint in the eager eye an electronic signal. There are lots of ways to play the game.

SPORTS

In sports, we are told, it is not who wins or loses but how the game is played. Although winning is everything, one is still allowed to win only within the rules. In fact, according to former West Point All-American Colonel Pete Dawkins, "To win by cheating, by an umpire error or by an unfair stroke of fate is not really to win at all." But Princeton football coach Jake McCandless pointed out that deception within the rules is worth a 240-pound tackle, a rare commodity these days at Princeton.

Sports, like all institutions fashioned by civilization, arose from earlier, more restricted if not more primitive, forms. People have always run for pleasure, wrestled for delight, thrown bits and pieces as far as possible. As time passed and life became less simple, such delights began to be hedged about with rules and regulations. Once a man chased a zebra or threw a stone or ran until he was exhausted. Slowly, ritual and regulation arrived. Contestants ran specially defined distances, started at the same time, ended in the same place. Stones were thrown in a special arena. Time and place and space became part of the village games as the village evolved into the town, the green into a playing field. Ultimately, there were even records and statistics and the recollection of specific rather than general past feats. Sports became institutionalized so that, like great cathedrals, it revealed in form the substance of society and by their impact helped determine the nature of that society.

Children around the world have long played various hiding games. These require a certain amount of ingenuity for success. They involve an exciting and charming battle of wits between hiders and finders, and they teach the young some of the basic principles of deception, such as camouflage and putting oneself into the mind of the opponent, as in the popular American games of Hide-and-Seek and Kick-the-Can. And all players learn that peeking is cheating. Even babies are taught the delights of hiding-finding by older kids or parents who teach them Peek-a-Boo. All the way from Peek-a-Boo to their card game of Cheat, children learn the principles of cheating.

Children of the Dogon tribe in Mali, West Africa, play a game that is quite unusual in that it even involves a certain amount of primitive sleight of hand. This game, called Sey, is played with a pebble and three hollows scooped in the sand. The hider takes up a handful of sand together with the pebble and fills each of the hollows. The watcher-finder must try to detect into which hollow the hider has dropped the pebble. A clever hider will attempt to make the load-move as natural as the other two, while the finder will try to detect any telltale differences. A *very* clever hider will, of course, try to simulate these telltale gestures. Cheating becomes the name of the game.

These village games evolved into town games and then national games and ultimately imperial games, always reflecting the values of their society, always imposing these values on the players. To cheat—and always, always, there have been those who cheat—violated the very nature of authority in society. To cheat, not to play the game that reflected the norm, indicated that there was another world, the world of deception, in which people did not play *the* game, *your* game, but their own, and always turned a pretty penny in so doing. The most poignant indication of the distance between the believer in the game as played and the fallen player is illustrated by the following short exchange:

> BOY: Say it ain't so, Joe!
> Say it ain't so!
> JOE: Kid, I'm afraid it is.

> —"Shoeless Joe" Jackson to a Young Fan after confessing to a $5,000 bribe to throw the 1919 World Series.

It is one thing to adjust the height of the pitcher's mound or hold the runner on third base by a firm grip on his belt when the umpire's back is turned—cheating both. It is another quite accepted maneuver to pretend to await a ball lost in the sun or lob a curve when a fast ball is anticipated—part of the game. But, but to Throw the World Series is the ultimate in cheating. That is a violation of the cathedral. Those tempted by money—and no one in recollection has been greatly tempted by anything else—truly cheat. They have not looked left and run right, they have not even coughed at the moment of truth at the Master's tournament or found a chink in the rules, they—true cheats—have SOLD OUT.

There are various ways of "cheating" at sports. The first is not only quite legal but also all but written into the rules. A quarterback must attempt to deceive the defense. They expect it. He is trained so to do. His coach has crafted such ploys for years. A football offensive player is programed to deceive by misdirection. There are, of course, other odd means to adjust the rules, but basically, like a magician, a quarterback attempts to deceive the defense, every time, each and every time he (or these days, she) plays the game. The deception is within the rules. Thus, an important variant is to explore the edges of those rules. In the crudest and most blatant forms, the owner of a baseball club with long-ball hitters tends to readjust his ballpark by moving the fences about a bit so that his left-handed hitters will zap it down the alley. Grass is watered to slow down ground balls by ground-ball–hitting opponents. None of this is "illegal"; it merely constitutes taking advantage of opportunity by those in a position to take it. With few exceptions, such maneuvers are still within the rules of the game.

Those games like cricket that insist that players deny themselves seldom leave room for such "expansions" of the rules, such novel interpretations. One of the crucial points of cricket is that it is a GAME where such cunning advantage is unwelcome. There has even been a fuss that some (non-English) bowlers bowl *too* hard. Not cricket, that; not playing the game. Americans, less reticent, tend to surround the game with regulations, rules, barriers and limits, assuming that these players will seek out and exploit the grey areas—will not only throw too hard but will benefit from so doing. Thus "deception" itself is a crucial aspect of American sports. A superior quarterback is one who can look left and throw right, align his team in a running mode, and pass unexpectedly. All quite proper. All within the written rules of the game. Still, legally, within the game, there are adjustments within the rules, alignments, options, that are not *exactly* covered by the rules. Not cheating, not exactly, only using the magician's "one-ahead" ploy of beginning before the audience is aware the act is under way. In football the offensive team wanders about, leaving a potential receiver on the sidelines (out of the play), then follows by the quick snap, the swift pass to the incredibly open receiver, the flash score. Fair? Well, it *was* legal . . . but deceptive. The defense cheat themselves by not contemplating this special option. Such "legal" game options are no different from Chess players who groan and moan, Bridge players that hem and haw, Poker players who mutter over splendid hands—the noise and confusion emitted to dazzle the opponent. The high hard one thrown by the relief pitcher that smashes into the ground in front of the plate intimidating the batter, or the flurry of punches by an exhausted boxer to postpone the inevitable.

Then there is plain old cheating. Some are low-grade forms such as holding a jersey during a rugby scrum, elbowing the runner next to you, "accidentally" kicking an unfortunately placed golf ball. All really are taking slightly unfair advantage, stretching one's position of advantage, to WIN. Ah, if only that were the only problem, for, in sports, as in games of chance, money lurks. While the extraordinarily eager player will try to win honestly—Richard Nixon's coach could never use him because in an excess of desire he always went off-side (to win, to win)—the true cheat wants to win or lose for personal advantage, most often monetary advantage. But not always, some are absolutely determined simply TO WIN, no matter how. And from the very beginning of sports, before parimutuel betting, before the pools, before any kind of gambling, there were those who felt that it was not how you played the game but who came home with the laurels.

THE LUST FOR LAURELS

The first Olympic games were held in Greece in 776 B.C. Although the ancient games were primarily a religious event, that did not deter cheaters. In one final bout of the pancratium event (boxing and wrestling for boys), an athlete killed his opponent. Ruling the deed was done deliberately, the judges disgraced the victor and crowned the corpse. A more serious scandal occured during the ninety-eighth Olympic game in 384 B.C., when boxer Eupolus of Thessaly was disgraced and fined for bribing three opponents to let him win. Later, a series of admonitory statutes called ZANES were erected outside the Olympic Stadium with the considerable monies collected from fines.

The Olympics were reintroduced in their modern secular version in the Athens Olympics in 1896. And cheating followed. At the 1908 London game British officials went so far as to lead the exhausted marathoner to the finish line and then carry him across.

The 10,000-meter walk in the 1924 Paris Games was won by an Italian who walked all the way to take his Olympic Gold. The only remarkable thing about this was that *all* his competitors were either cautioned or ejected for *running*.

Twenty-one-year-old Stella Walsh Walasiewiscz became the heroine of the 1932 Olympics in Los Angeles. Polish-born but American-raised, she opted to run for the Polish team and took the gold medal in the 100-meter dash. She subsequently took four other Olympic gold and four silver medals. At the age of forty-three she won her fifth U.S. pentathlon championship. In more than thirty years of competition, Stella won 1,100 awards. All were the result of fraud. When the sixty-nine-year-old athlete was shot and killed in December 1980 in an apparent robbery attempt in a Cleveland parking lot, an autopsy was performed. The autopsy disclosed that Stella was a man, albeit seriously underdeveloped in "her" male sexual organs. Nor was she even a hermaphrodite, a person with characteristics of both sexes, as she had no female organs—internal or external—and had predominantly male chromosomes. But Stella's reputation was built during the pre-World War Two days when there were no mandatory medical examinations of contestants.

Lightweight Greco-Roman wrestling at the 1960 Rome Olympics was clouded by the disqualification of the Bulgarian finalist for taking a fall to the Russian, Avtandil Kordize, in order to let the Soviet comrade move ahead of another contestant, a detested Titoite Yugoslav.

Officials can be wrong in judging fouls in sports like wrestling or walking, and the athletes often are not deliberately cheating when they foul an opponent but are just too enthusiastic. But everyone recognizes a cheat when they catch him using illegal equipment. The Soviet fencing team at the 1976 Montreal Olympics was very red-faced when the Red Army's 1972 silver medalist, Boris Onishchenko, lunged at his British opponent and clearly missed, yet the electronic scoreboard lit up like a Christmas tree. A quick frisk by the rightly suspicious judges revealed that Onishchenko was using a gaffed épée. The tips of competition épées are legally wired to the scoreboard and so are the metal chest targets of each competitor so that when the tip strikes the target an electric circuit is completed and the scoreboard registers a hit. Clever Onishchenko had illegally rewired his so that it would light up without a hit. But the Russian was too clever by far because, like a card cheat caught with a holdout machine up his sleeve, he was, as Shakespeare said, "Hoist[ed] on his own petard."

The Montreal games also saw the unsubstantiated claim by the American diving-team manager that the Russians had offered to have their judges award extra points to American diver Phil Boggs in his event if the Americans would get their judges to do the same for Russian diver Irina Kalinina in hers. Although the charges were dropped, this would have been a neat switch because no one would have suspected favoritism.

Drugs are a perennial problem at the Olympics as in most other sports events. A few athletes are invariably disqualified when illegal drugs turn up in their mandatory urine specimens. Most, if not all, weight lifters take steroids to improve musculature, but most discontinue the intake before the tests. American weight lifter Mark Cameron didn't at the 1976 Games and was disqualified. And some women athletes take both steroids and male sex hormones to improve their performance.

Basically, no matter how highly "professional" the Olympic contestants may be, those who have cheated do so to win, from which certain unspecified psychic and material benefits may flow. Another athletic contest, perhaps the most amateur of all, the Boston Marathon, offers only spiritual benefits—and a real laurel crown. Yet even there cheating has occurred. Twenty-six-year-old Rosie Ruiz qualified for the Boston race by reaching the finish line in the 1979 New York Marathon in just under three hours; she came in 663rd overall and 24th among the women runners. Next year she was the first woman at the finish line in the 1980 Boston Marathon, making her the unofficial world champion women's marathoner.

The publicity led quickly to disclosure of fraud going back to her New York qualifying run. During that race, a woman photographer had met Rosie on the New York subway where the marathoner said she had fallen out with a bad ankle after ten miles of the twenty-six mile race. The two women left their train near the finish line and just walked up to it. Another woman runner who finished a second ahead of Rosie testified, "When you run marathons, you become familiar with people you're running with. I passed several women near the end. I did not see Miss Ruiz. She did not pass me, and I did not pass her, and the chance of missing her was slim." Rosie also failed to show up on the videotapes of the final section of the run. Besides, her time was suspiciously fast, given her previous poor record. Thus, Rosie lost her New York Marathon finisher's medal and subsequently was declared no-win for the Boston Marathon, where, again, no one could remember seeing her in the race.

In point of fact no sport is so absolutely without the lust for laurels that someone won't cheat—even the lame, the halt, and the blind are not immune. For example, thirty-seven-year-old Mr. Ian Moor of England had spent nearly two months in training at York University, preparing for the National Paraplegic Championships scheduled for September 1979. He managed to win the discus throw from his wheelchair at the Greater Manchester Paraplegic Games, but he was discovered as a fraud when his photograph was published in the *Yorkshire Evening Press* and neighbors recognized their fully mobile local postman.

When more serious matters are at stake, it is hardly surprising that contestants tend to take not just maximum advantage but, if possible, unfair advantage. The officials of the annual Indianapolis 500 believe that all cars entered should have the same horsepower, to give an equal chance to every driver, and they write the rules accordingly. Some Indy 500 drivers, however, prefer a more than equal chance and extend the competitive spirit to having their mechanics beef up the "boost," the manifold pressure, to gain significant horsepower advantage. These teams are clearly out to win and shrug off the practice by saying, "You don't cheat, you don't eat." They also argue, "It isn't cheating unless you're caught." The young lad who took first place in the annual soapbox derby this past decade was also imbued with this philosophy. He simply installed a small, silent electric motor in his coasting machine, which gave just the extra amount of acceleration needed to beat the motorless cars he was competing against.

BALL GAMES AND THE GAMBLER

While some people will bet on any outcome, neither the soap-box derby nor even the Indy 500 has been a prime attraction for the gambler. Ball games are another matter, even baseball, the Great American Sport, the National Pastime. There have always been those in the game who cheated for advantage, to win. The spitball and the knockdown pitch are "illegal," but punishment is regulated. The philosophy is that it is not cheating unless the umpire catches you.

One of the more arcane methods to snatch an edge is to adjust the tools of the trade. The regulation baseball bat is made by turning down a solid piece of hardwood on a lathe. This is the way they come from the factories in St. Louis, but many do not long remain in their legal state. "Sure, there are guys who will 'fix' a bat for you," admits Yankee infielder Graig Nettles, explaining, "When it comes back, it's like a Mafia hit gun—no serial numbers." Nettles speaks with authority, for while hitting a routine fly ball against Detroit in 1975, his bat came apart, spewing out six childrens' rubber Super Balls. Seeing the small black orbs bouncing around home plate, the umpire called an automatic out, the official penalty for using an illegal bat, one that hits either farther or erratically.

"I played on a team at New Orleans in the minors," recalls Baltimore Oriole manager Earl Weaver, "where every bat on the club was corked. I hit six homers that season—every one of 'em in the one month before they found us out. The umpires raided our clubhouse like they were the Untouchables. They destroyed the bats in public, right on the field. I wanted to cry." Weaver explains that corking a bat is a simple matter of drilling down into the barrel, filling it with cork, plugging it, and sealing with plastic wood. "You can't spot a good job with a magnifying glass," he observes, adding, "You gotta saw 'em up to find anything."

"You can't yell 'Check his bat' every time a guy walks up to home plate," says Weaver, pointing out, "If you're wrong, then maybe the umpire won't check him next time you cry 'Wolf.'" Weaver recalls, however, that when the Orioles came up against Detroit first-baseman Norm Cash in crucial situations in the last inning, "a bunch of us would all yell, 'Check his bat.' Norm would turn right around, walk straight back to the dugout and switch bats before anyone could touch it."

This is all very well, but it does not greatly help the professional gambler who is interested in winning money, not games—not who wins or loses but the point spread is what matters. And it was only a question of time before the gambler would try to adjust the results.

By 1903, when the first World Series was played, baseball had become the American game. It had also become big money and that attracted the cheaters. A few players took bribes, but the World Series itself was clean, although crooked gamblers had tried to fix the first one when Boston catcher Lou Criger was offered an attractive bribe but turned it down. Then, sixteen years later, America was shocked by the so-called Black Sox Scandal.

The 1919 World Series pitted the Cincinnati Red Sox against the Chicago White Sox. The mighty White Sox were overwhelmingly favored to win, but bad morale plagued the team. The players hated owner Charlie Comiskey for his cheapskate ways. He grossly underpaid them and arrogantly welched on promised bonuses. Eight of his disgruntled players decided to cash in on the Series; for some it would be merely retirement pay.

Led by first baseman Chick Gandil and pitcher Eddie Cicotte, they approached bookmaker "Sport" Sullivan with a startling proposition. For $80,000 the eight players would throw the first two games. Eighty grand was big money and Sullivan also needed to raise a substantial fortune for the betting, so he brought in several other gamblers, who got the notorious Arnold "The Brain" Rothstein to bankroll the deal. The fix was in.

The players did their part, losing the first two games, 1–9 and 2–4, and going on to lose the Series by losing five of eight games. With over half the White Sox starting lineup trying to lose, these games were a comedy of errors—dropped balls, sloppy fielding, and fat pitches. Rumors of a fix spread fast, but when ace New York sportswriter Ring Lardner asked Cicotte directly, "How come the first two games were so lousy?", the pitcher blandly lied, "I was just off form." The self-serving moguls of baseball tried the usual shoddy cover-up, but Chicago sportswriter Hugh Fullerton broke the story.

A grand jury indicted the eight bribed players. The trial jury, however, was so partisan that it found all eight not guilty, despite open court confessions by both Cicotte and outfielder "Shoeless Joe" Jackson. The gambling syndicate made millions but cheated the crooked players out of almost half their promised bribe. Moreover, the new Commissioner of Baseball, Kenesaw Mountain Landis, banned all eight players from professional baseball.

Since then, organized baseball has taken the most stringent precautions to maintain an honest game—players had best not even be seen in the same room as professional gamblers or such devious people as racetrack owners (unless said owner also owns a ball club). Even superstar football players have been suspended not for cheating but simply for betting on games. And while it is not impossible, it's still *hard* to throw baseball or football games. Too many players must be involved and too blatant an effort by too few will hardly go unnoticed: just striking out or dropping the odd pass won't do. Much more amenable to fixing is basketball, where two or three conspiring deceivers can hold down the points in a victory ("we still won") to a forewarned gambler's advantage. Recently there have been two different kinds of scandals at opposite ends of the country: cheating to win at New Mexico and cheating for gain at Boston College.

Federal and state grand juries brought indictments in 1980 against New Mexico coach Norm Ellenberger and assistant coach John Whisenant for various types of fraud. Allegations of irregularities covered the period from 1976 to 1979. These included plans to bribe a junior college official to supply a forged transcript to keep one player eligible for the upcoming 1979–80 season. At least some of the twenty gamblers who were regulars in the team's entourage are said to have helped recruit players by paying $1,000 cash bonuses to the "amateur" athletes and giving them cash rewards such as $100 for a good game or $20 dollars for each free throw or rebound. Grades at the university were also manipulated to keep certain players eligible. Cocaine was supposedly supplied by a local politician. Other allegations revolved around fixed games, point shaving, double billing for expenses, pocketing money, and just about every other type of cheating. In the wake of all these charges and disclosures, the team dropped six players and suspended one other. Former assistant coach Whisenant complains, "We're indicted for what every coach is doing." He has a point, particularly when one considers that two thirds of the university's *football* players' credits for eligibility were questionable.

Unlike the University of New Mexico Lobos, who pulled almost every imaginable fiddle, the Boston College basketball team chose to specialize during its 1978–79 season. Their scam was "point shaving," deliberately holding back on scoring by the cheater-players. Two or three Boston College players were bribed by professional gamblers, being paid one to two thousand bucks each per game to shave points. At least five games were fixed this way in that season. For example, B.C. came to its December 1978 game with Harvard unbeaten in six games, while Harvard had an uninspiring 3–3 record. The Las Vegas "line" figured B.C. to beat Harvard by 12½ points. This meant that B.C. had to win by at least 13 points for the bookies to pay off to B.C. supporters. The small gang of Boston fixers bet heavily on Harvard and their bought players came through handsomely, B.C. winning by only 3 points, 86–83, so that Harvard backers who had bet the "point spread" won.

FIXING MATTERS, GAMBLERS' GAMES

Boxing

While enormous sums are bet on good games—all-American baseball, good old football, round ball and oval ball games—their reputation (somehow) remains pure. But no one expects boxing, for example, to be very pure. Unsavory characters abound, promising fighters collapse unexpectedly, and even the most famous from Sonny Liston to Ali himself, stay in their corner or quit in the midst of the fray as did Duran in the Sugar Ray Leonard title fight. Perhaps they had simply had enough; but boxing is studded with "tank jobs," so much so that while gamblers bet $500 million in 1946, in 1972 the figure was down to $75 million. Promoters appear dubious at best—one has been accused of involvement in a vast $20-million computer fraud—and no one can be sure of an honest match.

Yet boxing is capable of being an arena for the most elegant and legal deception. Muhammad Ali was a master of the art. Ali "psyched out" his victims with his seemingly outrageous "lip" and his audacious predictions, disconcerting them so that they would meet him in the ring at a disadvantage. According to José Torres, Ali's masterpiece of deception occurred in the world championship fight in Kinshasa in 1974 against George Forman. Forman had easily defeated Joe Frazier, a strong boxer who had already beaten Ali once and had only barely lost to Ali in their second fight by a narrow margin. Moreover, Forman had accumulated the amazing record of thirty-eight career fights, all victories, of which thirty-one were by knockout. Ali also knew that Forman had a *big* punch and he himself a light one. Even the bookmakers had Forman as the odds-on favorite. Despite all these descrepancies Ali won, easily and by a knockout. How? Everyone, including Forman, expected Ali to try desperately to "dance" out of trouble while hoping to land enough punches to win on points. Ali had other ideas; he chose to do the totally unexpected—the "impossible," or at least the unimaginable. The "greatest" even tipped his strategy twice. First, when asked before the fight what advice he would give Forman, Ali gave the seemingly absurd but in fact quite truthful answer, "Lay back and wait." Second, Ali's trainer, Angelo Dundee, made a show of going around the ring just before the opening bell and loosening all the ropes. To everyone's astonishment, Ali's brilliant strategy was just to stand and take Forman's punches, counting on his reflexes and the loosened ropes to minimize the damage while he got in enough counterpunches to wear down Forman. That final dramatic right-cross knock-down was merely the accumulation of all the other punches that Forman had been running into while he mistakenly thought that Ali was playing his, Forman's game. Yet Ali left the "game" as a pudgy, middle-aged man sitting on his stool, overweight and under a cloud. All boxing was under a cloud—still.

THE RACETRACK

The Horses

The American colonials began betting the ponies in 1665 when the New World's first racetrack opened on Long Island. The "sport of kings" rapidly spread through the old colonies and into the new states, taking place at regular tracks and county fairs and in locally improvised races. Fixed races were common.

A jockey can "pull" (hold back) a fast horse. Two or more jockeys can conspire to a "boat ride" (fix a race). A trainer can speed up a slow nag by "doping" (giving stimulant drugs) or by shocking a horse with a "battery" (a pole attached to a storage battery) just before it comes onto the track. Horseshoes of different weights ("wobble shoes") will throw the animal off stride and slow it. Owners can bring in a "ringer" (a different horse) to assure either better or worse performance than unsuspecting bettors would expect. More simple and less detectable, the horse can be overfed to make him sluggish or tired out by overexercising him before the race. Do this a few times and your nag starts getting sky-high odds; then, and this is today's most popular scam, let him go all out for a surprise finish in the money.

Honest tracks use various methods to detect these cheating techniques. The saliva test introduced in 1910 and the more recent urine test are effective lab methods to detect drugs. Some state veterinarians have been bribed to switch samples. But a few imaginative owners or trainers get around all this by making the horse an addict and then slowing its "normal" performance by withholding the drug the day before the race.

The saliva and urine tests were originally given only to the winners, there being no perceived profit to be made on the also-rans. Then, a few years back, some tracks offered that newfangled exotic bet called the superfecta in which the bettor collects if the four horses he bet in one race all finish in the order selected. As the superfecta is run with an eight-horse field, the crooks would bet on four horses in all their twenty-four possible combinations and then have a bribed vet dope the *other* four horses with a *depressant* drug. This drug, called acepromazine, will slow any 40-mph likely winner to a 32-mph sure loser. One of the crook's twenty-four tickets will be a guaranteed winner, and the odds on a superfecta are long enough that it will more than pay for the twenty-three dud tickets. Tracks now test *all* horses after each race.

Track judges watch for illegal tricks by jockeys, tricks such as crowding and whip-slashing. But many borderline stunts

go unnoticed, as with the flagrant jostling of popular filly
Genuine Risk during the 1980 Preakness.

The simplest and safest way to cheat at the track is to do it
alone. Next best is for one crooked gambler to bribe one
crooked jockey to pull one likely winner so the real odds secretly favor a weaker horse.

James Forman "Todhunter" Sloan became America's most
famous jockey at the turn of the century when he introduced
the modern streamlined riding style of discarding spurs and
riding high over the horse's neck. He was an elegant, rich,
high-living dandy, an American, who rode for King Edward
VII. Tod Sloan was also crooked. He bribed other jockeys to
pull their horses so he would win. Worse, he once took a bribe
from a group of gamblers to pull the King's horse at the
English Derby. For this last bit of impudent treason, Sloan
not only got himself permanently barred from riding in England but got all other American jockeys barred for a time
there as well.

To prevent ringers (substituted horses), all racing thor-
oughbreds must be registered with the Jockey Club. Moreover, they now have their upper lips tattooed on the inside
with their registry numbers. As recently as 1976, however, a
British court fined trainer Anthony Collins and builder Tony
Murphy the equivalent of $2,000 each for conspiracy to de-
fraud bookmakers by this tired old switch. Gay Future was a
four-year-old chestnut gelding, bred and trained in the Republic of Ireland. His track record was poor and merited
heavy odds when Collins bought him early in 1975. At the
same time Collins bought a fast Irish horse, also a four-year-
old chestnut gelding, and shipped it with Gay Future's documents across the Irish Sea to his stables in Scotland. In
August the real Gay Future arrived from Dublin and started

out in a mobile van for Collins's stables. On the way, however, the fast ringer was switched in from a second van into which the real Gay Future disappeared.

The conspirators formed a syndicate that began placing small bets on the pseudo–Gay Future with bookmakers all over London. They had laid out over $8,000 when the bookies took notice and stopped taking book on that horse. The ringer won by fifteen lengths and paid off a glorious ten to one. However, the syndicate only collected $12,000 of their $80,000 before the bookies stopped payment and started the inquiry that led to trial. Ironically the prosecution won its case because Scotland Yard's Special Branch, having earlier mistaken Collins and his Irish group for IRA terrorists, had already infiltrated the gang well enough to collect hard evidence of the racing fraud.

Cheating the Track

In the good old days, losers at the horse and dog races sometimes altered their losing tickets to look like winners. Others got away with printing counterfeits. Neither trick works today, as tracks have fast tests to detect such frauds.

Employees in the parimutuel room, figuring the odds, would occasionally "handle" the old-fashioned calculating machines to create a few extra winners that they could then claim as their own. They could get away with this by penciling in on the records an extra win, place, or show. Nickle-dime stuff and risky besides. In any case, the general introduction of modern computers by 1970 has eliminated this practice, making it impossible to cheat the track or the IRS standing greedily behind it. The electronic bookkeeping is just too fast and too tight and the instant display on the big

totalizer board on the infield is just too public to slip anything past. Or so it was thought until Jacques Lavigne figured
how to fix the parimutuel computer.

In the early 1970's Jacques Lavigne was clerking in the
parimutuel room at Flagler Dog Track in Miami, Florida.
With larceny in mind, he tried to figure some way to "manage" some of that floating money. But the newly installed
computers seemed impossible to cheat.

Then one day, while looking wistfully out at the infield
totalizer board, Lavigne suddenly perceived his opening. It
was what he did *not* see that mattered; the tote board was
missing something. The ever changing odds that let each winner know what his exact winnings would be were missing on
all the new and novel wagers such as the trifecta, a bet requiring selection of the precise one-two-three order of finish.
These new gimmick games were possible only because of the
power of the new computer, which could instantly calculate
the 336 possible trifecta betting combinations for the typical
eight-dog race. But the old-fashioned tote board didn't have
enough room to show such complications. Only after the race
does the tote board display the final odds on the trifecta and
its ilk.

Lavigne realized that the new computer interfaced with the
old tote board to create an opening for a superb scam. If the
computer could be made to switch tickets assigned to losing
dogs to winning ones, no one would be the wiser. The com-
puter-generated books would balance. The track itself (and
the IRS) wouldn't lose a penny. The legitimate winners
would still win, but only a fraction of their due. And even
then they would have no way of knowing that the final posted
odds, which were the only way for them to figure their earn-
ings, had been substantially reduced by dilution of the particular betting pools where they had placed their bets.

The theory was simple, but Lavigne needed confederates. He recruited the essential partner, the computer manager-operator, and for security reasons also brought seven men in to explain away any delays to track officials, to print the bogus tickets, and to cash them in at the ticket windows.

It was a smooth operation. The trifecta part of the computer was shut down secretly for only a minute while the outcome of the race was reported and they did the thirty-second job of flicking toggle switches to embezzle part of the real winners' loot. For example, in the race on 30 August 1977, the trifecta pool was worth $15,000. After the track and the state took its $3,000 the only real winner, Leon E. Rodriguez, was paid only $3,000, the remaining $9,000 going to four losers' tickets, which were switched to Lavigne. All this went on unnoticed in plain view of the public and track officials, as the computer room is behind a picture window in a public lobby.

This scam earned Lavigne's gang nearly $2 million over five years, until late 1977, when they were caught. The only reason they were even found out was that the computer operator bragged to his wife, who blabbed to a friend, who was, by unlucky chance, a bounty hunter, who in turn went directly to the track owner for a reward. Lavigne got two-and-a-half years.

And Other Beasts

Dog racing is a rather seedy sport, a kind of poor man's version of the horses. And yet the dogs used are an elegant breed, the greyhound. Except for its diminutive cousin, the whippet, which can't handle much distance, the greyhound at 41 miles per hour is the fastest dog of all and is outrun only by the cheetah, impala, and red fox.

Fixing dog races makes use of many of the same tricks used for the horses, particularly the use of ringers or giving the dog a heavy meal just before the race. Another stunt is to give the poor beast a hot enema. When dog tracks were first introduced in 1923 in America and in 1926 in Britain, ringers were as common as in the early horse races. Now all dogs must be registered and receive a "passport" listing points of positive identification. These days the game is pretty honest, much more so than in the past.

Although horses and dogs are the most popular racing beasts in America and Britain, people around the world will bet on almost anything that moves, including camels (in the Middle East), goats (West Indies), homing pigeons (Belgium and Britain), jumping frogs (California), lizards (Australia), tortoises (Asia), crabs (Puerto Rico), and rats (Ireland). They will also bet on any species that fights its own, particularly dogs and cocks.

Dogfighting was popular in the United States in the last century. A common form of cheating was surreptitiously to rub red pepper onto the coat of your dog, thereby blinding or generally upsetting the other dog during contact. To thwart this practice, the handlers would "taste" the opponent's dog, literally licking its coat to check for pepper. And to even up the effects of the common practice of drugging, the two handlers would sponge the saliva from the mouth of each dog and squeeze it into that of the other.

Although outlawed in most countries, the sport of cockfighting, in which one bird destroys the other with sharpened beaks and spurs, is played throughout Latin America, in rural America, and in the Philippines. Although cheating is almost impossible, the late Errol Flynn devised a way. Stranded and almost broke in the Philippines in 1932 with a physician friend, young Flynn and his associate decided to enrich themselves by fighting cocks. They bought some birds and these proved consistent victors. Flynn's friend had merely taken a bit of high potency Brazilian snake venom from his medical kit and applied it to the beaks. After winning a healthy profit, the future movie superstar was found out when an opponent's bird dropped dead after only one peck on its cockscomb. Flynn fled the country sans baggage.

In conclusion, for the artful deceivers, the W. C. Fields of the world, there are no games of chance, only more or less sure things. Of course, there are those millions of honest folk bidding three spades, putting the wee white ball into the hole, dunking the ball, or betting on black, who assume that rules are there to be obeyed. For them to win unfairly is not to win at all, to have no fun. They enjoy the odds, respect the regulations, benefit from the straight and narrow. They play the game for the game's benefit. Alas and alack, others, of course, do not. Some, like casino operators, run the game to personal advantage ("there is no free lunch"), others, such as the "spitter" in baseball or "holders" in football, stretch the rules to win fame or fortune ("it doesn't count if you aren't caught"), a few use the game as a means to money. These, the absolute cheats, leave nothing to chance.

In games of chance, more often than not money is involved. Players do win matchsticks and Master's points at cards, but money is truly the name of the game. In sports it is not simply that the immutable odds should (must) run as nature dictates, or that the table must be flat and the dice honest, as in the money games; in sports, the entire institution must be beyond reproach. The quarterback may deceive the defense— it's part of the game. Some leeway may be permitted—Jim Thorpe played professional ball when he was an amateur (of course, the Olympic Committee did not forgive him, but most

Americans did). Some violations are even admired, such as that of the cunning spitball pitcher. Some "violations," such as counting in blackjack, seem to be violations only to the loser—the casino. Yet the real cheats in bridge or badminton are to most an abomination. They spoil the game. True, those games played for money alone, such as poker, are usually considered less invulnerable, less sacred than sports. People *expect* people to cheat at cards, but they abhor the violation of the "Great Games," the National Pastimes. They are not, of course, surprised. They may even want to know the underlying principle of such deceit.

The Law of the Fix

Want to "fix" a sports event? Just bribe some players or officials, you say? Well, yes, but only if you remember the other side of the proposition. Bribery is a form of conspiracy and the unforgiving iron law of conspiracy is that the more people who are in the know, the greater the chances are of somebody squealing. How could eight Chicago White Sox players think they could conspire to take bribes to throw the 1919 World Series without someone blabbing? Two did blab. How could Jacques Lavigne suppose he could bribe eight men at the Miami dog track to fiddle the computer without someone talking—one did.

If you're the jockey on the favorite, bet incognito on the next-best nag, then pull your own horse without being too obvious, and nobody except yourself need ever know. But take a bribe to do the same and two people know—maybe lots more, because the gambler could have bribed other jockeys and may have partners. The risk of disclosure rises as the number of knowers increases.

This same rule applies to team size. The bigger the team,

the more players you must fix to be sure you've got the same PC going for you. This is the real reason few eleven-player football or nine-player baseball teams get fixed and also why so many that do so get caught. Conversely, it is the real reason so many prizefights are fixed yet so few get found out. It is not that football players are any more honest than boxers, it's just harder and riskier to fix even a third of a football team than all of one side in a prizefight.

Consequently, in sports, to eliminate the element of chance, think small, go in quickly, get out swiftly, do not make a habit of cheating. World-class cheaters do not appear in *books* or *lists;* they clip their coupons in quiet. They have not played the game but exploited it, adjusted the odds, rearranged the results, deceived the innocent, and banked the results.

CHAPTER 7

People and the Everyday World

♦ ♦ ♦

If a thing's worth having, it's worth cheating for.

— W. C. FIELDS

CHEATING IS NOT SIMPLY a matter for the stage or the gambling casino or even the battlefield but is, rather, a regular if recognized aspect of the everyday world. Nearly everyone at some time or other cheats a bit, tells the white lie for decency's sake or smiles instead of frowns. And always these maneuvers of guile fall under the rubrics of hiding and showing.

STYLE

1. **Hiding** (One's Light Under a Bushel)
   One seeks to smooth life's rougher spots and conceal the unpleasant, for secondary benefits or as a favor.
   a. *Masking*   One almost literally wears the anticipated

mask—the courtier's smile hiding boredom, jealousy, or malice. The poor live-in relation, the good sport, genial, kind, considerate, pleased, and amusing—what is the alternative? No one wants a surly live-in relative.

b. *Repackaging*   While it is relatively easy, with practice, to mask unpleasant reality, it is a bit more complicated to repackage one's personality so that the chap with the heart of gold appears to be a grouch, the later persona fashioned to hide an apparent weakness.

c. *Dazzling*   When all is *almost* clear, when observers recognize there is light under the bushel, the best that can be done is to hide what can be hidden—like the smile on the face of the tiger. When the irate parent announces, "This hurts me more than you" or the dentist insists, "This won't hurt" they—without much hope—are attempting to hide an unpleasant reality.

2. **Showing** (One's True Colors, Kind of)
    While much personal hiding is an attempt to make life easier, often the showing of the false has meaner motives.

    a. *Mimicking*   While a teenager may mask many real and novel feelings so as not to stand out, those who mimic reality must show and tell. Thus, the wife who says "Not tonight, dear, I have a headache" mimics illness to evade the not quite inevitable. When the boss dashes out on the diamond for the company's annual baseball game, he becomes (maybe) just one-of-the-boys.

    b. *Inventing*   Dissatisfied with reality, the malcontent creates a more desirable structure for himself: an elegant family, hidden money, splendid prospects, a grand past. In fact, one can become all but a professional or even shrink in size overnight.

Example: The Doctorate.

The doctorate strikes many these days as being a bit shopworn and pretentious, but its mystique is still with us, as witness Dr. Strangelove and his real-world model, Dr. Kissinger. However low it has fallen in general esteem, the doctorate is still a valuable item ("union card"). While at many academic institutions it no longer requires great mental effort to earn one, unfortunately it still takes much time and money. Consequently it should come as no surprise that a number of ambitious persons have decided to democratize this elitist process. In olden days, one had to dress the part and affect proper speech. The Aquarian Age of the radical 1960's ended all that; now half the doctors wear casual clothes and affect vulgar tongue. Consequently almost anyone can pass as a Ph.D., Sc.D., M.D., J.D., or any of the several other kinds.

There are four easy shortcuts to the doctorate. You can simply claim to have one; you can fake documentation; you can plagiarize; or you can buy one.

(1) Dr. A was a full professor in an Eastern graduate school for diplomats until the 1970's, when a faculty enemy phoned his university and learned his highest degree was an M.A. in librarianship. Mr. A was quietly told to resign.

(2) Dr. B was a full professor of accounting in a seedy southwestern business college until 1974, when a

bright administrator noticed that his prominently displayed diploma from a Japanese university was nothing of the sort. Again a quiet resignation.

(3) Dr. C was a world-famous specialist in Central Asian languages and literature in a major American university when a colleague accidentally discovered that the professor's prewar European dissertation read like an exact translation of an earlier scholar's dissertation. In this case, as Professor C had honestly achieved two decades of superb work of his own, he was told to take unpaid leave, do a real dissertation at Columbia University, and then return with all honors restored.

(4) Like Dr. D in Berkeley, there are the thousands of doctors who simply have bought their degrees from unscrupulous and unaccredited schools—a quick correspondence course often sufficing. Among the most common being churned out in America in the draft-dodging sixties were the many doctors of divinity, including some very odd divinities indeed.

Example: The Shrinking Woman.

The day of the supertall model is past. The fashion industry now prefers female models to be between 5 feet 8 inches and 5 feet 10 inches tall. That way, as Patrick, the public relations director of the Glamour Agency in Paris, explained, models more easily fit their clients' standard-size dresses. So what does an outsized woman do to get in and stay in the business? Simply lie about your height, as European high-fashion model Sandia advises. She is exactly 6 feet tall and attracts a lot of attention in Düsseldorf when she shops in the fashionable Königstrasse in her favorite 4-inch heels. Yet her official Glamour "composite" brochure lists her as 178 centimeters (5 feet 10 inches). In 1979 Christina Brand, ex-top model and now proprietor of Dublin's new Brand Agency, set Sandia up for her first job in Ireland. Describing Sandia over the telephone to a photographer, Christina said "five feet ten." Sandia got the job. She says, "Once they see me, they *never* send me away."

   c. *Decoying* When there is no hope for completely persuading the audience that you are truly a professional or even shorter, then there is still hope that misdirection will ease the dilemma. Thus, the scrooges of industry, while evicting widows and children and paying starvation wages in appalling conditions, also give freely to charity, endow universities and libraries, set up foundations—so they cannot be *all* bad. . . .

Apparel

1. **Hiding** One aspect of a person's style can be determined by dress (she is a nurse, he is a hippy, and that must be Woody Allen). And one aspect of dress is to hide, to hide a real self, to hide an unpleasant structure, to look one way but be another.

   a. *Masking* When a gaggle of teenagers rush past, they appear interchangeable, clad in the fad of the moment, safe if all look alike, fearful only of standing out, of a self to which they cannot yet be true. They are lost in their crowd, one penny among other pennies.

   b. *Repackaging* The portly English banker, like most

portlies, does not want to look stout. Pudgy is not pleasing. So with the help of a tailor in Savile Row his figure is hidden in elegant and expensive suits that repackage his adiposity.

c. *Dazzling* And what of the hopelessly fat lady who, too, seeks to be slender once again. A dressmaker may, like the tailor, help a bit, but the only real hope is to dazzle the viewer with quiet, elegant, soft clothes and a huge jewel, or even a giant black dog, to distract attention.

2. **Showing** Clothes, even the most functional, are mostly about showing. Uniforms (that do hide the individual) reveal occupation and often rank. Generals have stars, a hospital doctor reveals his place in the hierarchy by the cut of his coat. Clerks dare not wear handmade shoes even if they could afford to.

a. *Mimicking* It is possible to mimic reality for nefarious purposes—to avoid work or rob a bank. Few security guards stop a man with a mop or pail or investigate the chap with the clipboard. And few question the security guard until he reveals a gun and takes over the armored car.

b. *Inventing* Some inventions are minor showing of what does not really exist: false jewelry, fake furs (those that pretend to be real, not those that are "funny-false") and foam-rubber "falsies." More elegant are the alienated English teens who have invented a dress style—Punk—to outrage their olders and betters. Alas, the Punk Style is on the way to becoming first a uniform and then a means for other teens to hide from themselves.

c. *Decoying* At fashionable resorts the incompetent often mimic real tennis players or real skiers by wearing the most expensive and elegant of sports gear. At the moment of truth on the court or the ice, their fond hope is that their style will decoy the observer from their lack of substance (far better to remain suitably togged at the bar). Decoy-like Dazzle is the last resort, an effort to show *something* desirable.

Nearly everyone at some time or another, hides his or her real person or shows a false one, dressing to conceal or to confuse. Some few people, however, are always hiding; like Alec Guinness in *The Captain's Paradise,* they lead a double life in order to enjoy two families. Still others must do so in order to moonlight at a second (or third) job. These persons alternate between their various roles. For others, the covert and overt roles exist simultaneously. Thus, the "double agent" in the world of espionage lives a truly double life. Finally, some persons entirely drop their old identity and take on an entirely new one. They may do this to avoid being drafted into military service, as did thousands of young American men during the Vietnam War. They may simulate a new identity to avoid the police, as did Patty Hearst and the members of the SLA or the Baader-Meinhof Group. They may do this to avoid the retribution of mobsters, as do many underworld turncoats with new identities arranged by the FBI. They may do this to avoid assassination, as do hundreds of Soviet defectors with new identities arranged by the CIA or MI5. All of the above are using deception by simultaneously hiding their true identity and simulating another. The person who plans to hide chooses one of two basic strategies. Either, as above, he displays himself in the guise of another; or he conceals himself by choosing a place beyond surveillance.

Some hiding is rather straightforward: Albert looks like a hippy rabbi but he's a lawyer. In fact he is one of America's top lawyers on trademark infringement. His main job is working for the cartoonist R. Crumb collecting a six-figure sum annually as payment for infringements of Crumb's enormously popular slogan, "Keep on Truckin' " with the three odd cartoon characters striding along. But Albert *knows* he is Albert. Like Alec Guinness's captain, he goes from one "paradise" to another. Unlike the captain, however, he goes from one show-person to another real-person. The captain is real in both paradises. At times, the pretend character infiltrates the hidden reality and the impersonator forgets whether he is a police spy or a rebel as Father Capon did in Russia in 1905. The underworld informer must leave behind one reality and fashion another one. Usually only their families are aware of the new reality, but some hiders create communities that are aware of both realities.

Throughout history and across cultures various individuals and families have banded together in secret for mutual protection, power, or influence. The early Christians tried to evade persecution in the Roman Empire by dissimulating their religious affiliation; the symbol of the fish (from Christ the fisher of men) originated as a secret recognition symbol. The Manichaean community in medieval China simulated being acceptable Nestorian Christians. The original Mafia of Sicily managed by secret collusion to control the politics and economics of their island in the face of desperate efforts on the part of the Italian central government to extend its domination beyond the mainland. To this day, Freemasons in Spain, Italy, and Latin America operate with a very low profile but often remain united in their anticlerical politics. These groups hid for protection; other secret societies show to intimidate. Thus, the white-hooded figures of the Ku Klux Klan simultaneously hide identity and awe observers. They have invented a novel reality that enhances often marginal personalities and achieves a measure of power in society: clothes make the monster.

Sex

Perhaps in no personal arena is the shifting process of hiding and showing more fascinating than in the relationships between men and women. At the very, very beginning, in the Garden of Eden, Satan, in the guise of a serpent, lied to Eve, saying that God had lied in the reasons he gave for prohibiting the forbidden fruit. After that everything was downhill: the Old Testament is replete with tales of sexual deception. For example, when Abraham went to Egypt, he feared that Pharaoh would take his beautiful wife, Sarah, and kill him. Accordingly, Abraham hid Sarah by repackaging her as his sister. To be sure, it was an incomplete ploy: the Pharaoh believed the lie and spared Abraham, but he went ahead and raped Sarah anyway. The Pharaoh was more interested in sexual sensation rather than sexual love, where most cheating takes place.

Romantic love, the devoutly held conviction that a single person is the embodiment of all necessary delight, has long been recognized as a special form of madness. The perfect woman or man, the adored idol, cannot by definition exist, so that the victim of this delusion is in the grip of extreme self-deception: the whole world shifts, values are distorted, and priorities warped. When the idol fails to return this violent emotion, the victim of unrequited love suffers, however briefly, the agonies of the damned. Many cultures regard such emotion as a dangerous affliction that will lead to irrational actions, as Othello was led to murder. What happens is that the lover creates—invents by showing the idol to the beloved. If the sentiment is returned, if gradually the created idol is transmuted into a more realistic persona or to a degree becomes more like the idol, if there is a bit of luck, the invention becomes real, the delusion actuality—then the marriage or mating is both ideal and functional. If not, swift divorce or enraged violence ensue.

Beyond the phenomenom of cheating oneself in matters of love, there is considerable cheating in matters of seduction, where a false reality is woven about more sensual desires, promises made, futures sketched, love professed. To a degree, all is fair these days—especially if the lover loves as well as desires—unless the contemporary Casanova has absolutely evil designs. Seduction nowadays often is hardly seduction at all, but is rather a scattering of clichés to cloak lust, a lust merely local and temporary. Rejection, the obverse of seduction, dampens desire through delay and decent deceit: my mother is waiting up, not tonight my back aches, I can't handle intensity yet. Another focus of love, the deception of the partner, the once adored, is mainly a matter of hiding. It may consist of a maneuver that fools potential observers—"He could not be having an affair with her because he is gay"—but generally it consists of excuses, "staying late at the office" or of hiding ploys—meeting at a motel instead of a matinee.

In one special area, deception used to play an enormous part in Western love ritual: when abstinence was a cherished virtue rather than an oddity of religious orders. For deep-seated reasons best speculated upon by psychologists and anthropologists, most cultures treat virginity as a valued commodity. Most cultures will, however, settle for the convincing appearance if the physical substance is unavailable.

Brides were presumed to be chaste in prewar Japan and if the hymen was broken, virtue could be proved by means of a physician's certificate that the hymen had been torn on a bicycle ride. Application of ointment of alum could give a temporarily tight passage, simulating inexperience. Drastic remedial action was available from plastic surgeons specializing in the restoration of torn tissues.

In Western culture there has long been a small but steady market for virgin prostitutes. Brothelkeepers, eager to satisfy their regular customers, procured a steady supply of children and teenagers. Alum, a bit of fake blood, and clever acting assured client satisfaction.

In this case the anticipated experience was invented, but in other cases it could be mimicked. Brides in prewar Serbia were married off with an ironclad guarantee of virginity. Misrepresentation in this area was cause for immediate annulment, return of the bride-price, and disgrace for the false bride and all her family. The wedding took place at the home of the groom. During the long night, while the reveling guests thronged the courtyard, bride and groom would slip up to the bedroom. Satisfactory consummation of the marriage contract was signaled next morning when the groom's mother proudly hung out the bloodied bridal sheets for all to see and applaud. And they were *always* suitably stained, if not in the natural course of events, then, by custom, by a brother of the bride who would cut his arm to provide the required proof.

While romantic love and its consequences, lust and sensation, appear now to be matters between individuals, ritual and enforcing institutions have always existed. To create appropriate order, to ensure domestic tranquillity, rites of passage were established. Marriage is one of several major institutions invented by society to ensure conformity of its members to the group's values and norms of behavior. Churches, families, and some careers press marriage on the young, emphasizing the positive virtues of the product, one of which is a legal and social disguise for private sexual lives. Some marriages, however, disguise forbidden sexual arrangements or none at all. W. H. Auden was married for a great many years to Thomas Mann's daughter without ever contemplating consummation—he was a homosexual who had married her so she could flee Germany as a British citizen. Since the 1960's, underground newspapers and periodicals in the United States have included open solicitations for marriages of convenience, particularly to enable foreign nationals to gain permanent entry status. The Soviet Union has a similar situation for its own citizens who are subject to internal immigration restrictions. Thus students who come from Siberia to study in Moscow are required to return to Siberia; but many circumvent this by arranging a marriage in the capital to qualify for local residence papers, and then getting divorced soon after.

Divorce in a secular society has also become a matter of convenience. Some American couples get divorced at the end of the year to gain certain income tax advantages, remarrying in the new year. In Soviet Russia one out of every five divorces is phony, the couples separating legally to gain various economic or other benefits while continuing to live together. Such "rituals" have little relevance to the institutions of the past, largely because for many the rite has no metaphysical implications—the Church is cheated because belief cannot be imposed, the state is cheated because conformity to state values cannot be enforced. In fact, the cheaters feel that such institutions are themselves structures of deceit and self-interest cloaked in piety and patriotism.

Religion

There have nearly always been a few, and at times many, who have felt that at best organized religion was structured self-deception and at worst a fraud. The true believers who worshipped the sliver of the true cross did not seem to care that in all of Western Europe there were sufficient slivers to reconstruct many true crosses. The faithful accepted miracles as their due: Fatima really appeared, stigmata existed, water turned to wine, and monks flew through the air. In some cases these miracles, representing violations of the assumed natural order, became institutionalized exercises in self-deception, exercises that as the centuries passed and the skeptical grew in strength, increasingly appeared to be conscious—and condescending—deceits. In Naples, according to the faithful, at special times a vial of the blood of San Genarius turns to wine: the swifter the transformation, the better the wine crop will be: the slower the transformation, the greater the likelihood that the parishioners will riot—an institutional miracle of dubious validity, except to the true believers. Throughout history, however, there have been those who consciously deceive the faithful.

The first charlatan conjurers were probably priests. Although difficult to prove at this distance in time, there is strong circumstantial evidence that many of the benign deceptions of stage magicians are directly descended from some of the less scrupulous "miracles" of priests. Some writers distinguish between magic and magick, keeping the modern spelling for stage conjurers and reserving the old form for persons proclaiming supernatural powers. Whatever one believes about the supernatural or paranormal, many claims to supernatural powers are made by charlatans. It is certain that many early priests, shamans, and medicine men often patched out their religions with simple conjurer's tricks. Certainly some believe they can see the future in the bottom of a tea cup or hear tomorrow in the wind in the willows, but other seers see the advantage and cheat for effect.

Divination with a rod is prehistoric in origin and existed among many cultures. Originally using arrows, the priests and shamans gradually adopted various types of sticks, straws, and reeds. The latter-day descendent of the divining rod is the magician's wand.

Marco Polo (with the help of possibly the first ghostwriter, Rusticello of Pisa) recorded a hundred-year-old legend that looks circumstantially like priestly divining-rod fraud. It was on the eve of the battle between Jenghiz Khan and Prester John that would determine who would unite all the Mongols. Marco Polo retells the legend:

> Jenghiz Khan one day summoned before him his astrologers . . . and desired them to let him know which of the two hosts would gain the battle, his own or Prester John's. . . . They got a cane, split it lengthwise, laid one half on this side and one half on that, allowing no one to touch the pieces. And one piece of cane they called Jenghiz Khan and the other piece, Prester John. And then they said, "Now, mark; and you shall see the event of the battle and who shall have the best of it . . ." And lo! whilst all were beholding, the cane that bore the name of Jenghiz Khan, without being touched by anybody, advanced to the other . . . and got on top of it.

It would appear that the Mongol shamans were acquainted with the uses of the magician's invisible black silk thread. Certainly, if all is fair in love and war, there is reason to

suppose that Jenghiz Khan, a master of psychological warfare, had connived with his shamans to assure a "prediction"
that would give his warriors added confidence before battle—
what else is religion for?

The dictums of religion could also be tipped by invisible
magic in the service of love or lust. The vestal virgins who
served the Temple of Vesta in ancient Rome were expected to
be intact in fact as well as name. If they were not, painful
death was the punishment. They were not only adept at using
simple conjuring tricks to enhance their religious prestige,
and one of them probably resorted to a magic trick to save
her life in "proving" her doubtful chastity. When Tutia was
charged with having violated her solemn oath of chastity and
faced being buried alive, she beseeched the goddess Vesta to
witness her innocence by helping her perform a miracle. Filling a sieve at the Tiber River, she held it high and carried it
through the streets back to the temple without losing a drop.
Pliny and Valerius Maximus recorded that this seemingly
miraculous feat silenced Tutia's slanderers and proved to all
that she was indeed inviolate. It is likely that she used a simple gimmicked sieve of a type that her modern fellow magicians know as the "Foo can."

While there are no more fantastic sieves or shamans'
wands, people now speak in tongues, handle snakes, cure by
touch, hear the voice of God, have the gift of the future, and
find fate in the cards or through a glass ball darkly. Some
believe in the Power. Some sell snake oil as a cure. Some have
found a place within an organized church, others start their
own. And some, improbable as it seems, go too far. In Rome
in March 1981, the Reverend Domenico Bernardini, fifty-six,
who, at his own request, had been released from his vows
twelve years before by the Salesian Order because of mental

problems, was taken into custody along with two women. The three were accused of performing bogus exorcisms. They had tied up young women, covered their bodies with ice, and recited prayers, finally burning a sign of the cross on their foreheads. The police felt that they were not sincerely attempting to free the women of evil spirits—apparently no crime—but wanted to cheat them out of money. It seems that the women had been persuaded to donate their paychecks, totaling 50 million lire ($50,000) to the priest once they had been "liberated" from "demons." The police feared that other bogus "exorcisms" might still be taking place undetected in private houses in Rome—which seems likely if demons still abound. After all, there is money to be made out of demons still, and making money by fair means or foul has a history surely as long as that of organized religion.

Business

> MAN: How would you like to make a few honest dollars?
> W. C. FIELDS: Do they have to be honest?

Like every other human activity, business attracts the cheat, and as in every form of cheating there is hiding and showing.

1. *Hiding*   ("The Check is in the Mail")
   a. *Masking.*   When the auditor arrives, he finds neat and nifty records—and a quiet, confident embezzler who is certain that his theft will remain hidden.
   b. *Repackaging.*   Those who seek loans to save starving businesses wisely wear Gucci loafers and drive BMW's or, better yet, are driven in Cadillac limousines.

c. *Dazzling.* Everyone knew Ari Onassis had vast amounts of money, and where there is money tax chaps are sure to follow. But Ari's books revealed a business structure so complex, with companies within companies disappearing into Grand Cayman banks and holding trusts in Switzerland, that no one could figure out just *how* much money existed and *where* it was—perhaps even Ari did not know. And W. C. Fields hid *his* money in so many accounts in so many different banks that he confused even himself—some of it may still be there.

2. **Showing** ("Here is an Offer You Can't Refuse")

a. *Mimicking.* The most notorious of all business mimickers are forgers who seek to copy the genuine exactly. Some go even one better: "false" British sovereigns, used still as a medium of exchange in the Middle East, contain more gold than the real ones. There was once a nifty stamp forger who created rarities and sold them as fakes at a considerable profit, knowing full well that his customers would mark them up yet further and sell them as real. He was eventually paid to retire. Others are still out there turning out Dior creations, counterfeiting Billy Joel tapes, salting gold mines, painting late Picassos.

b. *Inventing.* There are those who have made a good thing of selling not simply stock certificates for IBM or General Motors but shares in fake companies. Why salt a gold mine with real nuggets when someone will buy a piece of paper that claims to be stock in the Real Gold Mine, Inc. Movie stars have purchased oil refineries—mostly a few old pipes lying about mimicking a real refinery under construction—and received glittering evidence of their share in the form of certificates. A fortune was made on salad oil because no one looked beyond the certificates to the empty oil tanks. Welfare cheats fashion new and needy personae. The California "Welfare Queen" was scooped up, along with numerous wigs, disguises, false driver's licenses, blank birth and baptismal certificates—and several fur coats. She had, it was estimated, bilked the state of $300,000 in payments for Aid to Families with Dependent Children, medical benefits, and food stamps. She had previously stolen some $250,000 in a Chicago credit card swindle in which real people's real credit worthiness was mimicked to buy all manner of items, including a kitchen sink.

c. *Decoying.* For example, the used-car salesman recognizes customer skepticism and emphasizes the gleaming paint work and flashy whitewalls to distract from the cracked cylinders and lead the eye away from the lack of tread.

In fact, said used-car dealer touches most of the bases of hiding and showing at one time or another: he hides scratches under paint and poor quality under polish, he dazzles with glittering description, he mimics a *real* bargain with patter and patina, invents a splendid purchase with inexpensive accessories and decoys with a special one-day cream-puff discount. He has hidden the awful by fashioning an image of desirability, and if he does not, his lot will be out of business and the customer clamoring for cream puffs down the street. There is, of course, as much self-deception in the purchase of automobiles as there is overt cheating. In other aspects of business, cheating is criminal and, these days, often complex. While there is a quite unjustified awe in the popular mind concerning computers, they are in theory quite simple machines quite willing to do as they are told and no more. If they are programmed badly—garbage-in-garbage-out (GIGO)—the results are awful and/or useless. If not, what one programmer can devise another may be able to exploit. Wells Fargo National Bank recently lost an estimated $21 million because there was a lapse between the times when one part of the computer informed another so that the "false" deposits were briefly real. The fail-safe mechanisms were thus decoyed by the mimicked real accounts or the invented new accounts and the conspirators grew daily richer as long as their inside man stayed on the job showing the computer the false.

For the average individual involved in business the used-car salesman does not really seem a cheat nor the Wells Fargo conspirators very far removed from everyday life. Real life consists of a salary check, a mortgage payment—and the annual demand of the Internal Revenue Service for an income tax payment. And there the hidden cheat in each citizen stirs. The IRS estimates that the government lost $35 *billion* dollars in revenue in 1976 to tax cheats and $50 billion dollars in 1979—and this in a country where people are assumed to pay their taxes. While the IRS tends to categorize the government's loss in terms of either unreported income or over-reported deductions, the same categories of cheating apply here too.

1. *Hiding* ("What income?")
    a. *Masking.* If there is no income, there can be no tax. So one may attempt to hide by simply not filing a return, which if there is no intent to defraud is quite legal. Tax cheaters who do this keep all income out-

side of IRS purview—but it is a difficult ploy to manage unless the citizen is self-employed and operates largely in a cash economy: gamblers, prostitutes, small craftsmen, or Murder Inc., for example. More effective is to file but to hide some of the untraceable income, such as payment by cash, tips, unreported cab fees, poker winnings.

b. *Repackaging.* Services that would normally be paid for in money can be repackaged as favors: you do my plumbing and I will cure your cold.

c. *Dazzling.* This is a last resort when the IRS suspects matters are not what they appear—dazzle them with an elegant accountant who, like the stripes on a battleship, will make the truth more difficult to determine (the more apparently honest the accountant, the more confused the IRS).

2. **Showing** ("What tax?")
   a. *Mimicking.* While double-entry bookkeeping is a crucial advance in Western economic practice, double books are equally vital for the cheat. One book mimics a reality that should persuade the IRS that little or no tax is owed, the other reflects the handsome undeclared profit that is to be spent with discretion.

   b. *Inventing.* The three-martini lunch is a legitimate deduction unless the martinis are invented. The same is true of massive gifts to charity, astounding medical expenses, the use of cars for business purposes—the whole range of invented deductions whose genuineness, if one is wise, can be proven by equally invented receipts.

   c. *Decoying.* When the IRS does begin to suspect that much is hidden and too much is showing, the only hope is to decoy the audit, make the investigator look left at the real medical bills in hopes that he won't pry right into those fictitious martinis.

Despite the huge losses in government revenues as a result of tax cheats, most cheating is small-time; nevertheless, it adds up. And the IRS audit investigators even attempt to maintain a sensible proportion in their investigations, reaping some five dollars for each spent on collecting what is properly due. After all, most tax cheats are not very good, there are just a lot of them.

Most fraud is low level, although this too has a cumulative effect. Shortchange the customer often enough and he will be short of change. Milton "Uncle Milt" Weiner, for example, is a sharp ex-Communist Party organizer, Spanish Civil War veteran, Army sergeant in the Big One, political columnist, and Sausalito bon vivant. Old Milt is a streetwise man and he gambles only occasionally, just for the fun of it. Yet this past summer he was the victim of a simple horsetrack scam at a local county fair.

Milt steps up to the two-dollar window, plunks down a twenty, and asks for two tickets. The parimutuel clerk feeds him two tickets off the machine and hands him a pile of bills, ones showing. As our unsuspicious hero turns away he vaguely notices two seemingly inconsequential things: no one is behind him in line and yet the ticket machine is grinding away again. A few steps later Milt counts his change and finds six one-dollar bills but no ten spot. Shortchanged, he steps back to the clerk, who blandly tells him sure, if the cash drawer is ten bucks over after counting up that night, he'll get his money back. At that point Milt tumbles—he won't see his ten bucks again.

No smart racetrack clerk will steal from the company's till, any more than a smart croupier or dealer will steal from the casino; he really doesn't enjoy having his arms broken. But he can shortchange a bettor and use his ill-gotten gains to buy tickets, five in this case. The till will balance, the house has windfall profits, the clerk may have a winner. And all because Milt, like most of us, neglected to count his change before leaving the window.

The innocent or unwary are swindled by their friends and neighbors with pyramid schemes, by the sly clerk at the checkout line, by the seller of raffle tickets, and most of all by their own greed or negligence. At times the unwary are not so innocent. In fall 1975, a shop calling itself only P.F.F., Inc., opened to a very exclusive Washington, D.C., clientele. It paid top dollar for any goods, from stereos and credit cards to illegal weapons—no questions asked. For $122,000 the store purchased 3,500 stolen items worth $2.4 million. Two hundred satisfied customers, including a moonlighting federal prosecutor, were sure that the Mafia had set up a lucrative fencing operation. They were all sorely disillusioned five months later when arrested by P.F.F., Inc., which then revealed that its initials stood for Police-FBI Fencing, Incognito. Actually the thieves had fallen victim, as did the Abscam politicians, to a con scheme, an attractive proposition that absolutely assures the victim will lose.

Con Games

> Suckers have no business with money, anyway.
>
> "Canada Bill" Jones,
> Mississippi Gambler

The difference between business cheating and the con is essentially that the con has fashioned an opportunity at one remove from real life—a bet on probabilities, a throw at a carnival, a game in reality structured without chance. There is really no game, there is no gambling, there are no odds however skewed, no hope once the victim agrees to play.

On the edge of the con lies the hustle, which, somewhat as the house percentage, assures that the player loses. Hustling isn't actually cheating, but it is deceptive. If our high schools taught a course in statistics instead of trigonometry or some other such impractical subject, you wouldn't find it so easy to hustle the following bets. All of these are called "proposition" or "angle" bets because, while common sense makes them seem like fifty-fifty propositions, the underlying statistics actually give the hustler a big hidden edge. If a sucker takes you up on the deceptive odds you offer, you're not cheating, he's just ignorant.

If you find yourself in a room with at least twenty-three persons, confidently offer even money that at least two persons present will have the same birthday. With twenty-three persons the odds just tip in your favor; with forty they jump to eight-to-one.

Driving in a car pool or loitering at a corner, offer a sucker even odds that the last two numbers on at least two of the next thirteen (or more) cars to pass will match. With thirteen cars the odds are slightly in your favor; with only twenty cars they shoot up to seven-to-one.

Offer even money that by turning up the top cards in two standard decks you'll eventually turn up at least one identical pair. The sucker thinks the odds are even, but the real percentage gives you a 26-percent edge.

If you want to move up from being a merely deceptive hustler to being an outright cheat, try some of the following proposition bets. These are sure things the sucker can't win.

Propose that with your back turned you can guess which side of a spinning coin will fall up. The sucker spins the coin but you are always right. You peeked in a mirror? A confederate gives you "the office"? No, you have gaffed an old coin with a natural-looking nick on the edge of one side and you *hear* the difference; the spinning coin runs *slower* on that side.

Propose that flies in the room will land on *your* sugar cube first and not on his. Sure enough, the flies avoid his and eventually settle on yours, always. The two cubes are gaffed with a drop of DDT on one side. On the pretext of moving the cubes apart after the sucker has picked his, you turn one DDT-side up; it will be avoided and the other chosen instead. Back in 1947 Las Vegas mobster "Bugsy" Siegel took his colleague Willie Moretti for two $5,000 fly bets at the Flamingo.

Conversely, don't ever bet with a man who proposes he can take the last match from a large pile of unknown number, each player removing from one through six matches at his turn. This is an old puzzler's game and the player who knows the right way to count has at least six-to-one odds going for him. Of course, if you also know the secret and are willing to use a little sleight of hand, you can work the "cross" and beat the hustler, once you know he has the right count, by palming a match from your previous draw and then pretending to remove it next turn. This throws his count off and you automatically win.

The classic site of the con has always been the carnival, where the knowledgeable can watch the art of those who never underestimate the American public and never go broke. The most profitable and safest crooked carnival "game" is called Razzle Dazzle or Razzle by the carnival grifters. It is safe because there is no need of a gaff that could give it away. If caught, the flat-joint operator claims an "error in arithme-

tic" and nobody can prove otherwise. The whole secret is in
giving the sucker a miscount. The very name of the game tells
it all; the sucker is confused by the dazzling profusion of
numbers. Consequently, the less audacious flatties call the
game by such unrevealing names as Bolero, Double Up, or
Ten Points.

Razzle Dazzle is the modern miniaturized version of the
now almost obsolete carnival game of Roll-Down. Today it is
played with eight marbles and an inclined board with sev-
enty-two or more holes, numbered from one to six. To win,
the sucker must score at least ten points. The sucker throws
the marbles from a cup and they settle into the holes. The
grifter quickly adds the values as he removes the marbles,
announces the total count, say 47, and compares that with
the prominently displayed scorecard that says 47 is worth
eight points. To win the sucker must score at least ten points.

Because of the way the numbers are laid out, the operator
can make an almost instant count so that if he sees that the
sucker has lost he can either miscount his score to make him a
winner, to lure him on, or actually let the sucker do his own
counting. Conversely, if the grifter knows it's a winning number, he just dazzlingly miscounts the total score.

As a con Razzle Dazzle is hardly elegant, although it is
sufficiently profitable to have appeared at almost all historical
carnivals on record. How much more exciting to lay bets at a
track on *absolutely* sure things—to "past-post." Here one places
a bet with a bookmaker on a winning horse *after* the race has
been run. Two or more persons are needed to work this scam,
and they are called "horse mobs." To past-post the mob must
get the race results before the bookie; and that is made possible by the legal prohibition against instant radio or wire reporting to bookies. The bookie joint must rely on illegal

smuggling of information, race by race, out of the track; and any cheat who can get that information just a bit faster is in business.

The most ingenious of all known past-posters was the Blondie mob, so-called because it consisted of five women, all blondes, in their mid-twenties to mid-thirties. During their brief but profitable fling back during World War Two they managed to cheat several Los Angeles bookies out of at least $1 million before their con was figured out and they retired. One of the gang had single-handedly taken a top bookmaker there for $100,000 in just four weeks. Operating in a lavishly furnished and completely soundproofed room in which his big bettors were sealed during the entire race, the bookie accepted bets up to the time he got the results, in other words for some minutes *after* each race had been run. He couldn't see how Blondie was getting her information, but after her winnings reached $50,000 he decided to hire magician John Scarne to ease his mind. After watching Blondie take his client for another two grand one afternoon, Scarne told him, "She's been past-posting you, and the guy who has been tipping her off is you!"

Scarne explained to the incredulous bookie that one of Blondie's confederates, knowing the winner in the just-completed third race, would phone in directly to the bookie to bet, for example, $50, $20, and $10 on another horse in a later race, and asked the bookie to repeat her bet. When he did so, Blondie overheard and added the first digits (5 + 2 + 1) to learn from the bookie himself that number 8 had just won.

Most past-posters depend on getting their information faster than the bookie. Once, and probably only once, did a very clever horse mob work the reverse by putting a time delay on the bookie himself.

This ingenious variation was pulled some years back against a Chicago bookmaker by a gang known as the Whitey mob. They tapped the bookie's incoming race-result phone line, tape-recorded the messages, bet the winners, and a few minutes later released the delayed information to the unsuspecting bookie. It is unlikely that the Whitey mob realized they had invented an entirely new type of deception effect. By creating an unperceived time delay, they notionally put time out of joint and produced an It's-Later/Earlier-Than-You-Think Effect or, simpler, the Time-Distortion Effect.

Real-world examples are very rare, although this time-distortion effect is sometimes used in fiction. It was first used fictionally in 1964 in the James Garner movie, *Thirty-Six Hours,* a clever thriller in which the American officer-hero is led to believe that, after being unconscious for a year, he has awakened in a postwar occupied Germany, now free to tell the secrets of D-Day. The hospital is, of course, a Nazi fake and the Allied D-Day landings are yet to come. The time-advance illusion was also the basis in 1967 of one of Desmond Cory's better "Johnny Fedora" spy thrillers, and of the horse-bookie scam that ends the Redford-Newman 1973 film, *The Sting.*

There is somehow a certain attraction in the con man, the last blithe spirit of America, living on wits and credulity, punishing only the greedy. Lovers of the con have a variety of classical heros, not the least of whom was Jefferson Randolph Smith, the most famous con artist of the last century. Born in Georgia in 1830, as a young man he went West, mastered the shell game, and soon moved up to Three-Card Monte. From there he branched out to become the shill in the Soap-Game Swindle, in which the spieler sells bars of soap at exorbitant prices, claiming that some have currency of various denominations wrapped inside. As shill, Jeff Smith would "buy" a couple of bars at five bucks each and with well-acted surprise "find" a twenty or a century in one. The spieler would chant: "Take your pick among the lot./Why not invest a fiver for a hundred spot?/The bacon's frying, come on the lope, come pick your bar of Lucky soap."

At this point Jeff Smith became known as "Soapy" Smith and opened his own crooked gambling house. In 1898 he joined the gold rush to Alaska and opened a saloon in Skagway. Always looking for a new way to skin a sucker, Soapy noticed that the successful miners paid good money to report their good fortune to anxious relatives in the States. The mails were slow, so Soapy bought a shack and set up a telegraph office. His many satisfied customers failed to realize that the wires didn't run out very far. "It's the gesture," Soapy cynically remarked, "They feel damn good, don't they?"

The masters of the con come and go. Soapy Smith's telegraph line to nowhere, the Sting, Abscam are stations along the road of deceit. And nowhere along that victim-strewn road could one hope to stop and not find a promising game of Three-Card Monte. Like the shell game, the only skill in Three-Card Monte lies with the operator. It is not a game but pure sleight of hand. The sucker hasn't a chance, ever. But it is always a pleasure to watch. Just pick any street of deceit. On the sidewalk at Fourteenth Street and Broadway in Manhattan, a young black man recently had a small table set up near the curb with his back to an illegally parked VW bug. A half dozen players and kibitzers gathered round. He was explaining the simple rules with quick patter and fast hands. He shows the three cards: both red aces and the queen of spades (always the queen of spades). "Now, follow the

broad," he says cheerily, "and you win. Turn over an ace an'
you lose." With that he turns the cards face down and starts
to shuffle them around. One shabbily dressed player who
thinks he has managed to keep track of the black queen plops
a buck down in front of the middle card. The "broad tosser"
matches it with a buck of his own, the sucker turns it over—
red ace! Again the old razzmatazz, and an older white man
dressed as a hard hat steps forward and puts down a five-spot.
Monte covers the bet and Hard Hat turns up—the queen! A
winner, except Hard Hat is a confederate or, as they say, an
"outside man." After a few more plays he is still the only
winner.

At this point, while Monte stoops below the table to get
some cigarettes out of his bag, a loitering ten-year-old black
kid in hand-me-downs leaps forward and with a lightning-
quick move of his hand crimps a corner of the queen. He
flashes a big grin and steps back just as the operator straight-
ens up.

He is actually a second confederate employing the crimp
gaff. On the next play a T-shirted college man invests ten
bucks on the crimped queen to discover it was just another
ace, Monte having switched the crimps when he picked them
up for the next throw. You might think that by betting on
either of the *uncrimped* cards that the sucker would have a
decent fifty-fifty chance of winning. No, for if he starts to go
for the queen, the operator will "accidentally" tip over the
board and declare a misdeal or a confederate will quickly bet
it first. All that is missing is "broad mob's," the traditional
lookout; perhaps the local cops just don't give a damn or
maybe they have been properly humored.

These cons *always* get their suckers by hook or by crook; *very*
seldom will a Monte man let a sucker win and then only if he

has a really ripe one he thinks he can lure into bigger bets. In the early seventies a gang of thirteen Monte teams around Times Square actually did pay off the suckers, but they were exchanging the suckers' real paper for their own counterfeit. Con men never lose. They only get caught, and that rarely. After all, suckers have no business with money anyway.

CHAPTER 8

Public Cheating: Politics, Espionage, and War

THERE IS an inclination in the West to assume that *real* politics—ours, democratic, decent, orderly and just—is the norm, while *theirs* consists of aberrations, either rigidly totalitarian or simply chaotically violent. While other governments may cheat the people of freedom or may collapse in a welter of secret plots, we hold elections in an open society where, if not the best man, at least the chap with the most votes comes in first. Cheating the people seems somehow more unfair (a peculiarly Western concept) to Americans or English than it does to Iranians or Russians. Americans understand that even a democratic state may from time to time have to cheat to defend itself, but then the victim is seen as an opponent and not as a citizen. All might be fair in love and war but not in democratic politics.

This is the ideal. The reality in most democratic states is that the political process runs more smoothly if the rules are bent to narrow advantage. In early America politicians realized that government by fraud was cheaper and easier than any other kind. Votes could be bought by cash, by promises, by goods in kind, by intimidation. Even the dead could vote. Political "machines" were fashioned to harness and maintain voting that would assure that the appropriate politician was in office. Once in positions of power the politician not only paid his debts but also himself. City halls were built at astronomical costs to the common taxpayer. In the case of the Teapot Dome scandal (1921) government assets drifted into private hands, and at times decent folk despaired. Occasionally deceit wasn't even necessary and the thieves were blatant. The politicians saw their opportunities and took advantage of them; and they made sure the people reelected them. Who could ask for anything more?

Still, on the national level, with the exception of a few major scandals and perhaps the election of 1876, which was "stolen" by the Republicans in a quite legal manner, matters were never as bad as in the grim days of local machine politics. Presidents and certainly congressmen might benefit from skewed election districts, purchased voting blocs, or regional dishonesty, but at one remove. Now and again the hand was caught in the till, but increasingly and generally, dishonesty in politics was the exception. Visibility and the violation of public trust made cheating in politics seem more intolerable than cheating in, say, business. This is partly what made Watergate so alarming: the spectacle of an American president cheating—not for money but for power.

A president embarking on a deceitful course does so like everyone else, by employing the Deception Planning Loop—intuitively in Richard Nixon's case. In 1972 his strategic goal was reelection, a prospect once the Democrats nominated George McGovern that to the disinterested seemed inevitable. Nixon, however, felt that not only was his political future in the balance, which was quite true, but also and most unlikely, that of the nation. Thus, his logic ran, various unorthodox means might be employed to assure the desired end. And from that came the break-in at Watergate. The first deception goal was simply to go in and out of the Democratic headquarters without being seen. The RUSE was to slip in invisibly at night, leaving no trace. And consider what might have happened if someone had said, "No, don't put that tape on the door." Once discovered, the RUSE penetrated, and the conspirators unmasked, the President's goal was to deceive the American public concerning the involvement of the administration. To maintain himself in office for the next two years—his Strategic Goal—Nixon donned one mask after another, sacrificing one conspirator after another. The most blatant and the most perfect RUSE of invisibility, absolute masking, occurred when the telltale tape recording was erased. Ultimately the RUSES of masking no longer proved effective. It was rather like hiding an elephant under a blanket and people simply believed that *something* was under Nixon's blanket. People would not buy the image he presented of a misunderstood man—his showing of the false through the channels of television and the podium of press conferences had fewer and fewer takers. The intended ILLUSION was not bought. Efforts to decoy the American people with crises abroad and urgencies at home, efforts to mimic past statements and present virtues, efforts to repackage the Old Nixon as the New faltered. At the very end he was reduced to dazzling when on the tapes the "smoking gun" was at last found. Yet there had been no real smoking guns, only a corruption of the system and, worse, an unnecessary corruption—for American politics is not a killing business.

When politics *is* a killing business recourse to deceit is more likely, because the punishment for failure is violent. There is a real argument that the use of fraud instead of force is a decent, moderating option. Sometimes such fraud is fashioned for personal, not especially violent, reasons, as when Potemkin, favorite of Tsarina Catherine the Great, had his serfs hurriedly throw up a series of neat, clean, pretty but fake villages to impress his monarch. Modern artist Christo began his career with a Bulgarian army camouflage unit one of whose tasks was hurriedly to redecorate train stations along the routes taken by foreign tourists shortly after World War Two: twentieth-century Potemkin villages. Often, however, fraud is a viable alternative to naked political force; it may also be a mask for future violence.

At many times in many places, a convenient means to change the balance of power has been simply to murder the powerful. For the conspirators the deception goal was to maintain normality until the moment of striking; a variety of ruses might be employed to mask intention, projecting the illusion of stability and calm until the assassin could strike.

Assassination—or, rather, its planning—is a covert and deceptive technique to undermine, gain, or hold power. It has been commonly practiced and with considerable flair in the Roman and Byzantine empires, at times in China, during the ancient Indian Maurya dynasty (325–183 B.C.), throughout the Italian Renaissance, in the medieval Arab world, in early twentieth-century Japan, and intermittently in the modern West.

Of the twelve Roman emperors between 53 B.C. and A.D.

96, eleven were targets of domestic assassination plots; six were successfully killed, two committed suicide before they could be killed, and only three survived. Eight of these rulers had themselves plotted the secret assassination of their opponents.

Of the 107 emperors who reigned during the Eastern Roman Empire's 1,058 years (395–1453), 23 were assassinated. In Venice between 1415 and 1768, the city fathers formally debated over 90 proposals for assassination. In the 50 years since 1918 there have been at least 218 assassination attempts directed against chief executives in 36 countries. Of these, 68 succeeded.

In every case the victim to some degree accepted the ILLUSION created by the conspirators that all was well. Even given the high probability of conspirators around the corner, the assassin's ILLUSION too often proved effective. For example, Julius Caesar was explicitly warned that the Ides of March were a time of danger, yet he failed to take self-protective action. Of course, in matters of cheating the assassin's was never a very elegant ILLUSION. All that needs to be done is to keep a knife sharp and allies at a minimum until the victim is vulnerable.

Matters become more complex when the stroke not only kills but assures power to the ambitious. Some have killed the mighty out of madness, others for vengeance; but, for the ambitious, murder is a means not an end—and may not even be necessary in a coup d'état.

The phrase *coup d'état* ("stroke of state") sounds as if it might refer to an act of brute force, a strike by the state. In fact the term refers to the reverse, a sudden effort to unseat the mighty. It is a strategic move of weaker subordinates to overthrow stronger leaders. It is a conspiracy, a secret plot. It relies heavily on deception to pull together enough human and material resources, individually impotent that combined stand a chance of success. But only if they can mobilize in secret and act with surprise. If successful, the coup is a triumph of fraud over force, of cunning deception over naked power.

At the level of national politics, it is sufficient to note that between 1946 and 1964 there were at least 88 attempted coups in 37 of the world's 118 nations. Of these attempts, 62 succeeded. Nor is the coup d'état a purely modern technique; for example, three of the first twelve "Caesars" (Nero, Galba, and Otho) were deposed by army coups. And 65 of the Eastern Roman Empire's 107 emperors were dethroned by revolts. The coup is not a Western specialty; the nine Liao Dynasty emperors of China (907–1125) had to fight off nineteen "rebellions" by their own closest relatives.

In a coup, the deception goal, secrecy until the last moment, is the same as in assassination, but the problem is more complex because more conspirators are involved and more resistance might be anticipated. Killing or capturing the ruler may not be sufficient for the coup's success; his supporters may rally, his people may refuse to be governed by others. Some cunning coup makers employ shrewd ruses that exploit people's assumptions. Proclamations of the new state are broadcast on television: a calm general reading from typed notes sitting at the presidential desk within the National Palace projects an ILLUSION of controlled power that the reality of a few dozen sweating officers huddled in three or four rooms in the capital directing their tanks and one regiment would not confirm. Some coups are arranged to take place with the maximum leader out of the country or up-country on vacation. All involve RUSES that hide the real intention of the conspirators until it is too late and most include RUSES of consolidation, displaying the false symbols of power to lull the people and dismay the old regime.

It is comforting that some RUSES within some politics do not rely on murder, on potential violence, on unforgiving politics, but aim at achieving justice, not power, by somewhat irregular means. One RUSE from ancient China involved a Strategic Goal, better governing, that was to be achieved by a Deception Goal, creation of warnings. This involved inventing a new reality by means of assembled CHARCS channeled through historic routes, which produced an ILLUSION whose acceptance achieved the original intention. In the West the process remained inscrutable for a long time.

Beginning with the Han Dynasty, 2,000 years ago, the Chinese published an official history of each dynasty. The collected *Twenty-one Histories* are a triumph of systematic collection of data. Each history includes long, detailed chapters on chronology, biographies, population, agricultural statistics, world geography, and so forth. They are a rich treasure for historian and sociologist alike.

In addition, each history includes a very curious chapter. It is called simply "Unusual Events" and is seemingly a mishmash of large and small catastrophes. Arranged chronologically, we read of each earthquake, flood, and drought that plagued the Chinese Empire. So far so good, as these were clearly events of immediate bureaucratic concern. However, the chapter also records such other unusual events as sunspots, nova, birthings of two-headed sheep, and sightings of geese flying backward over the Imperial Palace. This odd mixture of events long puzzled Western sinologists. What, they wondered, was the common factor among the categories and why would the Chinese scholar-officials have troubled to record, much less publish, such matters so meticulously.

The mystery only deepened when scholars cross-checked these events (each identified by date and place) against the surviving official provincial histories that were the original source of data for the dynastic historians. The cross-checks proved that the dynastic historians, scholar and gentleman each one, had deliberately faked many entries.

The historian is a detective and here was a mystery crying out for solution. Why had the records been faked? The first clue was that while the verified reports of floods, droughts, sunspots, and so forth were either properly random or properly cyclical as they should be, the faked events tended to cluster in time. With what, then, did these particular periods coincide?

For all its secularity, the Chinese empire was felt by the Chinese to be a mystical entity. Westerners call it China, but the Chinese called it *Chung-Kuo,* the "Central Kingdom," central being the word-picture ⊖ᴛ of an arrow in the bull's-eye of a target. To the Chinese, China was literally the center of the world. And, as the court astronomers established, the exact center of the center of the world was a point inside the Temple of Heaven in the capital metropolis of Peking. For the Chinese Confucian scholar-bureaucrats, this human world was mystically linked by and at that bull's-eye point to the heavens. Moreover, the Emperor, having ex officio the Mandate of Heaven, was a divine emperor whose primary official function was to keep China in harmony with the universe. Like the Pope in his infallibility, the Emperor embodied divine perfection when he appeared ceremonially in his bull's-eye Temple of Heaven. If the Emperor failed in his priestly duties he alone was responsible for putting China out of tune with the universe.

The price paid by China for any improper behavior by her emperor was that she would be visited by catastrophe. Disharmony would result in floods, droughts, earthquakes, and rebellions, and would be further signaled by monstrous births, sunspot activity—in short "unusual events."

Even such a powerful official as the prime minister could not tell a divine Emperor in so many words that he was mucking things up and should straighten himself out. But the court officials could subtly caution a wayward Emperor by bringing to his attention various "unusual events" that implied he was failing. In their urgent need to persuade an Emperor to change his ways, these officials did not hesitate to fake such omens as geese flying backwards over the very center of the world.

This new reality, although false, invented and shown to the Emperor, was a gentle and effective ruse—a far cry from the spectacle of a new president (ex-colonel) reading his proclamation from the previous president's office. Both, however, involve the same process displayed in the Deception Planning Loop and, more often than not, both prove effective. Cheating, whether violently or subtly, has regularly played a part in the political process. One aspect of politics, the acquisition of denied information, almost always involves deceit. In Nixon's case, the desire to know thy enemy, namely the Democratic National Committee, led him down the cheater's road, even though the intelligence was probably not necessary and certainly not worth the price. If rulers are convinced an enemy is real and avowed, most states, whether led by benign if misguided emperors or murderous colonels, feel that the risk of cheating is justified, that no price is too high to discover enemy intentions. Of course, over the centuries respectable institutions have been established to permit the relatively free flow of information. Diplomacy, with its rules and regulations and accepted canons, is still fragile, as the American experience in Iran indicated (all diplomats were seen by the Mullahs as spies, all fingers on the hand of Great Satan). And in truth, all diplomats *are* spies insofar as they report back what they can discover about the intentions of friends or potential enemies, and they are deceivers when they present their own government's policies in a fashion often less than truthful. "An ambassador," punned the seventeenth-century English poet and diplomat Sir Henry Wotton, "is an honest man sent to lie abroad for the good of his country." A little deceit is not such a dangerous thing as long as it is bounded by convention. But when a country decides that it would like more knowledge than can be conventionally acquired, cheating becomes institutionalized as espionage.

ESPIONAGE

While there have been vast technological advances, especially in the past fifty years, spies really have not changed much in the last several thousand years. One can still find them out there scouting out the land, listening to the mighty, prey to purchase or betrayal, always suspect no matter how successful. And the most successful are always those close to the seats of power and consequently the rarest.

Every intelligence service would dearly love to have someone close to the center of the circle. A classic means to that end is to plant a mole within a crucial enemy's apparatus, ideally early in his career, and wait for his promotion to a position of power and access to the center. Until activated the mole simply masks his potential, a penny among pennies. Then, having arrived at a position of influence, he mimics the normal bureaucrat that he was as a mole but no longer is. The British, all too often contemptuous of the crude and unsophisticated Americans, have had absolutely disastrous experiences with moles. These Soviet agents were recruited in the thirties in an era of university radicalism—Anthony Burgess, Donald Maclean, Kim Philby, and the recently revealed Tomas Harris and Anthony Blunt—came to positions of prominence during the Cold War; they revealed not only British secrets but also what they knew of the Americans. The difficulty the British establishment had in rooting out the moles was largely a refusal to believe in the possibility of the bad penny: how could decent chaps who went to the appropriate schools, wore the accepted uniform, suffered from acceptable vices . . . be spies? There were other British scandals and betrayals, but to have key members of your establishment working for years for your enemy was an intelligence defeat of major proportions. The Americans, by the way, unlike the British or Russians, have yet to discover a mole, which only convinces some of the intelligence community that they are still being duped.

Most spies are not moles but rather agents operating under a cover. They have many "names": a real name known to very few, a name within their agency for bookkeeping purposes, a code field name—Apple or Dragon—and a cover name. Deep cover agents may resemble moles in that they remain passive for years until their information becomes vital. In some cases, the real name and cover name are the same since no one would suspect the person of spying. For example, clumsy then, clumsy now, the British dispatched one Patrick Alexander, member of the Aeronautical Society of Great Britain, to spy on the aeronautical efforts of the Wright brothers and report back to the royal engineers. He managed to ingratiate himself with the two, received an invitation to watch the first flight at Kitty Hawk in 1903 but managed to lose his way and miss the event. More typical and far more successful was Israeli spy Elie Cohen who, using a cover of Kamal Amin Taabes of Syrian parentage born in Beirut and domiciled in

Argentina, arrived in Syria in 1962. He managed so well that
at the time of his arrest three years later by Syrian authorities
he was in line for appointment as minister of defense. His
cover was intact until the end, for he had been discovered
only by chance when one of his radio messages was sent while
the usual masking Syrian broadcast was silent.

Some spies are simple volunteers, come in through the window because of a pressing ideological commitment, for personal reasons (often unsavory), or simply for money.
Obviously, intelligence services prefer the motives to be idealis-
tic, but they take what they get. When what they get is insufficient, without moles or without an effective covered agency,
they recruit. Potential volunteers are pressed to support De-
mocracy or Communism or the Old Country. The disgruntled
are sought out, the greedy paid, and when all else fails, blackmail can be employed and often is. At times, "intelligence" is
purchased rather than a person who may have access to only a
single item. The Russians are particularly fond of purchasing
and, like many services, press money on even the idealist.

Matters become more complex when those who run agents
become more cunning, turning a discovered agent to work for
them instead of for his previous masters—who, if they discover
the RUSE, may turn the double agent into a triple (at which
point everyone involved begins to become somewhat confused). An effective double, however, is an enormous asset
and not a novel one. Machiavelli counseled, in effect, use your
enemy's spies and your own traitors by feeding them the false
false information you want the enemy to have. In this case the
"agent" has become a channel in transforming a deception
RUSE into an ILLUSION. The more difficult it is to acquire
information the more likely it is to be accepted as real—as
long as it is not *too* real. Intelligence that is so good as to be a
miracle is often suspect. The British ambassador's Albanian

valet in the British Embassy, Cicero, photographing the ambassador's documents and passing them on to the Germans
for money looked suspicious to the Germans. His information
was intriguing and the Germans were attracted. So much so
that not only did the Germans cheat themselves out of much
of his information but also cheated Cicero by paying him in
forged bills. This was probably just as well, since he had been
under British control almost from the beginning.

While spies continue to come in a variety of recognizable
types, the technology of espionage has not remained the same.
Radio, radar, photography, sonar, all sorts of electronic wiz-
ardry extend the range of observation and in turn spur innovation to limit that observation in a cycle of breakthroughs
and defenses. Of all new devices, the most impressive has
been the spy-in-the-sky intelligence satellite that can produce
photographs from hundreds of miles up that can show the
numbers on a license plate. A variety of techniques, such as
infrared photography, extend the satellite's powers beyond
those of the human eye—although clouds and camouflage and
even bad luck or poor positioning cause problems. In spy
fiction at least, the most intriguing item is the "bug," which
comes in all shapes and sizes and can make up what ineffec-
tual agents cannot supply. In Ottawa in 1955 the Canadians,
for example, placed bugs in the new Soviet embassy, rebuilt
after a fire in the old one. The Royal Canadian Mounted
Police, using information supplied by a Soviet defector who
had left the embassy in 1945, cased the new embassy. The
bugs went in but soon thereafter went dead—discovered by
Soviet intelligence experts. They in turn were apparently informed about the bugs by a double agent in the British security service, indicating that one mole is worth a passel of bugs.

Still, the bugs can be inserted in quite unusual false "realities" as well as in real embassies. A pet social espionage proj-

ect of SS Intelligence Chief Reinhard Heydrich, from late 1940 on, was his discreet, superbly appointed "Salon Kitty" or "House of Gallantry." Located on Berlin's fashionable Giesebrechtstrasse it was personally managed by SS-Brigadeführer Walter Schellenberg. The hostesses—recruited by Chief of Criminal Police Arthur Nebe, appropriately enough a former vice squad detective—were elite European prostitutes and patriotic German society matrons. To front their operation, the SS intelligence chiefs set up the famous Madam Kitty. The unsuspecting clientele comprised a significant proportion of the diplomatic corps (including Japanese Ambassador Oshima), visiting VIP's (including Count Ciano, Mussolini's son-in-law and foreign minister), and prominent Germans (including Foreign Minister Ribbentrop). The battery of microphones and recorders was shut down only during SS Obergruppenführer Heydrich's frequent personal inspections. This odd institution did manage to collect some valuable diplomatic indiscretions, but its main use was for the type of blackmail against colleagues by which Heydrich flourished. Unknown to his colleagues in this enterprise, SS Gruppenführer Nebe was pulling a private double-cross. He had been a determined and active secret anti-Nazi since 1938, the one exception in the senior SS ranks. Therefore, the intimate secrets of Salon Kitty were undoubtedly transmitted to Nebe by his handpicked ladies and from Nebe to his regular contact in the underground, Colonel Hans Oster, Deputy Chief of Military Intelligence.

The mysterious and murky world of espionage seeks not only to acquire real information secretly but to dispense false information in such a manner that the ruse will create the illusion of reality. The Russians might have been better advised to leave the bugs in place and plant the input. At a somewhat higher level of state purpose the false is shown not

simply to dazzle or decoy the opposition but to achieve a
specific strategic purpose that requires a deception operation
channeling disinformation. This may be black propaganda
ruining reputations by outright forgeries, fake documents, unspoken speeches, or the maneuvering of nonexistent military
units. In fact, the closer war comes, the crucial moment for a
nation, the more vital hiding military reality and showing
false assets or debits becomes.

WAR

In wartime, Truth is so precious
that she should always be attended
by a bodyguard of lies.

—CHURCHILL to Stalin at Teheran, 1943

Nations may want to cheat their potential enemies by
showing what does not exist just as they might want to hide
what does. It may be useful for special purposes for the foe to
think one weaker or stronger than one is. Certainly it is advantageous to start early, and one of the most effective long-
range ruses, identical to the magician's one-ahead principle, is
to establish a False Order of Battle. An Order of Battle, OB,
is useful army and airforce jargon for the list of units in any
given military force. For example, the overall German Order
of Battle on 22 June 1941, the eve of the invasion of Russia,
was 180 divisions: on the Eastern Front it was three army
groups, comprised of 123 divisions. Clearly the more details
the Russians had about the OB—how many divisions, how
large, how equipped, where located, and commanded by
whom—the better off they would be. During World War Two
the Allies over the years made many efforts to create nonexis-

tent divisions, moving them about, maintaining appropriate radio traffic, even assigning, albeit briefly, real officers to non-existent postings (to their great confusion). The greatest single strategic use of the fake OB was, as noted, the deployment of Patton's "army" during and before D-Day in 1944—an elaborate and long-lived RUSE that sought to channel the reality of this false army to the Germans as an effective ILLUSION by a variety of means (radio communication, false tanks and vehicles, unit orders, tank tracks, all the CHARCS necessary to present a real army).

On the other hand, it is at times necessary not to show a false-force army but to hide a real one. This is true to some degree in most battles, where intention, direction, size, and power are best cloaked, but it can also be true even before the war has started. This was the case when Germany was prohibited from rearming by the restrictions of the Versailles Treaty and was too weak to do so in defiance of their recent opponents. To avoid provoking military intervention by France and Britain from 1919 through 1934, the Germans systematically used deception to hide their growing strength. They wanted their opponents to underestimate their actual and illicit strength and particularly their very substantial capacity for quick mobilization, what today's arms controllers call "the fast breakout."

It became increasingly clear to France and Britain that Germany could not be kept "disarmed" forever—the fact was that Germany was far more armed, especially after Hitler came to power. Still, there was hope that German rearmament could be limited by treaty, but the Germans had been using the one-ahead principle for some time. Britain agreed in the Anglo-German Naval Treaty of 18 June 1935 to permit Germany to build submarines, a weapons system Berlin had been absolutely denied since the Versailles Treaty of 1919.

Britain assumed that it would take the Germans some while
to catch up in submarine technology, much less build the
boats. Yet, ten days later, the German navy *commissioned* four
brand new, modern U-boats. This seemingly phenomenal
construction speed was the end result of three RUSES that
had set the stage for German undersea rearmament: illegal
research and development in the 1920's and 1930's; covert
prefabrication of all U-boat parts; and prior construction of
the assembly sheds. In June 1935, Germany actually had a
submarine fleet secretly masked from British eyes that needed
only to be assembled. In ten days the first four were finished;
by the end of the year eight more U-boats had been commissioned.

By 1936 Hitler, preparing for what he sensed was inevitable war to redress the injustices of 1919, followed a dual policy of hiding certain special strengths and exaggerating other
assets. The huge ritual displays at Nuremberg, the parades of
tanks, the mass flyovers for visiting dignitaries, the bombastic
language, and the aggressive posture in European events impressed the unwary or the enthusiastic with Nazi Germany's
military capacity. The Rhineland was returned to the Reich
in 1936, and German units intervened in Spain on Franco's
side the same year; in 1938 Austria was annexed; and by the
time of the Munich crisis in the same year, Hitler had
marshaled sufficient force so that he was no longer forced to
rely for success on pure bluff. The next year Hitler did not
want simply more—another territorial demand, this time
from Poland—but war. He had bought off the Russians, isolated France and Britain, and was ready to strike. Yet while
he had during the thirties exaggerated many of his assets, he
had also shrewdly hidden a few for later effect.

The great German battleship *Bismarck* was laid down on
Hitler's orders in 1936 with a design displacement of 41,700

tons—a decisive 19 percent over its pretended London Naval Treaty limit of 35,000 tons. *Bismarck*'s secret lay concealed beneath her waterline. Announced as drawing only 26 feet, she drew 34. These 8 extra feet enabled her builders secretly to add 4 extra inches to what was to be 9-inch armor; 70,000 horsepower to the announced 80,000; and 3 knots to the announced 27-knot flank speed.

The *Bismarck* was thus the world's largest and best armored capital ship under construction in 1936. As this intelligence was not appreciated abroad, the German Navy gained a three-year lead over the British and American navies in battleship construction. She proved her superior strength in 1941 by simultaneously sinking the "mighty" old 42,500-ton British battle cruiser *Hood* and driving off the brand new 38,000-ton battleship *Prince of Wales.* Only months later did the British Admiralty conclude from new evidence that *Bismarck's* unexpected strength had been hidden in her misrepresented and misperceived draft.

What the Germans had done was simply mask the reality of the *Bismarck,* technically complex but theoretically simple. Much more elegant is to use scientific and technological research, development and production to induce the opponent to accept an illusion requiring wasteful countereffort. R & D may produce a "secret" weapon but it may also invent a false one, depending on what's required.

An R & D example with considerable present relevance was Operation RAINBOW. This was a CIA plan in the late 1950's to simulate an Anglo-American scientific-technological breakthrough. RAINBOW was intended to convince the Arab oil countries, who even then were engaging in a bit of oil blackmail, that the United States was on the verge of developing a revolutionary new energy source. The CIA's expectation was that if the existence of this simulated energy source were believed, the Arabs would greatly underestimate United States dependence on oil, giving American diplomats greater leverage in Middle East negotiations. This imaginative plan aborted when the CIA learned of independent technical reports circulating that proved such a source, even if theoretically possible, could not provide enough new energy to cut United States dependence on Arab oil significantly. This was in the fifties. Obviously any significant R & D breakthrough in energy production would be a serious factor in national security affairs of many countries—even if in time it became clear that the means was an illusion, not a reality.

The Soviet Union and her Warsaw Pact satellites attempt to play similar R & D games with the Americans and their NATO allies. As one might expect, they try even harder. These cold war ruses are directed by the KGB's Department D, for *dezinformatsia*. The KGB's satellite secret services, particularly the big ones in Poland, East Germany, and Czechoslovakia, participate in these efforts under the careful coordinating eye of their Russian parent.

In the late 1960's, the deputy chief of the Czechoslovak Interior Ministry's Department D was Major Ladislav Bittman. A loyal supporter of his country's "Communism with a human face," he fled to the West in 1968 at the time of the Soviet invasion. He was the first "defector" from the East who had personally served in deception work; in his book, *The Deception Game,* he has given us our closest look at Soviet deception planning and operations. Although his editor deleted the best material on R & D, Bittman has since described several such efforts.*

---

* Interviews with Major Bittman, 1972. See also Ladislav Bittman, *The Deception Game: Czechoslovak Intelligence in Soviet Political Warfare* (Syracuse, N.Y.: Syracuse University Research Corporation, 1972).

Every week or so someone in the Czechoslovak Interior Ministry would put forward a new suggestion about how to fool Western intelligence services about the directions that their research was taking. All such suggestions were given the most careful attention by Department D. All were highly imaginative, most were too expensive or too risky, and only a few showed real promise. However, even the most promising ones usually foundered because of the unwillingness of senior scientists to risk their reputations by contributing their names to an operation that they rightly felt would eventually get exposed as a hoax. And it was only their top men of science that the Russians or Czechs felt they could effectively use. Invented scientists would not do because the Western intelligence service would probably be able to learn that they were nonexistent dummies. Even the few junior scientists who were willing to cooperate would not do either, because they would lack credibility in the West without the imprimatur of senior colleagues or simply because they would be highly suspect.

Unable to gain the cooperation of prestigious scientists, Department D finally made one effort to launch their first R & D deception, running it as a strictly in-house job. They drew only on the technical advice of their own electronics experts. These experts suggested a plausible but unfeasible new type of electronic device to jam nearby radio communications. The target would be West German military intelligence. Department D then had its carefully planted rumor networks in West Germany spread the story that Czechoslovak scientists had secretly perfected this device.

Department D was initially very pleased to learn that West German military intelligence had fallen for this story and were hastily diverting some of their best scientific brains and much research funds to finding an effective countermeasure to this nonexistent jamming. Then the whole clever scheme backfired. Three Czechoslovak labs were also starting work on the same worthless project. They had learned of the research in West Germany from their German colleagues at international conferences and decided that Czechoslovakia would also need a defense against this imagined threat to her own military communications. It was too late for Department D to warn them off without causing a major bureaucratic scandal, so the labs were simply allowed to continue their efforts until satisfied that the original jamming device was not feasible.

In matters leading to war, the contemporary cheater for the state must contemplate not simply the traditional ruses of the battlefield commanders but also the potential for deceit on the technological battlefield. An Israeli Phantom pilot may cheat a Soviet SAM-7 by taking swift evasive action (a traditional military RUSE) or all Israeli pilots may benefit from sophisticated jamming techniques that mask the planes from the missiles' sensors. All of these problems first became crucial during World War Two in the ceaseless cycle of innovation, response, and discovery that Churchill called "the wizard war."

The British introduced their first synchronized radio pulse navigational system to guide their bombers to Germany in March 1942. This system, called *Gee* (for "Grid"), superficially resembled the Germans' *Knickebein* ("Bent Knee") beam navigational system, which the Germans knew the British had recently mastered.

To delay German efforts to fathom *Gee*'s simple secret and thereby immediately jam it, Dr. R. V. Jones devised an ingenious two-part deception scheme. First he simulated (showed the false) a navigational device called *Jay* that worked on the Germans' own *Knickebein* beam principle. He thereby hoped to flatter the Germans into mistaking this decoy for a sincere imitation. Second he simultaneously dissimulated (hid the real) *Gee* itself to make it seem the same as *Jay. Gee*'s disguise was both electronic (to fool the German radar stations) and physical (mislabeling actual components so that any re-covered by the Germans from downed bombers would be mis-taken for parts of an ordinary radio transceiver). Jones's German counterparts were so successfully duped that they did not introduce effective jamming of *Gee* for five months, two months longer than even the most optimistic British esti-mates had allowed for.

Even more impressive was the successful diversion of Hitler's secret rocket bomb attack in 1944. This Luftwaffe V-1 campaign against London pumped in 2,340 of the terrify-ing "Flying Bombs," which killed 5,500 and seriously injured 16,000. There would have been as many as 50 percent more casualties if it hadn't been for the Germans' persistent misper-ception that most of the hits were overshooting their intended aiming point, Tower Bridge, at the geographical center of the great metropolis. In fact, most bombs were falling short, onto the much less densely populated southern suburbs.

To adjust range, the Germans depended on individual time-and-place bomb reports from their spies in London. Un-known to them, *all* their agents were under British control. Taking full advantage of this fact, Dr. R. V. Jones conceived and designed a scheme of plausible agent reports (faking the timings but consistent with any enemy aerial photoreconnais-sance evidence) that induced the Germans to steadily readjust their real aiming point ever further short of their intended one. By the end of the campaign, the Flying Bombs had been lured four miles south of their original bull's-eye.

The British, however, did not have things all their way. Operation CROSSBOW was Britain's World War Two effort to counter Hitler's super "Victory" weapons. British Intel-

ligence, particularly its photointerpreters (PI's), took pride in
their ability to locate the various launch sites prior to their
deadly activation. This target information was used to plan
69,000 Allied aerial sorties that unloaded 122,000 tons of
bombs at the high cost of 450 aircraft and 2,900 airmen. Yet
more than a quarter and probably at least half of this pro-
digious effort was wasted on obsolete targets. Indeed, not only
was the entire 28,000-ton effort from January through May
1944 wasted, but at no time were delays imposed on German
launch-site preparations before they actually opened fire.
This sorry record for the PI's was not only unsuspected at the
time, it is still largely overlooked by the historians and
memoir writers.

The Germans' original "Flying Bomb" installations (called
"ski sites," "large sites," and "supply sites" by the British PI's)
had become obsolete that January. They were henceforth su-
perseded by the well-camouflaged "modified sites," which the
PI's failed to detect until they began firing in June. Instead of
simply abandoning the old sites, the Germans continued to
simulate normal activity around them; and for five months
the Allies expended their entire CROSSBOW attack on these
now worthless targets, one of the larger of which had been
appropriately renamed Concrete Lump. Even after the new
"modified sites" revealed themselves in June through their
activity, CROSSBOW still gave the old sites high target
priority.

The British PI's were adept at identifying *decoys*, that is,
dummy installations simulating real ones at alternate loca-
tions. However, the PI's were quite unable to identify *lures*.*

---

* A decoy simulates a real target but in an alternate place, exaggerating value by
simulating high payoff or value. A decoy is a pure case of dazzle in that it creates
ambiguity of place. A fisherman's lure does not simulate another, real object, it
merely draws attention to itself. A hunter's "decoy duck" is actually a lure as well.

Indeed they were seemingly unaware of the very possibility of lures. The lure exaggerates value by simulating a significant payoff where there is little or none. This kind of baited trap is what French military theorists call an *abces de fixation.* Lures are much more difficult to detect than decoys because they are real (not dummy) objects. The lure is the real thing, only its function is faked, therefore camera imagery alone is not enough to uncover the hoax.

The cost to the Allies of the failure of CROSSBOW was tragic. The consequence for postwar American politics was incalculable, for among the many young airmen killed in this useless effort was Joseph P. Kennedy, Jr., whom his influential father was grooming as future President instead of brother John F. Kennedy. To this day the many Kennedy biographers have not realized that young "Joe" was lured to an unnecessary death—heroic, but pointless.

Not all advanced technological cheating was electronic—other British wizards had found a means to read the German secret ciphers, known as ULTRA. But to mask their possession of ULTRA, no British countereffort could be taken solely on the basis of this knowledge. The enemy must be kept convinced that the secrecy of his troop, plane, and ship movements had been compromised by conventional intelligence tradecraft.

The Royal Navy, for instance, often got timely notice of the movements of enemy warships and convoys. To keep the precious secret of ULTRA, the Navy operated under the vexing constraint that none of these tempting targets could be attacked at sea unless it could be made to seem that some other intelligence source had reported the movement. Therefore, when ULTRA was used, it was necessary either to send out search planes and let them be seen on these very nonaccidental sightings or to have it seem that a radiodirectional finding fix had occurred. Consequently the German enemy attributed its frequent naval losses to either visual or radio detection. A major instance of faked visual reconnaissance triggered the Battle of Cape Matapan when, in 1941, zeroed in by ULTRA readings of Italian naval ciphers, a Short Sunderland flying-boat scouted the Italian fleet flagship at close quarters.

Still another type of alternate intelligence source, ship watchers, was deceptively simulated on the eve of the second battle of Alamein in 1942, when ULTRA reported that Field Marshal Rommel was about to receive vital supplies, particularly petrol, carried in five Italian transports from Naples. But the usual aerial reconnaissance ploy was out because the ships' route was fogged over. Nevertheless, ULTRA's chief security officer, Group Captain "Freddy" Winterbotham, believed these targets were of such high value that a comparably high risk to ULTRA was perhaps warranted. Only Churchill personally could decide. The Prime Minister, in full agreement about the danger of compromising ULTRA, authorized the attack. In the event, four of the ships were intercepted and sunk at sea and the fifth was destroyed in harbor before it could offload. Rommel's Afrika Korps was crippled at its most crucial moment.

The Germans were highly suspicious and radioed an order for an urgent postmortem. The possibilities to be investigated were specified as radio insecurity, traitors, or as Winterbotham had feared, compromised ciphers. On reading this intercepted message (ULTRA got it too!), Winterbotham recalls that he "took the precaution of having a signal sent to a mythical agent in Naples, in a cipher that the Germans would be able to read, congratulating him on his excellent information and raising his pay." ULTRA was safe.

Perhaps one of the most interesting of British RUSES accepted by the Germans as an ILLUSION was *Moonshine II,* a case of going to the well a second time that paid off. In mid-1944 the R.A.F. introduced *Moonshine,* an airborne radio transceiver that amplified radar pulses to make the one carrier aircraft simulate a swarm on the German radar sets. To discriminate, the Luftwaffe was forced to produce more sets, and this effort took them over twelve months before the British abandoned *Moonshine.*

Over a half year later and after additional rounds in the "wizard war" of electronic innovation, the British had the audacity to reintroduce this tired device. They knew the German radar experts would soon tumble; but they reasoned that, as the Germans would be expecting the next newfangled state-of-the-art "black box," they would be momentarily confounded by half-forgotten radar signals. Consequently, *Moonshine II* was trundled out one last time on 6 June 1944, to join the premier performances of several truly innovative electronic deceptions concealing the Allied armada sailing toward Normandy. Incongruity was enchanced by using *Moonshine II* in a new context: mounting it on a few small boats to simulate a vast approaching fleet. In theoretical terms the British had sent out a revealed RUSE through novel Channels to create an ILLUSION that the Germans failed to recognize in time. Seen differently, British cunning rather than technological advance cheated the Germans because the Germans were inclined to cheat themselves. And in any case, if the Germans had not bought the ILLUSION, little of consequence would have been lost, which is not always the case in deploying strategies of deception.

One key, if intuitive, American effort, as noted, came later in the war, in December 1944, when a major Dazzle RUSE was effected. As the Allied lines in the Battle of the Bulge were crumbling before Hitler's surprise offensive (his last throw before final defeat), General Patton promised Generals

Eisenhower and Bradley that he could rush his powerful Third Army north to stop the enemy advance. Time was of the essence, so Patton's urgent movement orders to his corps and division commanders went out over his radio nets "in clear" (uncoded), despite the certainty that the German radio intelligence teams would overhear.

Everyone involved knew it was too late to mount any conventional deception operation. Nevertheless, General Bradley turned to Captain Ralph Ingersoll, then in temporary charge of Bradley's Twenty-first Army Group's "special" (i.e., deception) plans section, which was called, for cover, simply Twenty-third Headquarters Battalion. Bradley ordered Ingersoll to do anything possible to conceal Patton's crucial movement. Inspired by the recent example of the vast confusion to German intelligence engendered by the unintentional scattering of the American airborne units on D-Day, Ingersoll invented an unprecedented RUSE, one that he did not even class as a deception, which he thought meant to make the victim certain but wrong. Instead he chose to make the enemy merely uncertain, confused, and hope for the best.

The Twenty-third Headquarters' Battalion's radio operators normally spent their time simulating notional (i.e., invented) units. For the next twelve hours, however, Ingersoll had them imitate real units, specifically the nine divisional, three corps, and one army headquarters under Patton. And they did this four times over for each headquarters. In effect they presented German intelligence with five General Pattons, each approaching from a different direction. Of course the Germans immediately realized what was being done, but they were still dazzled by the four fake armies weaving around the one real one. In the event, the Germans were able to keep track of only one of Patton's advancing divisions. The others were either lost entirely on the German battle maps or, worse, mislocated. Consequently Patton was able to gain substantial tactical advantage and he went on to break the back of the *Wehrmacht*'s last offensive. Since the practice had come before the theory, Ingersoll never knew he had fashioned a Dazzle RUSE from conventional alternative Charcs, channeled it by open radio communication, and succeeded in forcing the Germans to accept the ILLUSION.

In war, in espionage, and even in conventional politics, cheating is ever with us. The Russians surprise everyone by moving into Czechoslovakia or Afghanistan and not into Poland. The British are yet again surprised to learn of treachery in their intelligence service. American congressmen are surprised to learn that the friendly Arabs bribing them are part of an FBI ruse. Everyone's ILLUSIONS are shattered—more interesting until that fateful moment ILLUSION for the cheated is Reality, partly because the Russian deception planners, the sly mole, or the FBI agents have devised elegant RUSES sent through appropriate Channels—but partly because the cheated *want* to believe. Sloth or complacency or greed or arrogance lead to self-deception, which is a universal characteristic of man and one that makes counterdeception, the thwarting of cheating, so difficult. Too often the prepared mind is prepared to be cheated.

PART III

CHEATING
THE CHEATERS

♦ ♦ ♦

Dictum sapienti sat est.
(A word to the wise is sufficient.)

CHAPTER 9

Illusion and Reality
in the Arts

♦ ♦ ♦

If there is such a thing as a basic
human quality, self-deception it is.
—COLIN M. TURNBULL

THE ITALIANS as always, have an apt epigram in matters of
cheating: *"Non è vero, ma ci credo."* ("It isn't true, but I believe
it."). Why would one consciously, rationally, prepare one's
mind to be cheated? At least in magic, the audience while
wanting to be cheated—to see the ILLUSION, not the
RUSE—accepts that a trick is a trick and not a miracle, not
reality, and applauds the ILLUSION that cannot be denied
while knowing it is a RUSE. In the case of *real* self-deception
the viewer insists that there is no RUSE, that ILLUSION is
Reality; nowhere is this more evident than in the arts. Samuel
Taylor Coleridge poetically called such cheating "the willing
suspension of disbelief." Without such an act much of the
magic of the arts would be lost, the ILLUSION torn aside to
reveal the RUSE. Yet over the centuries these ILLUSIONS
have become so accepted, so delightful, so *real,* that few
viewers consider that much of art is built on cunning RUSES.

In some cases, film, for example, the ILLUSION of movement is achieved by a physiological RUSE: the eye sees movement as the frames flicker by and cannot detect each flicker
even by an act of will. In other cases, the prepared mind is so
prepared that it is all but impossible, for example, not to see
depth in a realist painting, although the eye *knows* that such
perspective is an ILLUSION. And in many cases, the prepared mind chooses to accept the ILLUSION—that the hoof
beats of the Lone Ranger's Great Horse, Silver, on the radio
are real, or that Clark Gable is Rhett Butler standing before a
real Tara plantation. In some cases a character, such as Sher-
lock Holmes, becomes realer than real, an ILLUSION all but
transformed into Reality.

> Those things that are most real
> are the illusions I create in my
> paintings.
>
> —DELACROIX, *Journal*

All pictorial representations are demonstrably false—ILLU-
SIONS, the most false of all are those professing to be "realistic," to be truly representing real objects (nudes or apples or
seascapes). A picture plane is flat, there is no depth except
what the painter tricks the eye into accepting; but the eye,
not by inclination but by training, is eager to seize the ILLU-
SION. And then, having been satisfied, inclined to deny that
there is any RUSE. This is true not only with depth but with
all aspects of "realistic" painting. In nineteenth-century
paintings, tree trunks *obviously* were brown as they were in
nature. A new realist, who painted outside from real tree
trunks, was forced to place a violin against the trunk to show
that tree trunks were not brown; rather, the conventions of
painting made them brown and the viewer preferred to accept the evidence of the inside easel rather than that of his

own eyes outside. In any case, the more "lifelike" the painting or sculpture, the more false is the image. The only painting that is realistic has been developed in the twentieth century with nonobjective art (various schools of "abstract"—Picasso or Leger or the Fauves, still create ILLUSIONS, even if in Cubism space is flattened out almost to the picture plane). In nonobjective art some works are clearly of geometrical origin (stripes or circles) and a few of these make use of human physiology to give an illusion of movement or in a few cases, nausea (real, not aesthetic) but most remain geometrical. They are squares of paint on flat canvas. The other tendency is not to produce any recognizable forms (the eye may see clouds but the painter is not painting illusions of clouds) so that the painting is itself alone. That is all there is to a work by Jackson Pollock or Franz Kline—paint and canvas, the shapes are themselves, nothing more. There is no attempt at creating an ILLUSION. There is no "picture" in the traditional Western sense: one of the reasons that the average viewer finds it so difficult to *see* what modern painters are about.

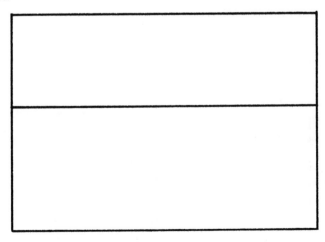

There is no difficulty in seeing that this drawing is *only* a line across a white picture plane. Even when the line is entitled *Horizon,* the eye can choose or not to see depth.

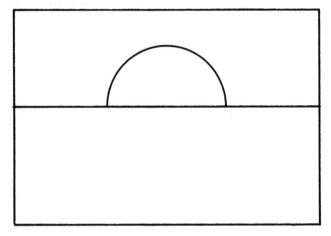

When a half circle is added to the line (and no mention of a horizon) the eye can refuse to consider depth. When the drawing is entitled *Sunrise,* the first response is to see depth—the viewer looking uphill (the ILLUSION) to the setting sun. With some but not much effort the picture plane can be returned to a flat surface—a line and a half circle.

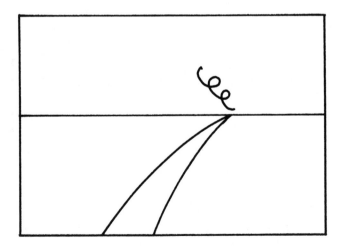

Without a title it is possible to see this as a picture plane divided by a straight line with two curved lines in the bottom half and a squiggle in the top. Once, however, the viewer discovers that the title of the drawing is *The 7:15 Commuter Train Seen at 7:16,* it is almost impossible to avoid the ILLUSION of depth.

The innocent viewer seldom realizes that these ILLUSIONS may actually create his idea of reality. Greek columns are made to seem straight by widening them slightly at the top. The flag of the French Republic with its three vertical stripes of blue, white, and red seems to be a banner divided into three equal parts. This is not so, for the nature of the human eye requires that for the stripes to *look* equal they must have a width-ratio of 30 to 33 to 37 for the blue, white, and red. Many contemporary artists are aware of the nature of illusions, and in fact fashion art works in comment on this. A Jasper Johns sculpture looks exactly like a Ballantine Ale can until one gets close and realizes it is painted bronze. A similar approach was taken by the French painter René Magritte in his "The Wind and the Song." His drawing of a pipe is labeled, quite accurately, "This is not a pipe." It is a few lines on a flat plane that the viewer *insists* is a pipe and can not make his eye flatten out into a completely abstract shape. Magritte's most famous work involves paintings of impossible real-life visions crafted with great "realist" care—an illusion presenting the viewer with an ILLUSION inside it.

Like the Op artists, who can make the viewer physically dizzy by recourse to physiological knowledge, other artists confound the eye with "impossible" ILLUSIONS. Dutch printmaker M. C. Escher was fascinated by such visual ILLUSIONS. Until his death in 1972, he produced a magic world of delightful yet somewhat disturbing woodcuts and lithographs depicting metamorphoses between living beings and inanimate objects, topological tricks (such as his giant ants crawling on an endless Möbius strip), and bizarre symmetries such as those in his most famous work, *Day and Night,* which is a strange mirror-image that vibrates with reversed meaning, regardless of which side of the picture you look at first.

Of all Escher's works, the most unusual are those in his series called *Impossible Buildings.* One, titled *Waterfall,* at first glance appears to show a pleasing old-fashioned waterwheel. Then, while the eye scans, it becomes bizarre for, although the water flows downhill at every point in its course, the stream comes full circle to discharge itself at the *top* of the wheel. It is the perfect plan for a perpetual-motion machine.

In *Belvedere,* the best-known of his Impossible Buildings, Escher proves he fully understood how he got his ILLUSIONS. A clown sitting at the base of this odd structure is seen puzzling over an equally odd cube. This, as Escher knew, is a geometrical curiosity called the Penrose Square.

The Penrose Square is the prototype of Escher's Impossible Buildings. It is also the prototype for an entire class of visual ILLUSIONS. Conventional landscape and still-life paintings seek on a two-dimensional surface to give the illusion of a third dimension, depth. Depth is simulated by various art conventions, including overlapping figures, deepening tones, and the use of lines that converge at infinity creating the illusion of perspective. The wondrous thing about the Penrose Square is that it is, indeed, only a triangle square, but one that *looks* as if it *should* be a cube. It is deceptive because its incongruity lies in the fact that it is a two-dimensional object that cannot exist in three dimensions. Thus, while Escher's *Waterfall* is indeed a perfect two-dimensional plan for a perpetual-motion machine, it cannot be transformed into a three-dimensional working model.

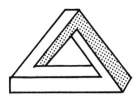 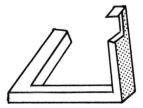

Architects, like painters and sculptors, sometimes create visual ILLUSIONS. Unlike painters and sculptors, however, they need not do so, as their structures are "real." Architectural ILLUSION is only an afterthought.

By siphoning two million *livres* ($15 million) out of the treasury, Louis XIV's superintendent of finance, Nicholas Fouquet, in the seventeenth century erected at suburban Vaux-le-Vicomte the finest château in all France. The house itself was magnificent, and the garden was vast, stretching over two miles from the front door. Landscaped by André Le Nôtre, the distinguished designer of the Jardin des Tuileries, the gardens at Vaux-le-Vicomte provided an extraordinary illusion. By means of an ingenious system of perspective applied to the waterways, pools, fountains, and shrubs, a person walking away from the château got the illusion that it remained close.

The housewarming in 1661 included King Louis XIV, who, noting that Fouquet's home was finer than his own and learning that it had been paid for by treasury funds, had the show-off arrested three weeks later by the musketeer D'Artagnan on charges of embezzlement. By expropriating Fouquet's shrubbery, statuary, architects, and team of 900 artists, masons, sculptors, tapestry weavers, and carpenters, the king outdid Fouquet by building the palace of Versailles.

Sir Christopher Wren was a true Renaissance man and one

of England's finest minds. He made major contributions to mathematics, astronomy, physics, and even physiology; but his enduring fame is as England's greatest architect. When frustrated and plagued by lesser minds in the accomplishment of his building projects, he never showed anger, never once in his ninety-one years exercising the prerogative of the architect-engineer to utter a curse. What he could not win by sheer force of authority he won by tactful agreement, followed by simply going ahead and doing it his way. By whatever sly means, he always had his way.

To celebrate his election to Parliament in 1688, Wren built a handsome new town hall for the city of Westminster, a section of London. The Mayor, however, was nervous. He feared that the upper floor, a meeting hall, might crash in upon his ground-floor office. The mayor demanded two additional stone columns to give extra support. Although Wren knew they were structurally unnecessary and mere aesthetic clutter, he complied. The mayor could look up at the massive columns, reassured of his safety and that of his official family. Neither the mayor nor anyone else realized that it was all a practical joke—an ILLUSION. Not until two and a half centuries later did workmen on a high scaffold observe that the columns supported nothing: they stopped just short of the ceiling.

Wren repeated this hoax when supervising the construction of the guildhall in Windsor (designed by Sir Thomas Fitch). Under pressure by the city council to add extra columns on the open ground floor, Wren finally complied, but again the columns were dummies. Mostly, however, as in the case of the gardens at Vaux-le-Vicomte, the ILLUSION is open, the RUSE known, but the eye tricked into accepting it—architectural magic. In the Palazzo Spada in Rome, Francesco

Borromini created an ingenious ILLUSION (an architectural trompe l'oeil) by the use of perspective within a bit of waste-space in the garden adjoining the Palazzo Massari. The depth of the resulting visual tunnel is multiplied more than four times by Borromini's use of light and the spacing of columns to enhance perspective. Standing in front of the tunnel the delighted eye refuses to accept the *real* space. It is not so much a case of the willing suspension of disbelief as it is the case of being offered a RUSE impossible to refuse.

All literature is ILLUSION as well. This is true not only of fiction but of nonfiction. The written word necessarily distorts the reality it attempts to depict because of two profound limitations inherent in the medium. First, words are only approximate representations of their real-world models. Second, language is linear and one-dimensional. We take language so much for granted that it comes as a surprise if we confront its real nature. For example, what do you see in the following figure?

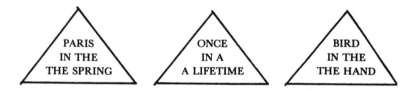

Did you notice the redundant article? The article appeared twice in each phrase ("the the," "a a"), but few readers notice. Psychologist Richards J. Heuer, Jr., writes, "This is commonly overlooked, because perception is influenced by our expectations about how these familiar phrases are normally written."

Words are abstractions and therefore necessarily only partial representations at best. And what of the linear nature of writing—all writing, whether left-to-right, like English, right-to-left, like Hebrew, or top-to-bottom, like Chinese; whether set down in letters, characters, or hieroglyphs. Our thoughts can, perhaps, sometimes be less linearly structured, as when in moments of insight we simultaneously entertain two or more images. But when we attempt to verbalize those images we must do so word-by-word-by-separate-word across time. Language is, if you will, a kind of one-dimensional Penrose Line striving to create the ILLUSION of a Penrose Square trying, in turn, to represent some real three-dimensional object or event.

Puns and paradoxes are literary devices that exist only in language. They do not exist in nature, which is never ambiguous and cannot be paradoxical. The pun implies an ambiguous reality, the paradox an impossible one; but the incongruity in both cases is purely literary. Incongruity cannot exist outside our minds.

Words can only suggest the images, smells, tastes, and feel of a scene, an object, or a person. Thus, all attempts to portray character necessarily fall short of depicting a whole person. At most we get what the author chooses as the "relevant" facts, but relevancy is in turn determined on the basis of some abstract theory about the nature of character. Whether they are the stick-figure fictions of hack writers or the richly textured portraits by the greats, all characters are incomplete vignettes, ILLUSIONS accepted by the reader as real.

Life does not have a story line or plot. These exist only in literature to satisfy our strongly ingrained aesthetic or moral need for things to be tidy or fitting or dramatic. The English short-story writer W. Somerset Maugham defined the short-story genre as a story with a beginning, a middle, and an end. Here again is a linear development that does not necessarily match reality. The same is true regarding our need for happy or tragic endings, when life provides few endings ("catastrophes") and fewer of those few that are anything more than happy or tragic episodes.

All detective fiction is deliberately deceptive in plot as well as substance. The plot is a RUSE and its structure is intended to deceive the reader. This is true of all mystery stories and spy thrillers that are not mere adventure narratives. The writer is the deception planner and the reader his or her target. The author manipulates the clues to the puzzle in precisely the same way any other deceiver does.

In the simplest format, most common in the detective short story, the solution depends on identifying the one suspect that possesses the opportunity, a motive, or some special capability—such as sufficient strength to move the corpse—that draws suspicion. Red herrings abound, becoming usually little more than "noise" in which the one crucial clue is buried, barely noticed. These are gimmick stories. The more sophisticated stories and novels weave a complex set of narratives that are more highly deceptive.

Few mystery writers have a clear notion of how they go about threading in the element of deception that distinguishes their genre of fiction from all others. They are artists, not theoreticians. Even those critics and scholars who have analyzed the field have been unable to spell out anything more than a few crude guidelines about building suspense and camouflaging clues. The mystery field, large and popular as it is, has no theory of deception. But it could.

The single most insightful remark about the deceptive element in the field was made back in 1948 by one of the master mystery writers, Raymond Chandler. This British-born American said, "The most effective way to conceal a simple mystery is behind another mystery. This is literary legerdemain. You do not fool the reader by hiding clues or faking character à la Christie but by making him solve the wrong problem."

Chandler's statement not only suggests an analogy between mystery plotting and the magician's sleight of hand but goes one sure step further to identify *what* must be done; namely, making the reader solve the wrong mystery. Chandler only just missed telling us *how* to achieve this goal. As with most other forms of deception, the detective story depends on blending hiding and showing. In this case, the clues to the real narrative are hidden while the clues to the cover story are prominently displayed.

Three exceptionally good recent examples of sheer misdirection in the thriller genre are Len Deighton's *The Ipcress File* (1962), Nicholas Luard's *The Orion Line* (1976), and Charles McCarry's *The Secret Lovers* (1977). These have added interest because each author had himself served as a professional intelligencer before turning to the writing of thrillers. Deighton was in Air Intelligence in the R.A.F. Special Investigations Branch from 1947 to 1949; Luard was in a British army special sabotage and intelligence unit that took part in clandestine border operations during the 1956 Hungarian Revolution; and McCarry was in the CIA, from 1958 to 1967, as an intelligence officer in Africa and Asia.

The theater represents another accepted ILLUSION, the audience knowing that the play is not the real thing but only a "pretend." Erasmus noted, "To destroy illusion is to ruin the whole play." The theatergoer accepts with alacrity acts that begin "ten years later" and have fantastical stage sets, rather as operagoers accept that the roles of beautiful young women may be sung by large, middle-aged ladies. Even those most cunning of illusionists, the magicians, tend to suspend their analytical eye when before a legitimate stage.

Accompanied by eleven colleagues, the American master magician Dr. Harlan Tarbell attended a performance in the nineteen-twenties of *The Charlatan,* starring Frederick Tilden as Count Cagliostro, the famed eighteenth-century alchemist. They sat in the audience, amused by the melodrama and the several simple tricks (recognized RUSES) used by Tilden to enliven his show. Then, suddenly, the villain, a lawyer, maneuvered the hero into a dilemma where Cagliostro must either back down in disgrace or accept a challenge by his enemy to a public test of his magician's skills under conditions risking almost certain exposure.

Cagliostro, like Houdini two centuries later, accepts the challenge. In full view of the villain and his gang of skeptics, the magician displays his apparatus: a handful of sand, a flowerpot of clear glass, a tall paper cone, and a seed. The lawyer carefully inspects each of these items and shows them to his cronies (and to the audience beyond the proscenium). They are plainly exactly what they seem to be and otherwise empty. Cagliostro then proceeds to pour the sand into the pot, plant the seed in it, cover it with the cone, and step back. The lawyer again rudely intervenes to verify that he has not been tricked. Cagliostro then steps forward and confounds his enemy by raising the magic cone to reveal a full-grown rosebush.

While the rest of the audience cheered Cagliostro's vindication, the twelve magicians sat amazed. They had come expecting to watch an actor use a few obvious old tricks but saw instead a new master magician so skilled that he had sur-

prised even them with a great innovation in the otherwise
jaded "Indian Mango Tree" ILLUSION.

The professional magicians simply could not detect how
Tilden had done this trick without the usual recourse either
to an assistant who covertly passes the flowerbush to the conjurer or to some gimmicked container from which the conjurer, working alone, produces it. Some wholly new principle
seemed involved. Confronted after his performance, Tilden
was delighted but surprised that he had deceived a panel of
experts. He frankly confessed that he was *only* an actor, and
cheerfully explained his "obvious" deception plan.

Tilden knew better than the magicians how thoroughly a
theater audience can be led to "suspend disbelief." So Tilden,
as actor, had audaciously and blatantly chosen the enemy of
the hero for his assistant. Thus the lawyer, while checking
Cagliostro's apparatus to "verify" it was empty, simultaneously, as Tilden's fellow actor, "loaded" the empty paper
cone. Tilden's variation on the old Mango Tree trick used the
usual assistant but masked this fact by a psychologically deceptive twist. While most magician's assistants are overtly
part of the act, a special subtype called the confederate is not.
Tilden's innovation was to apply the accepted theatrical convention of actor/role to blend his actor-assistant with his role-
villain, to give Tilden a psychologically invisible confederate.
Tilden was not attempting to fashion a Ruse-within-a-Ruse
to fool any potential magicians in the audience but simply to
create an EFFECT that the average viewer would accept as a
magical ILLUSION.

If the theater is an ILLUSION, how much more so are
radio plays, where the only channel is sound. If deprived of
sight, we are peculiarly subject to illusion when confronted
with a theatrical production; it is, so to speak, theater for the

blind. We then depend only on our sense of hearing, and that is our most deceptive sense. Radio drama (indeed any kind of all-sound production) is the ideal example. The sound effects are recordings or gadgets. A technician in the studio shakes a sheet of stiff steel and the radio listener hears thunder; inverted cups struck in a certain rhythm upon a board are perceived by the unaided ear as the beat of horses' hooves. The actors too can easily create ILLUSIONS on radio that are not possible on stage or TV. The audience hears a large cast of characters, but it is only three or four actors, each simulating two or more speakers by merely changing voice. The audience hears a young boy—his voice is simulated by a grown woman. Mel Blanc was "the man of a thousand voices," including Bugs Bunny, Sylvester, and Tweety Bird in the cartoons. BBC radio audiences of the 1950's heard, say, the comic character of Bluebottle on *The Goon Show* and seldom realized that this part (and others) was freely traded off among the three talented Goons (Peter Sellers, Spike Milligan, and Harry Secombe). Radio can even transmute fiction into nonfiction. Fancy becomes perceived as fact. This was proved most dramatically one Sunday night in 1938 when Orson Welles created an ILLUSION so much more realistic than even he intended that this accidental effect usually is mislabeled as one of the all-time great hoaxes.

Orson Welles was then a gifted young actor and stage director. CBS broadcast his repertory company, The Mercury Theater, for one hour every Sunday evening. For its next show, the company wanted to perform the famous science fiction tale by H. G. Wells about an invasion from Mars, *The War of the Worlds.* The company puzzled over how best to translate this bit of nineteenth-century narrative into a radio play. In the process of revision to become Welles's radio script, Wells's short story emigrated from Britain to America in both setting and language, was updated to take place in the near future, and was entirely rewritten into a documentary format, specifically as a simulated news event.

The live broadcast on October 30 began with its standard identifying announcement and theme music, then segued into a fictitious orchestra said to be playing in the ballroom of the Park Plaza Hotel (which did not then exist in New York City). Thenceforth, except for the regular commercial breaks with their reidentifications of the true program, the "ballroom music" was periodically interrupted by "news bulletins" and "eyewitness reports from the field" that told a fast-breaking story of the conquest of the American East Coast by invaders from Mars.

One would think that this mix of the real and expected with documentary-type "news" would have kept the ILLUSION within rational bounds, but it did not. The normally more popular Edgar Bergen–Charlie McCarthy show playing opposite featured an unknown singer and hundreds of thousands switched dials in time to catch just the simulated news bulletins. Even thousands of regular Mercury Theater fans were gradually taken up in the ILLUSION. Police and radio stations were flooded with calls and thousands began evacuating their homes. The producers had not intended that the radio-ruse be bought as reality instead of ILLUSION, but in this case disbelief had hardened into certainty.

In the case of films there are no real people on stage or real sounds coming out of a radio but merely frames of film rushing past at speed with appropriately dubbed sounds. Yet here, too, the audience makes believe for the course of the film, small children are *really* frightened of Frankenstein, women cry at the death of the heroine, boys feel bigger, and a young man falls in love with the girl star Jodie Foster of *Taxi*

Driver and went out and shot the President to impress her. Even those films attempting to be most realistic are subject to the same artificial limitations of plot and characterization common to the novel. Some of the more elegant directors in the history of cinema have used film not simply to create a special effect, an ILLUSION of stopped time or stream of consciousness, but rather to make it obvious to the viewer that the medium was illusory. René Clair, the French poet and director noted, "The cinematic art starts with illusion." Why show a door closing, if it is enough to hear it slam? As a critic noted, Clair was involved in a process of pictorial and aural forgery and the result was more compelling as ILLUSION than the films of the realists.

In that most abstract of the arts, music, there may be a place for odd tricks played on the ear or ILLUSIONS that sounds made by instruments mimic those of nature; but, by and large, music is what it is, like nonobjective painting. Yet while there are only rare musical forgeries, this too is an ILLUSION, for the nature of sound is such that we identify Beethoven's Fifth Symphony or the Beatles' "Yellow Submarine" by recalling sounds past and anticipating sounds to come. When the music is very alien to us, from Asia or the Middle East, this identification is difficult because the music often sounds to the Western ear like noise, not melody.

If art is all ILLUSION, aesthetic forgery, then there is some comfort in considering that science seeks the truth, reality, that both scientific practitioners and observers regard self-deception as a potential disaster on the road to discovery. Scientists at all times and places have, like most humans, been deceived by their own arrogance and pride, their commitment to the comfortable, their reluctance to speculate further than the first triumph. If a major scientific theory represents the conventional wisdom, most scientists will first try to discard contradictory discoveries or reluctantly attempt to fit them into the existing framework rather than discard the received wisdom. The dream of the artist is to make something new, but the flawed scientist does the reverse, often seeking to avoid the new under the assumption that reality is already to hand. In fact much of Western science is constructed on several assumptions—that the universe is complex but not malicious; that there is a real, explicable reality; that the rules don't change; that the simplest explanation is best (probably right—a variant of Occam's Razor). When there are too many "facts" to fit a theory comfortably, there is an uneasy feeling: since the universe is not malicious then the existing explanation is not simple enough, not adequately elegant—something is wrong. Cheating is not an intention of the scientific method, whereas it is the only means of the artist. The scientist's ILLUSIONS may be more compelling than reality, but they are still ILLUSIONS, cheating by mutual consent.

CHAPTER 10

Hoaxes and Self-deception in Art and Science

♦ ♦ ♦

I am grateful that I fooled the
experts and convinced them, if
anonymously, that I was a worthwhile artist and not a picture-
postcard sketch artist.

—HANS VAN MEEGEREN
(Dutch art faker)

IN THE WORLD of willingly suspended disbelief, the cheat
sneaks in on tippy toes. There is almost no recorded classical
disc that has not been run through the mix repeatedly to
erase the errant (artificial is better, live is error pocked). To
make takes *better,* greater and greater liberties are taken with
reality, ILLUSIONS are proffered. Audrey Hepburn did not
sing the songs in the film *My Fair Lady,* Natalie Wood did not

sing her songs in *West Side Story,* and Deborah Kerr did
not sing hers in *The King and I.* Young opera singers are
brought into recording sessions, sworn to secrecy, to sing the
high notes that famous older singers can no longer manage.
And these are just adjustments; most rock music exists only in
dubbing and mixing studios, and even the live music concerts
are electronic (not to mention light and flash) shows. The
audience may know this is the case—and much of the audience seldom has heard real musicians, playing real music, in
real halls without electronic aids. But this is the system. No
one *feels* cheated even if the edge of conventional ILLUSION
has been breached. The record of Beethoven's Fifth is not a
fake ILLUSION to most listeners but only a more effective
ILLUSION, yet the RUSE has been doubled: not only is the
nature of music and the recording art involved but also the
restructuring of the real to add to the ILLUSION.

Once the first small steps have been taken, the rush downhill to deceit and outright cheating, not only in terms of the
medium but in terms of reality, follows. The very cunning let
others run off while they stay at the top of the hill cashing
checks. Salvador Dali, one of the most famous of contemporary artists, as far as the more stringent critics are concerned,
has painted nothing of consequence for a generation and perhaps little of significance even before that. Yet he has become
an industry, enormously popular for good reasons, and well
paid—an old man incapable of managing his affairs or lifting
a brush. As the years have passed Dali has devised a means to
let others cheat on his behalf. Year after year he signed blank
sheets of paper—what easy, profitable work it was. For example on 3 May 1973 it was confirmed that he had signed four
thousand sheets weighing 760 pounds. The next year French
customs stopped a truck loaded with 40,000 sheets of blank

paper. What Dali was doing was allowing others to cheat with his name. The signature was real but everything else imprinted on the paper was a fake: color reproductions dusted with gilt but with an *authentic* Dali signature. Dali cheated himself in destroying the reality of his work. More to the point, the potential buyers were going to cheat themselves in accepting that the signature was more important than the art work. Dali was allowing anyone to "make" a Dali. In an almost reverse ruse the great Italian surrealist De Chirico, who had switched from an avant-garde painting style to romantic fantasies, despised by the critics and his previous public, repeatedly denied the authenticity of his earlier paintings. Did you buy an early De Chirico? He disclaimed it. Painters with a vast output often forget what is theirs and what is not. Picasso was an example of this. But De Chirico knew more or less what was his.

At least Dali and De Chirico were involved with real (more or less) art. In the arts and sciences, as elsewhere, there are those quite willing not to slip in on tippy toes but simply to cheat. Mostly in painting, the cheaters tend to mimic the real, showing realistic illusions rather than inventing an entirely new body of work.

The famous mid-nineteenth-century French landscape painter, Gustave Courbet, was extraordinarily prolific. Valued in their own day, thousands of his paintings are preserved in numerous public and private art collections. But most of the estimated 28,000 paintings attributed to him are fake. Whatever the true number of counterfeits, Courbet holds the world's record as the most-often-faked artist. Because his signature always commanded a good price Courbets have been faked for over a century. Also he was easy to copy.

There are too many Courbets. There are also too many

paintings bearing the signatures of Vermeer, Picasso, Matisse, Utrillo, and Corot. Anything of value will be faked, if it can be faked or, rather, if someone can figure out how he can do it. And some forgers are very, very good as painters but are just not too original.

A magnificent oil painting was reported discovered in a Paris attic in 1937. The prestigious Boymans Museum in Rotterdam purchased *Christ and the Disciples at Emmaus* for 550,000 guilders ($270,000) after it had been judged by top experts to be a genuine work by the seventeenth-century Dutch master, Jan Vermeer. Vermeer's reputation shot up and some critics began comparing him with Rembrandt. What joy then in the art world when several other lost Vermeers appeared during the war. *The Blessing of Isaac* and *Last Supper* went to private collectors for $500,000 and $800,000. *Christ's Ablution* fetched a similar sum and went on public display in Amsterdam's Rijksmuseum. *Christ and the Adulteress* was sold for $850,000 to the avid German art connoisseur, Hermann Göring, who proudly displayed it in his lavish Karenhall estate outside Berlin. This purchase eventually led to an investigation that solved the mystery of the source of these "lost" paintings.

After World War Two Reichsmarschal Göring was tried for war crimes by the Allied authorities in occupied Germany. Göring's huge art collection became fair game for recovery by the original owners. It became evident that Göring was less a gourmet of art than a gourmand, who greedily extorted many of his finer pieces. During this recovery scramble, the Dutch government claimed the Vermeer as its own and demanded punishment of all Dutch citizens connected with the sale of this national treasure.

One Dutchman brought to trial in 1945 was an obscure,

fifty-six-year-old painter named Hans van Meegeren. He admitted he not only had informed the Nazis of the whereabouts of *Christ and the Adulteress* but had also acted as middleman in arranging the sale. Given the evidence and his own confession, Van Meegeren's sly defense was that he was not guilty of collaboration because he had cheated the Nazis by selling a worthless painting. He then told the incredulous court that he, van Meegeren, had painted *Christ and the Adulteress*. Moreover, he disclosed that he was the painter of all the recently "discovered" Vermeers. To prove this claim, he offered to paint one more "new" Vermeer. In his own studio, under police guard and watched by art experts, he proceeded to do just this. The art world was stunned and the court convicted him only of "forgery" and sentenced him in 1947 to a mere twelve months in prison. He died two weeks later of influenza, his nearly $3 million net profit still in a Swiss bank account.

Before he died, van Meegeren fully disclosed (to those who would pay) why and how he had carried out his giant hoax. Frustrated, he said, by lack of recognition, "I conceived the idea that I would copy the style of a great painter and duplicate it so perfectly that the imperious rulers of the art world would accept it as genuine." He selected Vermeer because, "He was a great, although lesser-known artist. Little mention of Vermeer is in the books. Unlike other artists whose works are catalogued, Vermeer can have many 'lost' paintings newly discovered. Also unlike Da Vinci or Rembrandt, the experts are not that familiar with Vermeer. It is easy to fool them with a Vermeer."

Van Meegeren knew that any work purporting to be a Vermeer would receive the closest critical examination and a battery of modern laboratory tests, including microscopic analysis, infrared photography, X-rays, quartz lamps, and chemical analysis. Each of these tests was designed to detect fraud by detecting one or more of the incongruities that distinguish every false object from its real model. He managed to circumvent all of these potential pitfalls. He did not copy, mimic, existing *works* (doubles lead to the inevitable conclusion that one is a fake) but freely "created" new or "lost" works in the *style* of Vermeer. To do this he drew upon his background as an art historian and closely studied all available Vermeers in galleries and equally carefully researched the techniques and materials available to a seventeenth-century painter in Delft.

To fabricate his first masterpiece, *Christ and the Disciples at Emmaus,* van Meegeren purchased a large oil, *Resurrection of Lazarus,* by a minor seventeenth-century artist. He then cleaned off most of the original artist's paint to get an authentic canvas that would pass microscopic test. He even left several patches of the old painting that he could work his own paints around. These original pigments would, of course, be fully authenticated by X-ray and chemical tests.

In addition van Meegeren took great care in forging his own paints. Using the same techniques as Vermeer, he made green by grinding up lapis lazuli, radiant red from the dehydrated bodies of the Mexican cochineal beetle, and added white lead to brighten the hues of other colors. To create darker hues and shadings, he even added mud, as had Vermeer. These carefully forged paints would also pass the chemical tests.

Finally, he baked his painting to give it the hardness of dried-out old paint. This would get it past the hardness test. Thorough drying also simulated the "Rembrandt patina" or *craquelure,* that minute crackle in all old dried oils. This would pass microscopic examination.

When he deemed his painting fit to pass, he approached a leading art attorney with the lie that he was acting for a famous European family that, having fallen on hard times, wished to sell a few Vermeers in their collection but would only do so under guarantee of anonymity. All payments would be made directly to Van Meegeren as their sole agent. "That," as the forger explained, "is how they were sold and how I received my payments." Van Meegeren's fourteen forgeries had passed all the anticipated tests.

If van Meegeren was the master forger of one Flemish painter, de Hory was the master of many French moderns. Moreover, he was the most wide-ranging art forger of all time. Until 1946, Elmyr de Hory, a well-born forty-year-old Hungarian expatriate living in Paris, had little success in selling his own rather unimaginative painting. That year, Lady Malcolm Campbell mistook an unsigned de Hory drawing for a Picasso and bought it from him for £40 sterling. When he learned his "Picasso" had fetched £150 sterling from a London art dealer, de Hory turned to counterfeiting high-priced, modern French works on a very large scale. He did it to make money and to prove to himself that he was a fine painter.

His repertoire spread from drawings and gouaches to lithographs and oils and from Picasso to Matisse, Rénoir, Modigliani, Derain, Vlaminck, Braque, Bonnard, Dégas, Laurencin, Cézanne, Dufy, Chagall, Léger, van Gogh, Toulouse-Lautrec, van Dongen, Marquet, and Gauguin. Sales were made to leading galleries on every continent except Australia. The only major artists that de Hory never painted were Klee (not, to de Hory's mind, "a great painter"), Utrillo, Corot (already overcopied), and Miró ("Even the real Mirós look like fakes.").

De Hory lived high on his fraud, although systematically

fleeced by his even less scrupulous agent-managers. Then, in 1968, he was finally exposed; he had left a trail of clues too long and too easy to follow. Although he had a good eye for the styles and techniques of those he imitated, some experts began to recognize his own style underlying the others. Also, he and his agents were often too impatient for quick profit to brother with the right paper, canvas, stretchers, or paints. Hounded by his litigious agents and fearing extradition to France, the cheat killed himself in 1976 with an overdose of barbiturates.

During his twenty-two-year career at art fakery de Hory produced and sold over one thousand counterfeits. Since his death his forgeries have become collectors' items in their own right. Today, with de Hory's real signature of "authentification" on the back, they sell for from $800 for small drawings up to $10,000 for major oils. The present market value of this master forger's life work has been estimated at over $30 million.

Although de Hory revealed all his secrets when caught, he admitted that in his heyday in the mid-1960's, "I did get a little bit annoyed" when New York painter David Stein pleaded guilty to counterfeiting works by Picasso, Matisse, and Chagall and revealed how he preferred Lipton's tea for "aging" paper and how he used a sunlamp to dry his watercolors. "I thought," de Hory complained, "that's very indiscreet to give away so many trade secrets. Now everybody's going to jump on the bandwagon!"

When not pressed to make a quick sale, de Hory took much care to make his counterfeits look authentic. He studied originals in museums and galleries and photographic blow-ups to get the brush strokes and paint thickness just right. He used the best Lefranc colors and matched these to the paints peculiar to particular artists. He bought yellowing and properly watermarked prewar paper. When he couldn't get the prewar paper he would buy new but old-style paper. He bought old oil paintings from the Flea Market and, using an alkali solution, cleaned off the worthless painting to get an authentic old but blank canvas. To simulate the crackle of old dried oil paints, he used a special restorer's varnish. He had a carpenter copy an authentic prewar French stretcher (the wood frames on which the canvas is stretched before painting) with its distinctive joins and wedges. He would then "age" it with oils and colors.

Art works, particularly works by famous artists, have a history, and history means documentation—bills of sale, certificates of ownership, official stamps, descriptions in auction catalogues, and letters of authentication by well-known critics or the painters themselves. De Hory and his managers and agents made or bought all of these appropriately forged documents. Their most clever method, an entirely original one, began by buying rare art books with tipped-in color prints of masters and a description such as "Modigliani, Reclining Nude, 1918, oil on canvas, 92″ × 118″, signed lower left corner, Private Collection, Paris." De Hory would then paint a work to those specifications, have it photographed and printed on the same paper stock as in the original portfolio and substitute it for the print of the original painting. The unsuspecting buyer got not only a "signed Modigliani" to hang on his wall but an impressive coffee-table book that seemingly proved the picture's fame as well as its authenticity.

The art forgers start with an enormous asset beyond their skills and research. Collectors *want* to possess the rare. The Metropolitan Museum in New York *wanted* to own and display the huge Etruscan warriors that graced their hall, statues far larger in size than any known Etruscan work and statues now withdrawn, almost reluctantly, and banished to the basement, when the Museum finally accepted that they had been made in Italy in this century. People want a Corot or a Rembrandt. Museums want a David. Museums feel they must accept a Uccello of dubious provenance or a Modigliani on the cusp of fakery. The shrewd museumgoer from time to time will notice that the famous David has its title tag changed, that the number of Rembrandts in the Dutch School room has been reduced, that the last generation's purchase is not to be found on display. Greed to have, show, possess is enormous, even on the part of staid institutions, so that stylistic inconsistencies, curious bargains, novel discoveries of lost, unknown work disarm the prepared mind. The avid collector awaits, salivating, the RUSE that will be seized as reality, better to believe and to own and to show *this* Corot than have no Corot at all. It is not even a case of the Italian proverb *"Si no è vero, è ben trovato"* ("If it isn't true, still it's well founded"): even if there is smoke, ignore the fire. I need it: so it *must* be real. The cheater need only satisfy the perceived need with an ILLUSION.

It is not only the great art works, the Vermeers or Picassos, that engender such a perceived need. Anything rare and desirable, beer cans or custom stamps or baseball cards, while hardly art, may attract the forger. In crafts, in applied arts, in any arena where people make special things for special people, the forger lurks, creating ILLUSIONS. As fast as markets develop for antiques and these objects acquire value, the counterfeiters are sure to follow. Modern Egyptian potters have done a thriving business since the 1920's producing "ancient" ceramic jewelry. Greek potters turn out passable imitations of ancient pottery, which is then "discovered" in tombs and other old ruins. Modern Japanese blacksmiths will forge the treasured *katana* or so-called samurai sword, particularly those by the more famous old sword makers like Goro Masamune.

Conversely some *real* objects acquire added value by misrepresentation. Thus, original eighteenth-century Chippendale furniture underwent a revival in England between 1850 and 1870, which produced a flood of reproductions from his *Director.* Today, many of these genuine one-century-old antiques are misrepresented by dealers as genuine two-centuries-old Chippendales. "Real" is relative.

Some objects defy forging because the original technology was so sophisticated that its results can't be duplicated. For example, no one has yet been able to reproduce the finer Chinese Shang Dynasty bronzes. These magnificent cast bronzes have a crispness of detail (due to the "lost wax" process) that defeats the putative forger.

All the old but not yet antique "collectibles" have first their "reproductions" and then, as prices climb, their counterfeits. Revived interest in Art Nouveau in the psychedelic 1960's soon brought about the appearance of fakes on the market. The revival of Art Deco in the 1970's brought fakes with it as well. Interest in American Indian art has choked the market with fakes, some particularly fine ones coming from an artisan in Oregon. A large foundry in San Francisco produces fine replicas of Remington bronzes for the less discriminating.

Cheating with physical things is hardly surprising—art forgeries are an institution in Western society—but it is and has been possible to cheat in all sorts of esoteric fields. Rhetoric, the art of oratory developed by the classical Greeks and perfected by the Romans, has been widely recognized as a vehicle for misleading audiences. The logical errors, false

analogies, and other deceptive practices of rhetoric were recognized at the time. Moreover, as early as the first century
after Christ, the analogy was made explicit between the deceptions of rhetoric and magic, when Seneca the Younger
characterized the conjurer's sleights of hand common in his
day as being similar to oratorical tricks. Both, he wrote, were
"pleasing deceptions, harmless to those who do not know
them, and without interest to those who do." Two centuries
later, Sextus Empiricus drew the same analogy in admitting
he was as deceived by sleight-of-hand performances as he was
by false arguments, "which only have a show of being sound,
although we cannot say exactly where the catch is."

Fallacious, misleading argument is, of course, not a monop-
oly of professional orators. We are all amateurs at this ourselves and either use or are victims of various oratorical tricks.
In the twentieth century the rise of technology has made possible the extension of oratory RUSES, nowhere more effectively than on television, where images are lovingly created.
At least behind the mask or the deceitful mimicking the decent lurks some sort of reality, if unsavory. In written literature—physical things again—pure invention may hold sway.

Entire new works of literature have been counterfeited and
ascribed to a famous author or a newly discovered genius.
Old works are reworked, translated, or copied outright and
ascribed to the plagiarist. And there are always those with a
mind prepared for the new and novel, the undiscovered. First
prize for sheer self-deception must go to the French nineteenth-century autograph collector who paid good money for
a collection of what purported to be Cleopatra's love letters.
The forger had been careful to write them on real papyrus,
but he had written them in French.

One of the first writers of a fiction-as-fact book was a

twenty-five-year-old Frenchman who called himself George Psalmanazar when he appeared in London in 1703. There he posed as a native of the island of Formosa (now Taiwan) and claimed to be a recent convert to Christianity. Psalmanazar did not look "oriental," but this raised no serious question about his imposture because few Europeans of the period had ever met a Chinese or Japanese, much less a Formosan, and the contemporary literary descriptions and illustrations of Far Easterners were about as inexact as those being painted of European travelers at the same time by Japanese and Indian artists. Psalmanazar was invited to Oxford to teach "Formosan," a language he promptly invented, beginning with a fabricated alphabet. This, in turn, enabled him to fulfill his next commission at Oxford, a "translation" of the Holy Bible. Lionized by the curiosity-seeking British aristocracy, Psalmanazar then wrote and in 1704 published *The Historical and Geographical Description of Formosa.* An immediate bestseller, this tome gave credulous Britons an outlandish and entirely imaginary account of the mysterious island. Wined and dined in a manner befitting his assumed role, Psalmanazar finally exposed himself—posthumously, in his last will and testament.

Psalmanazar was essentially interested in his own advancement and his forgeries went down in history as quaint conceits. This is not always the case with literary forgery. In the ninth century, as noted, the *Constitutum Constantini,* the so-called Donation of Constantine, one of the most important political and religious documents for the next nine centuries was published. The 3,000-word document purported to be from Constantine, the first Roman emperor to become Christian and who made Christianity legal throughout the empire. In his supposed Donation, Constantine gave the Pope tem-

poral control over the entire world and secular authority over
Europe, including Constantinople (later called Istanbul). The
document emerged from the archives of the Roman Catholic
Church at a time when Rome was in desperate conflict with
the Eastern Orthodox Church, and several Popes continued
to cite it throughout the Middle Ages in support of their
church's temporal claims. Public doubts about this work's
authenticity emerged in the fifteenth century and gradually
grew until the late eighteenth century, when Voltaire could
call it without scholarly contradiction "that boldest and most
magnificent forgery." One key to the final exposé was that the
Donation referred to New Rome by that name, over a decade
before the real Constantine coined the term in founding his
capital.

The most famous contemporary author of nonreality is
Clifford Irving, whose impact has hardly been as great as that
of the producer of the Donation of Constantine. He is more in
Psalmanazar's class, if not quite so elegant—a true child of his
time. And unlike Psalmanazar's, Irving's RUSE was discovered while he lived. Reflecting nine years later on his world-
famous hoax-autobiography of Howard Hughes, he told
ABC-TV's Pat Collins in 1980 that it had failed because of
poor planning. "It was," he admitted, "a day-to-day adventure. I never knew what was going to happen next. That's no
way to plan a crime." This bit of self-criticism is correct and
his months in prison confirm it. However, despite his ama-
teurishness, Irving nearly got away with the most audacious
and profitable literary hoax of the century.

Irving's disclaimer to the TV viewers of America that he
lacked "a highly developed criminal mind" is too modest. He
had been putting in a certain amount of training in that
direction prior to the Hughes hoax. Irving was not noted for

his truthfulness and was known for covert cheating on his four wives and deceiving his several lovers. An early fascination with the secret and devious world of espionage led him to write his fourth novel, *The Thirty-Eighth Floor,* as a thriller. It had also been overly inspired by his friend Irving Wallace's recent novel, *The Man;* but as Irving's ex-lawyer would later say, Clifford Irving freely "used the friends who had trusted him." On his island home of Ibiza, he was a friend and admirer of Elmyr de Hory and the author in 1969 of the notorious art faker's biography, appropriately titled *Fake!* Moreover, Irving was impressed by de Hory's example of how easy it could be to fool experts. Later, in collaboration with Richard Suskind, he wrote a shoddy nonfiction book on spies, aptly titled *Spy.* Writer-researcher Suskind himself had once drifted close to plagiarism in his nonfiction book on the crusades.

None of Irving's books sold well and he was always short of money, so short that he never got around to paying de Hory his promised half of the royalties for his biography. Irving was now out for big money. When the name of the mysterious Howard Hughes reemerged in the news in late 1970, he sensed that his publishers, McGraw-Hill, would pay big money for the elusive billionaire's autobiography. So Irving decided he would write the autobiography of Hughes in the accepted as-told-to style. Knowing he would never get the cooperation of the subject, he would just have to tell it to himself. He figured that Hughes had withdrawn so much from the world that he would be unlikely to come out of hiding enough to expose the hoax.

Being a bit lazy, Irving enlisted Suskind as his researcher, and between the two they managed to cull much material from old books, news clippings, and government files. Irving, too busy to read or Xerox the materials in the Library of Congress, simply tucked them under his overcoat and walked out. Although this research turned up a mass of data, it was not only stale but entirely lacked the kind of intimate detail that could bring the subject to life. The novelist was quite prepared to invent colorful incidents, but then he got a windfall. On 12 June 1971, Irving got his hands on a draft manuscript of Noah Dietrich's biography of Hughes.

Dietrich had been Hughes's right-hand man for over thirty years, until 1958, when Hughes fired him and went into total seclusion. With Jim Phelan ghosting, Dietrich had produced a rough draft of a biography of Hughes containing a wealth of intimate anecdotes and monologues—just what Irving needed to flesh out his stick-figure picture of Hughes.

Dietrich's manuscript had been "lent" overnight to Irving by Dietrich's literary referral agent, Stanley Meyer. Irving admits that he pirated two unauthorized Xerox copies. Both Meyer and Irving gave sworn testimony that they had met by accident. The fact that Meyer had not only passed this manuscript to Irving without the author's knowledge but also all along had been leaking it chapter by chapter to Hughes's own lawyer suggests some other dark design, one still unexplained.

However he came by it, Irving now had a very big "property" indeed. By the beginning of 1972 his enthusiastic publisher, McGraw-Hill, had paid one "H. R. Hughes" a whopping advance on royalties of $750,000, of which about $50,000 plus $15,000 for "expenses" went directly to Irving as ghostwriter. McGraw-Hill felt safe because they would immediately recoup all that and more with $250,000 from *Life* magazine for serial rights, $400,000 from Dell for the paperback rights, and $325,000 from the Book-of-the-Month Club.

During the year Irving claimed he was interviewing Howard Hughes all over North America, the eccentric principal was holed up twenty-four hours a day in his penthouse suite atop the Britannia Beach Hotel in the Bahamas. To lend plausibility to his interview claim, Irving actually traveled to the pseudo-meeting sites he named. Unfortunately, this alibi began to crumble when Baroness Nina Van Pallandt admitted that during their cozy stay in Oaxaca, Mexico, Irving was away from her once, just once, and then for only two hours, not nearly enough to cover the time he claimed to have spent there with Hughes.

More decisive woman trouble occured when a Swiss bank leaked the crucial information that the "H. R. Hughes" who was busily depositing and cashing McGraw-Hill's checks was female. "H. R. Hughes" was actually Irving's wife, Edith. Using rare published copies of authentic documents bearing Hughes's handwriting, Irving had taught his wife to forge the famous signature. Irving did much better, forging long handwritten letters from "Hughes" to himself and to McGraw-Hill. Not satisfied with some of his early efforts, he later substituted first one, then a second set of better imitations. No one noticed the substitutions and no less than three top document experts passed these forgeries as authentic.

It took the real Mr. Hughes's telephone interview on 7 January 1972 to set investigators really digging. Within two months *The Autobiography of Howard Hughes* was scrapped and Irving, Suskind, and Edith confessed.

Irving's aborted effort triggered a journalistic hunt for other recent literary hoaxes. Reasoning that McGraw-Hill had proven its gullibility with the Irving fiasco, the reporters started their hunt with that publishing house. They soon hit pay dirt when it was discovered that McGraw-Hill's recent best-selling, *Memoirs of Chief Red Fox,* was also a hoax. Its colorful accounts of American Indians, including the infamous Wounded Knee massacre, had come not from the old chief's memory but from a book published in 1940 by Indian expert James McGregor.

The key in both McGraw-Hill dialogues of deceit had been greed. The "authors" were supplying such tempting RUSES that sensible editors looked no further. Certainly there was money to be made in some art frauds; in one special case it was fake tunes to be played, but not for money. Perhaps a new Beethoven symphony or more Bach cantatas might spin off profits somewhere, but in music most cheating is concerned with pirated discs rather than forged compositions. There is, however, one splendid musical hoax, cheating for art's sake.

Fritz Kreisler was the world's most celebrated violin soloist from the end of the nineteenth century until World War Two. While in his early twenties, in Vienna, he decided that the existing repertoire of music for the unaccompanied violin was too small for his big talent. To remedy this perceived deficiency, Kreisler began in the late 1890's to write his own music. However, he chose to ascribe it to the then obscure, long dead composers Couperin, Francoeur, Porpora, Pugnani, and even Vivaldi, claiming that he had personally discovered the manuscripts "in libraries and monasteries while visiting Rome, Florence, Venice, and Paris." Musicologists and music critics at the time judged Kreisler's "discoveries" to be "little masterpieces." They remained undetected and quite unsuspected until 1935, when Kreisler casually confessed his composership to Olin Downes, music critic of *The New York Times*. While most of the duped experts were outraged, the music-loving public took this gentle hoax in high spirits.

Cheating within the arts is based in large part on the desire by the victim to be deceived. It is undertaken for an entire spectrum of reasons, for pleasure and profit, for power, and in God's name. In the sciences there is less scope for deceit. The goal is truth, which may (but seldom does) reward the discoverer with vast sums or enormous prestige. Both are possible. Pure discovery may lead to patents and a Bentley, while Nobel Prize winners are now folk heroes. The temptation in the publish-or-perish world of contemporary research science is there: truth may need a nudge. Gregor Mendel, for example, may have given his statistics a bit of a push in order to get genetics off to a flying start. Some have gone a bit further than nudging.

Sir Cyril Burt died in 1971, acclaimed as the father of British educational psychology. His widely published scholarly research on IQ was powerful ammunition for those who argued that because IQ was strictly inherited, no amount of public monies to upgrade environment or education could raise the IQ of any child—particularly the children of the poor. Sir Cyril's fame and knighthood were based on two major studies. The first reported a forty-year survey of 40,000 London fathers and sons verifying that IQ invariably followed the father's occupational (i.e., class) status. The second and more impressive study was an in-depth account of fifty-three pairs of identical twins who had become separated in childhood, one being raised poor and uneducated, the other well-to-do and with good education. This was an ideal sample because identical twins have identical genes. If the hypothesis that genes alone determine IQ, then such twins will test equal in IQ regardless of any differences in cultural or educational experience. Sir Cyril's twins dramatically confirmed this hypothesis.

In 1976 two American professors exposed both of the late knight's landmark studies as fraudulent. Subsequent investigations in Britain confirmed details of the fraud. The father-son survey had never been made. Of the twins study all data on the twenty-four pairs collected before World War Two had been destroyed in a 1941 German bombing raid and Sir Cyril fabricated his elaborate statistics from memory. The other thirty-two twins he claimed to have studied after the war simply did not exist.

At present the medical research field seems to be undergoing a veritable crime wave of cheating in research. At least eight major scandals were exposed during the seventies and several more are currently being investigated. In all, some thirty researchers have been caught faking data and otherwise cheating on federally funded medical research projects. There was the psychiatrist whose psychoactive drug research "laboratory" contained only two items, a large executive chair for the psychiatrist and a kindergarten chair for his visitors, the last of whom was a Federal Drug Administration auditor who concluded that the doctor had been cheating the FDA for the past seven years. A Boston University researcher faked cancer patients' charts to make it seem they were doing much better than they actually were. A researcher with the Sloan-Kettering Institute for cancer was caught faking skin-graft experiments that "proved" cross-species transplants could take. He had simply painted the impressive black spots on his white mice and the white spots on black mice. Investigators suspect that this medical research "crime wave" has been under way for many years but has only come to be recognized because of better reporting during the past decade. Moreover, they admit that the cases detected are probably only a fraction of those that have occurred. The usual explanation is typified by a Massachusetts General Hospital press release, which explained their own recent sorry experience on the grounds of pressure of competition for grant money. However, the cheater himself, Dr. John C. Long, who had reported a "breakthrough" on culturing cancer cells, admitted that it "was the gradual loss of my sense of responsibility as a scientist. Science is based on a sense of trust and I violated that. I simply was impatient to get on . . . so I reported work that I had not done."

The greatest of all known scientific illusions was created not to give truth a nudge or to get ahead but simply as a hoax without authorship. Someone—and after generations of investigation no one is yet sure just who—created an entirely novel type of early man, the Piltdown Man, whose remains indicated a cross between man and a higher ape (not surprising since those were the bones that had been aged, combined with human bones, and planted). A whole generation of physical anthropologists struggled to fit the Piltdown man into their evolutionary schemes before the ruse was revealed. Aesthetically it was a triumph far beyond "breakthroughs" that cannot be repeated in other laboratories or "inventions" that fail in field tests.

Inventions, often not very "scientific," are always a means to rewards because they are likely to fill a perceived need, just like a Corot, and are snatched up as illusions. Gullible citizens and governments have squandered fortunes in the elusive search for such impossible discoveries and inventions. This search began with the belief of the medieval alchemists that they could transmute lead to pure gold. All they needed was the "philosophers' stone." And not a few charlatans claimed to have produced it, claims that continued into the early part of this century, to the profit of these pseudo-scientists. As recently as 1974 Dr. Andrija Puharich claimed in print to have seen Uri Geller transmute base metal into gold by sheer "psychic" effort.

Self-proclaimed chemists and physicists have also made money on phony processes for making precious stones such as diamonds and sapphires out of dust and turning water into gasoline. In almost all these cases the trick lies in the ability of the "inventor" to make an unnoticed switch. Put water in the gas tank, crank up the engine, and it fires right up—fed from a small concealed tank of real gas. It helps if the charlatan pretends to paranoid fears that someone will "steal" his secret, thereby giving him plausible excuse for not allowing close examination of his apparatus until after the sale. From the nineteenth century to the present, other inventors have been selling everything from perpetual-motion machines to death rays. Some of these men are quite genuine cranks, sincerely seeking their individual impossible dream. Others are unscrupulous and have not hesitated to supply faked evidence of their success.

In 1916, two years into World War One, with only more futile slaughter facing them on the bloody western front, the British army was interested when a young man showed them blueprints for a death ray. "It'll save a million lives and end the war in ten days," he boasted. He was a twenty-eight-year-old Scot who said he was Dr. James Shearer and had taken his doctorate in the medical-electric field from the University of Washington, D.C. Although dressed as a captain in the Army, he was in fact only a sergeant in the corps, a position that gave him access to the materials to build his cover story of a fake commission with a fake degree from a fake university with fake plans and fake equipment.

A laboratory demonstration was scheduled for a group of

observers ranging from a general down to a single medical laboratory assistant. Shearer set up his bizarre apparatus (patched together from junked X-ray equipment) and placed a caged rabbit at the far end of the lab, some fifty feet away. The general was delayed, but Captain Doctor Shearer insisted the experiment go ahead, arguing that the machine was "warmed up." He pointed it at the rabbit and flipped switches and twirled dials while the machine buzzed and sparked. At first Shearer acted impatient, then apprehensive. Would he succeed, all wondered. Then, after three or four long minutes, triumph! The rabbit suddenly squealed, collapsed, twitched, and died.

As the impressed observers left the room, the young lab assistant casually picked up the dead beast and started out. "Bury it," Shearer ordered, as the assistant followed last. Disobeying orders, the curious assistant took the corpse to his own lab where tests soon revealed the true cause of death: strychnine.

Small wonder that Shearer had insisted the "experiment" not await the general. The gelatine capsule containing the lethal poison was timed to dissolve about fifteen minutes after being forced down the animal's throat. It would have been embarrassing had the rabbit died before the machine had even been switched on. The court-martial put Sergeant Shearer in prison for three years. This is the longest recorded sentence ever served for killing a rabbit.

Killing a rabbit, painting another Picasso, buttressing the Rock of Peter with forged parchment, writing new Vivaldi violin pieces, all are RUSES that go forth across the channels of deception with one great asset. The waiting audience, the potential purchasers of the RUSE, has a perceived need—they badly want what they are about to receive. They need the Corot on their wall or the Vivaldi on their phonograph or the ray smashing into the rabbit. And they get it, for their prepared mind is exploited. In the process, money may be made or reputations enhanced. Sometimes no one is the worse off, or the deceived are justly cheated, sometimes not. In the honest arts one must deceive, disbelief must be denied. In the not-so-honest arts and sciences, the cheater has the advantage more often than not. All the people may not be fooled all the time but the right ones are cheated for the desired end. The depressing evidence is that all the people can be fooled some of the time, but a mind prepared to test the ILLUSIONS for RUSE is better prepared for reality than those who, knowing or unknowing, seek to be cheated. There are precautions.

EPILOGUE

Counterdeception

♦ ♦ ♦

Be frustrate all ye stratagems of Hell
And develish machinations come to Nought.

—MILTON, *Paradise Regained*

Basic Principles and Considerations in Matters of Deceit:

1. Those Who Expect To Be Cheated Can Be.
2. Those Who Do Not Expect To Be Cheated Will Be.
3. Those Who Can Not Be Cheated Are Not Worth Cheating.
4. There Is No Free Lunch.
5. A Word To The Wise Is Seldom Sufficient.
6. It Is Not Who Wins Or Loses But The Name Of The Game That Matters.
7. Truth Is The Best Lie.
8. There Never *Has* Been A Free Lunch.

The assumption that someone out there intends to cheat

you is never unwarranted but is not of especial value. *Everyone* has been, can be, or will be cheated and to have a prepared mind may only assure the inevitable. The problem is to discover what is *really* going on, not what seems to be going on. Whole professions and trades do little else than seek reality. Their counterdeception techniques are routine. Lawyers, chemists, physicians, public health experts, police detectives, editors, museum staffs, anthropologists, psychologists, historians, survey researchers, counterintelligence officers, cryptanalysts, and automobile mechanics want the truth, just the truth. When truth seekers fail to detect deceit, murderers walk away from "accidental" deaths, audiences applaud forged dramas, students read faked history, viewers are awed by hoax Picassos, and the innocent clatter down the street in counterfeit Guccis. Carbon dating may expose the Piltdown Man, X-rays the fake sculpture, and lie detectors deceit. Torture may lead to the Truth and chemical analysis to criminal indictment. Yet any system of protection or detection devised in matters of deception can be thwarted. You *can* fool all the people—or certainly the ones that matter. Thus a Prepared Mind must be Pessimistic.

9. To Be Is To Be Cheated.

The process of discovering how one is to be cheated, how one is being cheated, how one will be cheated *(Counterdeception)* may be one small step toward reality.

10. What You See Is Never What You Get.

If nothing more, one can at least know *how* deceit is achieved. Unlike nature, complex but not malicious, cheating is malicious and divisible into nifty categories. All cheaters attempt to mislead about only nine kinds of things singly or in any combination. These are the types of things that can be hidden or shown:

PATTERN
PLAYERS
INTENTION
PAYOFF
PLACE
TIME
STRENGTH
STYLE
CHANNEL

Pattern.   The most comprehensive category is that of pattern. As noted detective-story writer Raymond Chandler said, "The most effective way to conceal a simple mystery is behind another mystery." Specifically, Chandler pointed out, one deceives or cheats by making the victim "solve the wrong problem." In other words, the cheater has created a false pattern, parallel to but different from his real design, and presented it in such a way as to misdirect the victim's attention and interest away from the real pattern.

Players.   Who are the principal characters in the cast, the main actors? And what are their real roles as opposed to their professed ones? Magicians deceive their audiences and gambling sharps their suckers by using confederates. Intelligence services run their agents and confront double agents and triple agents in a bewildering drama where, often enough, no one knows who is friend or foe.

Intention.   This category comprises events, actions, operations or communications, all of which can be hidden or shown. Will a certain event occur? Hitler bluffed Britain and France about his intention to seize the Rhineland and he deceived Poland and Russia about his intention to invade Poland. Similarly, Russia has deceived Japan, Czechoslovakia, and Afghanistan about its intentions to invade. The con man masks his intent to deceive.

Payoff. The cheater can deceive his victim about the ascribed value, the consequence that he assigns to his intended action. Payoff is the value option, that is, the payoff of any intention can be disguised so that it is misperceived as being either relevant or irrelevant. If relevant, then the value of the payoff can be misrepresented as being either higher or lower than it really is. A lure exaggerates value by simulating high payoff where there is little or none.

Place. Where does the action take place? At what point, in what area, from what direction, to what place? Nowhere or somewhere, and if somewhere, then here or there? Wolfe deceived Montcalm about the direction of his secret approach to Quebec in 1759. A radar-jamming screen confuses the enemy about the final target of the incoming bomber wave. Which silo has the real missile, which the dummy? And which walnut shell or which hand hides the con man's pea? A decoy simulates a real target but in an alternative place.

Time. When is the intended event to occur? Never or sometime? And if sometime, then later or earlier? The magician's "one-ahead" trick is an its-later-than-you-think trap, the real trick having already taken place long before the moment it is shown to the audience, who suppose it to have just occurred. The Allies caught the Germans napping on D-Day 1944, Hitler having been deceived into believing the invasion would occur sometime later. The boy who cried wolf unintentionally lulled the shepherds into an its-earlier-than-you-think trap. Similarly, and to the same effect, Hitler deferred his invasion of France in 1940 no fewer than nineteen times.

Strength. What are the capabilities of a player, his degree of coercive power, force structure, amount of clout, level of morale? Is he stronger or weaker than portrayed? Virtually disarmed after the Great War by the Versailles Treaty, Germany at first managed to cheat by hiding some of its military strength, pretending to be weaker than it was. Then, after 1935, Hitler successfully pretended to be stronger than he was to bluff his way to some cheap victories.

Style. How is the thing done? By what procedure, tactics, fashion, or manner? Or by means of what technology, devices, gadgets, gimmicks, weapons, tools? The horse nomad's "Parthian shot" was a surprise in its day. The cheat can be either innovative or conventional in his style yet pretend to be the opposite, thereby unbalancing his victim. Similarly he can appear to be active or passive, cooperative or competitive, aggressive or defensive.

Channel. This is the means for communicating information about the other eight categories. The cheat can sometimes play games about the reliability of the information channels open to his victim, planting false information to make reliable ones seem unreliable and vice versa.

Remember, wandering about with a head full of Payoffs and Patterns, Charcs of Deceit, Dazzling and Decoying, and the odd Deception Loop, remember:

1. It Is No Better To Be Cheated Than To Cheat, And Less Fun.
2. No One Promised Life Would Be Fair.
3. Believers In The Free Lunch Suffer From Indigestion.

4. *Dopo il fatto, il consiglio non vale.* ("After the fact, advice is useless")—Why Didn't Someone Tell Me!

Unfortunately, in cheating:

5. The Mind Prepared To Be Cheated Is Sure To Be Cheated. But Not Every, Every Time.
6. There May Be A Cat In The Bag.

Nature may not cheat but man does—to be human is to cheat and be cheated. The clever mind, prepared or not, can be cheated more easily than the simple. The avaricious mind will cheat itself. The wise mind, here prepared, taking *"consiglio,"* will at least know the rules of the game. Good luck. You might just need it.

Index

Achilles, 19
acoustical deception, magic and, 253–55
Aguinaldo, Emilio, 42–43
Alexander the Paphlagonian, 259
Alexander, Patrick, 364
Alexius I Comnenus, 25, 26
Ali, Muhammad, 313, 314
Allenby, General, 81, 84
"alternative goals," principle of, 40–41
Anderson, John Henry, 259
Angle Principle, 250
Anna Comnena, 26
Apollodorus of Athens, 18
apparel, cheating and, 328–32
architecture, illusion in, 389, 391–93
Argamasilla, Joaquín María, 234
arts
    hoaxes and self-deception in, 403–21
    illusion and reality in, 385–402
    See also painting; theater, *etc.;* names of artists
assassinations, 357–58
Auden, W. H., 335
authorized cheats, 208
Auzinger, Max, 252
Bacon, Friar Roger, 249
baseball, cheating and gambling in, 308–12
Belisarius, 24
Bergen, Edgar, 255
Bernardini, Reverend Domenico, 338–39
Bevan, Colonel J.H. "Johnny," 84
Bible, guile in, 17
Binet, Alfred, 46
Bishop, Washington Irving, 261

Bittman, Major Ladislav, 372
"Black Art," 252
Black Sox Scandal, 309–10
Blackstone, Harry, 230, 252, 269
Blanc, Mel, 399
bluffing in games, legal, 281–85
Boer War, 42
Boggs, Phil, 305
Borromini, Francesco, 293
Boucher, Guillaume, 238
boxing, fixing, 312–13
Boyce, John, 257
Bradley, General Omar, 380
Brand, Christina, 328
Brenon, John, 239
Bruce, Robert, 32
Buchwald, Art, 95
Burt, Sir Cyril, 421–22
Busby, Jeff, 236
business, cheating in, 339–45
Byzantine Empire, 24–26
Caesar, Julius, 22, 358
Calchas (prophet), 18, 19
Caligula, 294
Cameron, Mark, 306
camouflage, 53
Campbell, Captain Gordon, 80
Campbell, Lady Malcolm, 49
Cardano, Geronimo, 287
cards, cheating at, 285–93
    at Poker, 291–93
    signaling, 287–91
Carson, Johnny, 243
Catherine the Great, Tsarina, 357
Caulfield, Royal Navy Captain F.W., 43
Chandler, Raymond, 47, 396
characteristics spectrum (CHARCS), 65–69
    war application of, 90

Charlemagne, 26
Cheaters Test, 99–203
cheating. *See* theory of cheating;
   names of games, sports people, etc.
   also see everyday cheating;
   magic; war
China, history of dynasties in,
   360–62
chivalry, 27, 31–32
Christie, Dr. Richard, 98, 99, 201
Christo, 357
Churchill, Winston, 76–77, 84,
   374, 378
Cicotte, Eddie, 310
Civil War (.S.), 39–41
Clair, René, 401
Clarke, Brigadier Dudley Wrangel,
   84, 221, 222, 223
Clute, Ced, 236
cockfighting, 320
Cohen, Elie, 364–65
collectibles, counterfeits of, 412–13
Collins, Anthony, 316–17
Collins, Pat, 416
Colorni, Abram, 243
Comisky, Charlie, 310
computer cheating, 298, 318–19
condottieri, 34
confederates, 232
con games, 345–53
conmen, 218–20
Constantine, Emperor, 59
Cory, Desmond, 350
Cotni, Baruch, 263
Cotton, Charles, 294
counterdeception, 427–32
coups d'état, 358–60
Courbet, Gustave, 405
covers, 52
Cowell, Joe, 292, 293
Criger, Lou, 309
Crumb, R., 331
Dahl, Roald, 289
Dali, Salvador, 404–405
Dandolos, Nick "The Greek,"
   288–89
Dares the Phrygian, 18
David and Goliath, 21, 37
Davenport Brothers, 260

Da Vinci, Leonardo, 407
Dawkins, Colonel Pete, 299
Dayan, General Moshe, 55
dazzling
   characteristics of, 66
   in humans, 55–56
   in nature, 50
deception/deceit/deceivers
   counterdeception, 427–32
   profile of deceivers, 97–226
   structure of deceit, 45–74
   test, deceivers', 99–203
   See also duplicity; theory of
      cheating; *aspects of deception*
Deception Planning Loop, 71–74
De Chirico, Giorgio, 405
decoying
   characteristics, 67
   in humans, 59–60
   vs. luring, 376n
   in nature, 51–52
de Hory, Elmyr, 409–11, 417
Deighton, Len, 396
Dessoir, Dr. Max, 267–68, 269
dice, cheating at, 294–95
Dickinson, Thorold, 210
Dictys of Crete, 18
Devant, David, 240
Dietrich, Noah, 418
Dimbleby, Richard, 262
disclosure, magician's defenses
   against, 265–67
dissimulation, 61. *See also* hiding
doctorates, cheating for, 326–27
Döbler, Ludwig, 239
dogfighting, 320
dog racing, 318–20
Donation of Constantine, 415–16
doppelgänger, 57
Douglas, Mike, 261, 262, 263
Downes, Olin, 420
Downs, Thomas Nelson, 266
Doyle, Sir Arthur Canon, 260
drugs, cheating with
   at Olympic games, 306
   at race tracks, 315
Dundee, Angelo, 314
Dunninger, Joseph, 260, 261, 288
dupes, profile of, 97–226

duplicity, nature of, 13–226
  applied theory, 77–96
  deceit, structure of, 45–74
  guile, prevalence of, 15–44
  profiles of deceivers and dupes,
    97–226
Duran (boxer), 313
Edward VII, King of England,
  316
Eisenhower, Dwight D., 380
Ellenberger, Norm, 311
Erasmus, 396
Escher, M. C., 389–90
espionage, 363–68
everyday cheating, 324–53
  apparel and, 328–32
  business and, 339–45
  con games, 345–53
  religion and, 336–39
  sex and, 332–35
  style and, 324–38
Fairbanks, Douglas, Jr., 221
Falconi, Signor, 238
Falkenhayn, General, 81, 82
Faraday, Michael, 257
Fawkes, Isaac, 238
fiction-as-fact books, 414–20
Fields, W.C., 298, 340
films, illusion in, 209–11, 400–401
Fischer, Bobby, 282
Fitch, Sir Thomas, 392
Fleming, Ian, 221
Fleming, Peter, 221
Flynn, Errol, 320–21
Forman, George, 313, 314
Fouquet, Nicholas, 391
Fox Sisters, 259
Frazier, Joe, 313
Frontinus, 23, 24
Fullerton, Hugh, 310
Funston, Colonel Frederick, 42–43
FUSAG (Army Group Patton)
  ruse, 91–93
gaffed equipment, cheating at
  games and, 295–99
games, cheating at, 271–99
  cards, 285–93
  chance, games of, 272–73
  comparative sucker scores, 279

dice, 294–95
  established betting charges,
    272–73
  house percentages (list), 276–79
  legal hiding, bluffing, and lying,
    281–85
  mechanics of, 295–99
  prevalence of, 279–81
  Vigorish Test (sucker quotient),
    273–76
  See also con games; sports; *names
    of games*
Gandil, Chick, 310
Gardner, Martin, 260
Garner, James, 350
Geller, Uri, 223–26, 232, 234–35,
  241, 248, 257, 260, 261–65,
  268, 290, 424
George III, King of England, 259
Gideon, 20
Göring, Hermann, 406
Goldin, Horace, 240
Gordon-Gordon, Lord John, 219–
  20
Gould, Jay, 218–20
Greeley, Horace, 219
Guicciardini, Francesco, 35–36
guile, ruses of war and, 15–44
Guinness, Alex, 330, 331
Halsey, Admiral, 221
Hannibal, 22
Hasted, John, 241
Hay, Henry, 231, 247, 265–66
Hearst, Patty, 330
Heller, Robert, 239
Henderson, Lietenant Colonel
  G. F. R., 41–42
Henry V, King of England, 32
Henry the Fowler, 29
Hepburn, Audrey, 403
Heuer, Richards J., Jr., 393
Heydrich, Reinhard, 367
hiding
  in humans, 53–56
  legal, in games, 281–85
  in nature, 49–50
Hitler, Adolf, 83, 213–14, 369,
  370, 375, 379
Hobbes, Thomas, 36

Hocus Pocus Junior, 230
holdout machines, 297
Homer, 18
Houdini, Harry, 216–18, 234, 260, 285, 397
Hughes, Howard, 416–19
Ibn Khaldūn, 28
illicit cheats, 208
illusion, characteristics spectrum of, 68–69. *See also* film; magic; theater, etc.
Ingersoll, Captain Ralph, 380, 381
inventing
  characteristics of, 67
  in humans, 58–59
  in nature, 51
Irving, Clifford, 416–19
Irving, Edith, 419
Jackson, General "Stonewall," 41
Jackson, "Shoeless Joe," 310
Jenghiz Khan, 28, 29–30, 337–38
Jeune Ecole, 36
John, Emperor (John the Good), 26
John, Prestor, 337
Johns, Jasper, 389
Jones, Dr. R. V., 374, 375
Joshua, 17
Justinian, 24
Kalinina, Irina, 305
Katterfelto, Gustavus, 238
Kempelen, Baron von, 238
Kennedy, John F., 377
Kennedy, Joseph P., Jr., 377
Kepplinger, P. J. "Lucky Dutchman," 297
Kerr, Deborah, 404
King, Admiral Ernest J., 84
Kissinger, Henry, 248, 326
Kolta, Bautier de, 252
Kordize, Avtandil, 305
Kreisler, Fritz, 420
Kreskin, The Amazing, 260, 288
Kline, Franz, 387
Kublai Khan, 31
Landis, Kenesaw Mountain, 310
language, illusion in, 393–96
Lardner, Ring, 310
Lavigne, Jacques, 318–19, 322

Lawrence, T. E. (Lawrence of Arabia), 15, 81, 82, 84
Leger, F., 387
Lenin, V. I., 45, 83
Le Nôtre, André, 391
Leonard, Sugar Ray, 313
Leo the Wise, 24–25, 27
Liddell Hart, B. H., 83, 84, 94
Lincoln, Abe, 97
Liston, Sonny, 313
literature
  counterfeits in, 414–20
  illusion in, 393–96
Long, Dr. John C., 423
Longstreet, General, 40
Lopez, Bishop Ruy, 282
Loren, Sophia, 262
Louis XIV, 391
Luard, Nicholas, 396
Ludendorff, General, 60
luminous readers, 298
lures, 376n, 377
lying, legal, in games, 281–85
MacArthur, General Douglas, 94
McCandless, Jake, 299
McCarry, Charles, 396
McClellan, Union commander, 40
McDonald, Mike, 99
McGovern, George, 356
McGregor, James, 420
Machiavelli, Niccolo, 35, 36, 99, 365
Mackler, Gregg, 243
magic, 211–12, 216–18, 229–70
  disclosure, defense against, 265–67
  "forcing," methods of, 246–48
  mind readers, seers, psychics, etc., 259–65
  senses, deceiving, 249–58
  technology and chronology of, 238–41
Magritte, René, 389
Magruder, General, 40
Mahābhārata poets, 21
Mann, Thomas, 335
Marceau, Marcel, 253
Marchand, Floram, 258
Marco Polo, 337

Marcus Aurelius, 23
Maria Theresa, Empress, 238
Marshall, General George C., 84
Marx, Karl, 203
Maskelyne, John Nevil, 259
masking
   characteristics of, 66
   in humans, 53–55
   in nature, 49
Mauborgne, Major Joseph O., 290
Maugham, W. Somerset, 394–95
medicine, hoaxes in, 422–23
Meinertzhagen, Major Richard, 81, 82
Méliès, Georges, 210, 240
Mendel, Gregor, 421
Meyer, Stanley, 418
mimicking
   application in war, 77–80
   characteristics of, 66–67
   in humans, 56–58
   in nature, 50–51
mind reading, or "mentalism," 259–60
misdirection, 230
modeling, fashion, cheating in, 327–28
Montcalm, Marquis de, 37
Moor, Ian, 307
Moretti, Willie, 347
Morgenstern, Oscar, 283
Mulholland, John, 231
Murphy, Tony, 316
"muscle reading," 261
music
   counterfeits in, 420
   illusion in, 401, 403–404
Napoleon Bonaparte, 38
nature, physical cheating in, 48–52
Nebe, Arthur, 367
Neoptolemus, 19, 20
Nettles, Graig, 308
Newman, Paul, 350
ninja, 20, 21
Nixon, Richard M., 248, 303, 356, 362
nomadic cavalry, 28–29
Normandy, invasion of, 85–89

Northrup, F. S. C., 209
nuclear strategy, 94
Octavian, 22
Odysseus, 18–19, 21
Olympic games, cheating at, 303–306
   drugs and, 306
Onassis, Aristotle, 340
Onishchenko, Boris, 305
optical illusions, 209
Oster, Colonel Hans, 367
Otto the Great, 29
Overlord, Operation, 84, 85, 88, 89,
Palyaenus, 23
painting
   forgery in, 404–13
   illusion in, 386–89, 390
Patton, General George, 56, 91, 369, 379, 381
Penner, Joe, 212
Pershing, General John, 84–85
Phelan, Jim, 418
Philadelphia, Jacob, 238
Philippine Insurrection, 42
physical cheating in nature, 49–52
Picasso, Pablo, 387, 405, 409
Pinchbeck, Christopher, 238
Pinetti, Giovanni, 238, 259
plants, 232
Pliny, 338
Poker, cheating at, 291–93
politics, cheating and, 354–63
Pollock, Jackson, 387
Potemkin, 357
Psalmanazar, George, 415
psychological cheating by humans, 52–60
   hiding, 53–56
   showing, 56–60
public cheating, 354–81
Puharich, Andrija, 262, 424
Quintus Symrnaeus, 18
racetrack, cheating at, 314–21
   cheating the track, 317–19
   horses and, 314–17
   other animals and, 319–21
radio plays, illusion in, 398–400

Rains, Brigadier General Gabriel, 40
Raleigh, Sir Walter, 232
Rameses II, Pharaoh, 17–18
Randi, 260, 261
Rannil, John, 255
rebel and rogues, 203–205
  rebels persona, 205
  rogue persona, 204
  test for, 203–204
Redford, Robert, 350
religion, cheating and, 336–39
Rembrandt, 406, 407
Renaissance, Italian, 33–34
repackaging
  characteristics of, 66
  in humans, 55
  in nature, 49
Retz, Cardinal de, 212
Robert-Houdin, Jean Eugène, 239, 258
Roberts, Lord, 42
Robinson, William Ellsworth, 252
Rodriguez, Leon E., 319
rogues. *See* rebels and rogues
Romanus Diogenes, 25
Rommel, Field Marshal, 378
Root, Elihu, 220
Rothstein, Arnold "The Brain," 286, 310
Ruiz, Rosie, 306–307
ruses of war, prevalence of guile in, 15–44, 89
  characteristics spectrum of, 67–68
SALT, 94–95
samurai, 20
Sandia (model), 327, 328
Sarfatti, Dr. Jack, 241
Scarne, John, 280, 281, 285, 288, 349
Schellenberg, Walter, 367
science, hoaxes and self-deception in, 421–26
Scott, Reginald, 46
Scott, Sir Walter, 45
Selbit, P. T., 217, 240
Seneca, 47
senses, deceiving of, magic and, 248–49

acoustical deception, 253–55
smell and taste, 258–59
tactile deception, 255–58
visual deception, 249–53
sexual relationships, cheating and, 332–35
Shearer, Dr. James, 424–25
Sherman, General, 41
showing
  in humans, 56–60
  in nature, 50–52
Shtrang, Hannah, 263
Shtrang, "Shipi," 261–62, 263
Siegel, "Bugsy," 347
signaling, cheating at cards and, 287–91
Simon, John, 229, 249, 258
simulation, 61. *See also* showing
Sloan, James Forman "Todhunter," 316
Slydini, Tony, 243
smell and taste, deception of, magic and, 258–59
Smith, Jefferson Randolph, 350–51
spiritualism, 259–60
sports, cheating and, 299–323
  ball games and gambling, 308–12
  fixing gamblers' games, 312–23
  Indy 500, 307–308
  law of the fix, 322–23
  marathons and, 306–307
  Olympic games and, 303–306
  racetracks and, 314–21
Stalin, Joseph, 213–14
Stassen, Harold, 221
Stealth bomber, 95–96
Stein, David, 410
Stodare, Alfred, 239, 252
Stone-Age hunters, 16
stratagems, deception in war and, 88–89
structure of deception, 47–52
  how to cheat, 70–71
  planning loop, 71–74
style, everyday cheating and, 324–28
Sullivan, "Sport," 310
Sun Tzu, 15, 21

Suskind, Richard, 417, 419
tactile deception, magic and, 255–58
Taft, Keith, 298
Tamerlane, 28
Tarbell, Dr. Harlan, 397
taste illusions, 211
tax cheating. *See* business
Taylor, John, 241, 263–64
Thackeray, William Makepeace, 287
theater, illusion in, 396–400
Thot, 16–17, 18
theory of cheating, 45–74
    application of, 77–96
    CHARCS (characteristics spectrum), 66–69
    deception planning loop, 71–74
    how to cheat, 70–71
    psychological cheating by humans, 52–60
    physical cheating in nature, 49–52
    structure of deception, 47–52, 61
Thorpe, Jim, 321
Thynne, Major Oliver, 223
Tilden, Frederick, 397–98
Tobin, Thomas W., 239
Torres, José, 313
Trojan-horse ploy, 18–19
Uston, Ken, 298
van Meegeren, Hans, 407–409
Van Pallandt, Baroness Nina, 419
Vegetius, 23, 24
Vermeer, Jan, 406, 407, 408, 409

Vernon, Dai, 236, 245–46
ventriloquism, 254–55
Verus, 23
Virgil, 18
visual deception, magic and, 249–53
Voltaire, 416
von Clausewitz, General Carl, 38
Von Moltke, Helmuth, 214–15
von Neumann, John, 283, 284
Walasiewiscz, Stella Walsh, 304
Wallace, Irving, 417
Walters, Barbara, 262
war, application of theory of cheating in, 77–96, 368–81
    illusions and ruses, 89
    prevalence of guile and, 15–44
    specific deception goals, 86–88
    stratagems, 88–89
Watergate, 355–57
Wavell, General, 83–84, 222
Weaver, Earl, 308–309
Weiner, Milton, 344
Welles, Orson, 399–400
Wells, H.G., 399
Whaley, Dr. B. Stewart, 98, 244–45, 268–70
Whisenant, John, 311, 312
Winterbotham, Captain "Freddy," 378
Wolfe, Major General James, 37
Wolseley, Colonel Garnet J., 39
Wood, Natalie, 403
Wotton, Sir Henry, 363
Wren, Sir Christopher, 391–92
Xenophon, 21